By Defeating My Enemies

Charles XII of Sweden and the Great Northern War, 1682–1721

Michael Glaeser

'This is the Century of the Soldier', Fulvio Testi, Poet, 1641

Helion & Company

**In memory of the men, women, and children – soldiers and civilians –
who lost their lives during 21 years of war.**

Helion & Company Limited
Unit 8 Amherst Business Centre
Budbrooke Road
Warwick
CV34 5WE
England
Tel. 01926 499 619
Email: info@helion.co.uk
Website: www.helion.co.uk
Twitter: @helionbooks

Published by Helion & Company 2020
Designed and typeset by Mach 3 Solutions Ltd (www.mach3solutions.co.uk)
Cover designed by Paul Hewitt, Battlefield Design (www.battlefield-design.co.uk)

Text © Michael Glaeser 2020
Illustrations © as individually credited
Maps drawn by George Anderson © Helion & Company 2020
Front cover art work by Patrice Courcelle © Helion & Company 2020

Every reasonable effort has been made to trace copyright holders and to obtain their permission for the use of copyright material. The author and publisher apologize for any errors or omissions in this work and would be grateful if notified of any corrections that should be incorporated in future reprints or editions of this book.

ISBN 978-1-913336-46-2

British Library Cataloguing-in-Publication Data.
A catalogue record for this book is available from the British Library.

All rights reserved. No part of this publication may be reproduced, stored in a retrieval system, or transmitted, in any form, or by any means, electronic, mechanical, photocopying, recording or otherwise, without the express written consent of Helion & Company Limited.

For details of other military history titles published by Helion & Company Limited contact the above address or visit our website: http://www.helion.co.uk.

We always welcome receiving book proposals from prospective authors.

Contents

Timeline	v
The Royal Line of Sweden	vii
The Family of Charles XII of Sweden	viii
1 *Stormaktstiden*: the Swedish Empire up to 1682	13
2 Childhood: 1682–1697	25
3 A King Without Concern: 1697–1700	33
4 The Carolean Army under Charles XII	42
5 First Battles, 1700–1702	53
6 The Venture Into Poland and Saxony, 1701–1707	73
7 The March to Russia, 1707–1709	92
8 Poltava, 1709	110
9 Exile, 1709–1714	121
10 Rearguard, 1714–1717	135
11 Death in the Trenches, 1718	150
12 The Warrior King Reassessed: 1718 and Beyond	166
Conclusion	173
Appendices	
I Personality, Traits, and Myth	176
II The Vanity of Human Wishes	182
Colour Plate Commentaries	183
Select Bibliography	184

Acknowledgements

The support and encouragement of others is critical to any book writing endeavour. I owe a debt of gratitude to many individuals and institutions and believe a mention here is the least I can do.

To the University of Sheffield for providing me with a life changing experience, Stephen Kling Jr for giving me my first opportunity to write about Charles XII, Alex Burns for allowing me to be a guest author on his wonderful Kabinettskriege blog, all of my colleagues at Southern New Hampshire University, Sabaton and the concept album that started it all, Charles Singleton and the Helion staff, Peter Holmgren and the Lif Compagniet, Roger Castle for kindly donating his time to review the draft, my family, and my wife Susan. Thank you all.

Timeline

A selection of important dates in the life of Charles XII.

Date (Old Style)	Event
17 June 1682	Birth of Charles XII
January 1688	Birth of Ulrika Eleonora the Younger
26 July 1693	Death of Ulrika Eleonora the Elder
5 April 1697	Death of Charles XI
14 December 1697	Anointment of Charles XII
February 1700	Saxon troops march into Livonia, start of the Great Northern War
24 July 1700	Landing at Humlebaek
7 August 1700	Treaty of Travendal, Denmark exits the war
17 November 1700	Skirmish at Pyhajoggi Pass
19 November 1700	Battle of Narva
8 July 1701	Crossing of the Düna
8 July 1702	Battle of Kliszów
20 April 1703	Battle of Pultusk
14 October 1703	Capitulation of Thorn
1 July 1704	Stanislaus Leszcynski declared king of Poland
27 October 1704	Battle of Punitz
13 September 1706	Treaty of Altranstädt, publically revealed on 4 November, Saxony exits the war
15 April 1707	Charles XII and Marlborough meet
21 August 1707	Convention of Altranstädt, Charles XII secures Protestant rights in Silesia
3 July 1708	Battle of Holowczyn
December 1708	Death of Hedvig Sophia
7 January 1709	Assault on Verpik
17 June 1709	Charles XII struck in foot by bullet, fever sets in
27 June 1709	Battle of Poltava
30 June 1709	Swedish army surrenders at Perevolochna
21 July 1709	Charles XII arrives at Bender
10 July 1711	Treaty of Pruth
31 January 1713	Skirmish at Bender, the *Kalabalik*

27 October 1714	Charles XII leaves Ottoman territory
10/11 November 1714	Charles XII arrives at Stralsund
November 1715	Death of Hedvig Eleonora
5 November 1715	Battle of Stresow
13 December 1715	Charles XII evacutates Stralsund and returns to Sweden
February 1716	Launch of first Norwegian campaign
8 September 1716	Peter I calls off invasion of Sweden
October 1718	Launch of second Norwegian campaign
27 November 1718	Capture of Gyldenlove bastion at Fredriksten
30 November 1718	Death of Charles XII at Fredriksten
26 February 1719	Burial of Charles XII in *Riddarholmskyrkan*
9 November 1719	Treaty of Stockholm between Sweden and Hanover
21 January 1720	Treaty of Stockholm between Sweden and Prussia
3 July 1720	Treaty of Fredriksborg between Sweden and Denmark
30 August 1721	Treaty of Nystad between Sweden and Russia. End of the Great Northern War

The Royal Line of Sweden

Order of dates marks the following: Birth-Accession-Deposition*-Death

* if applicable

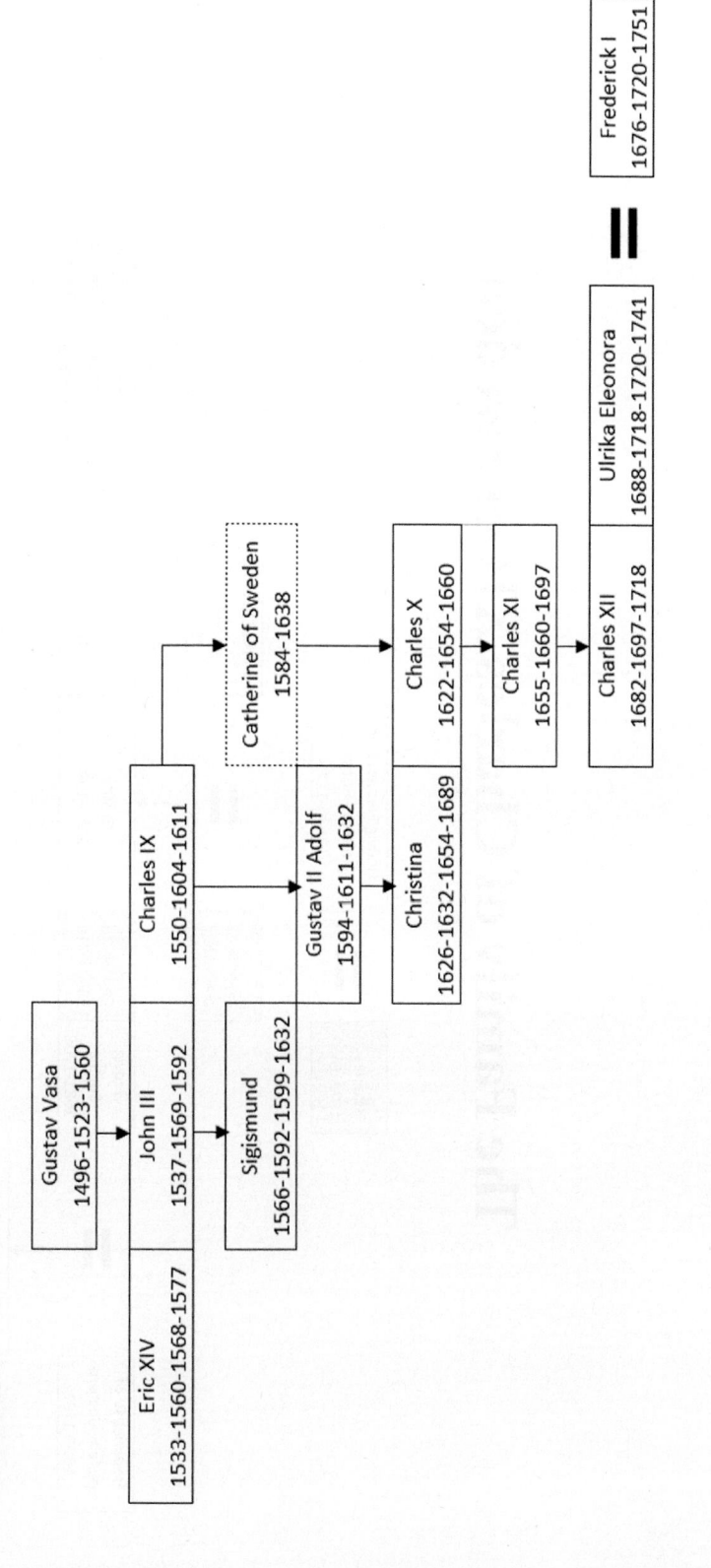

```
Gustav Vasa
1496-1523-1560
        │
        ├─────────────────────┐
        │                     │
Eric XIV              John III
1533-1560-1568-1577   1537-1569-1592
                              │
                      ┌───────┴───────┐
                      │               │
              Sigismund          Charles IX
              1566-1592-1599-1632  1550-1604-1611
                                      │
                              ┌───────┴────────────┐
                              │                    │
                      Catherine of Sweden    Gustav II Adolf
                      1584-1638              1594-1611-1632
                              │                    │
                              │              Christina
                              │              1626-1632-1654-1689
                              ↓
                          Charles X
                          1622-1654-1660
                              │
                          Charles XI
                          1655-1660-1697
                              │
              ┌───────────────┴───────────────┐
              │                               │
        Charles XII                    Ulrika Eleonora   =   Frederick I
        1682-1697-1718                 1688-1718-1720-1741   1676-1720-1751
```

The Family of Charles XII of Sweden

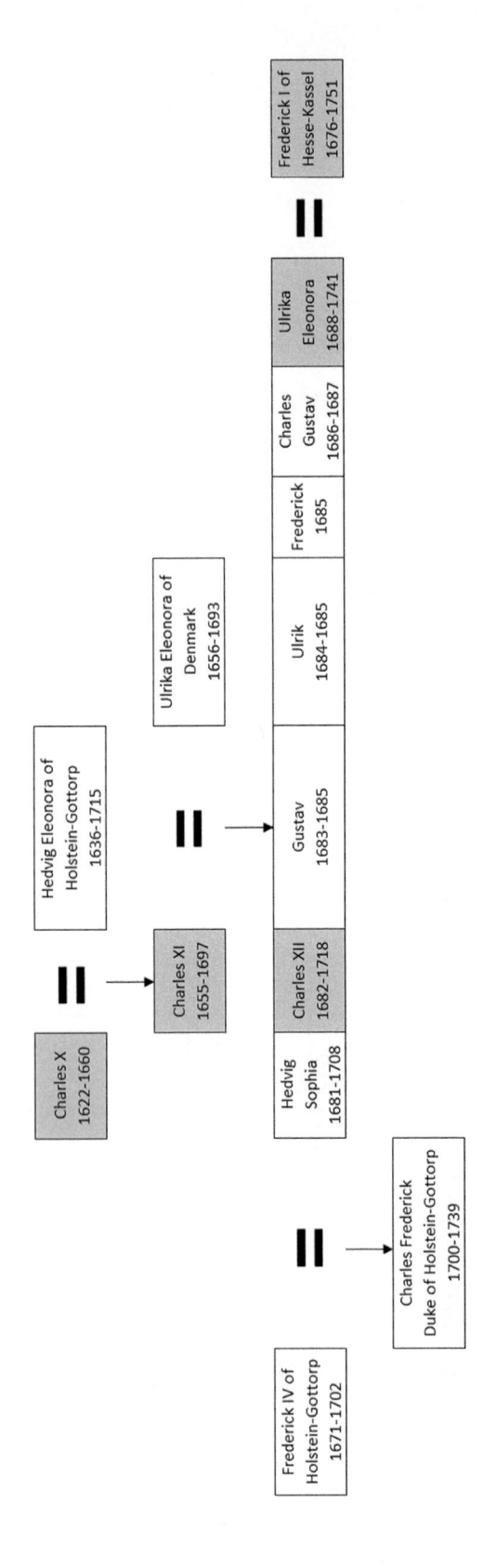

Charles X
1622-1660

=

Hedvig Eleonora of Holstein-Gottorp
1636-1715

→ Charles XI
1655-1697

=

Ulrika Eleonora of Denmark
1656-1693

→ Children of Charles XI and Ulrika Eleonora:

- Hedvig Sophia 1681-1708
- Charles XII 1682-1718
- Gustav 1683-1685
- Ulrik 1684-1685
- Frederick 1685
- Charles Gustav 1686-1687
- Ulrika Eleonora 1688-1741

Hedvig Sophia 1681-1708 = Frederick IV of Holstein-Gottorp 1671-1702 → Charles Frederick Duke of Holstein-Gottorp 1700-1739

Ulrika Eleonora 1688-1741 = Frederick I of Hesse-Kassel 1676-1751

Introduction

"Were Socrates and Charles the Twelfth of Sweden both present in any company, and Socrates to say, 'Follow me and hear a lecture on philosophy' and Charles, laying his hand on his sword, to say, 'Follow me and dethrone the Czar', a man would be ashamed to follow Socrates."

Samuel Johnson in a conversation recalled by his biographer, James Boswell[1]

Any student of the Great Northern War will have encountered Charles XII in some capacity. The King of Sweden is an omnipresent figure who is intrinsically linked to the war that would become his singular obsession for the remaining 18 years of his life. As Sweden's only monarch born to absolutism, his hand in the kingdom's affairs, for better or worse, left a recognisable imprint on all areas of historical interest – the export of iron, privateering in the Baltic, the production of emergency coinage, Swedish–Jacobite intrigues, regimental drill, and the implementation of foreign policy, to name a few. To most, Charles is best known for his direct leadership of the Swedish army as it stormed across Central and Eastern Europe from Copenhagen to Narva and Warsaw to Leipzig. A coalition of states, each negatively affected by Sweden in the past, united to open three fronts against an unproven king who inherited the throne at the age of 15 just three years prior. Charles famously put aside the fineries of court and marched off to war. While not a martial visionary like Gustavus Adolphus, he was nevertheless master of the battlefield for the first eight years of the conflict. He favoured aggressive tactics applied to both the infantry and cavalry, developed an eye for advantageous terrain, and exploited enemy weak points as soon as they were identified. He had a talent for using feints to disguise his intentions and could march his armies at a frenetic pace over terrain thought to be impassable. Charles notably fought from the front at a time when other monarchs were leaving the field to their generals. In doing so, he endured the hardships of war alongside his men which fostered loyalty, courage, and an *esprit de corps* that became synonymous with being a *Karoliner*. He played with death, surviving four bullets before the fifth decided the game in his 36th year, giving him the distinction of being the last European monarch to

---

1 James Boswell, *The Life of Samuel Johnson*, vol. II, (Boston: W. Andrews and L. Blake, 1807), p.500.

die on the field of battle. Ultimately the enemies proved too numerous and the odds too great, though they were arguably bolstered by the obstinacy of a king who would shun peace offerings unless he was provided with the restitution and security that Sweden demanded. The empire he strove to defend and maintain was lost and the overseas territories divided among the victors while his own legacy, forever tied to the end of Sweden's "Great Power Period", remains open to interpretation even 300 years later.

Many readers are introduced to Charles XII through the writings of Voltaire and his 1731 classic *Histoire de Charles XII, Roi de Suede*. It is a biography worth reading but with a caveat that the King serves as a motif – that military glory is fleeting and disgrace and ruin can follow despite being endowed with all of the positive virtues desired by man. To Voltaire, Charles was "... perhaps the most extraordinary man ever to walk the earth, who possessed all the great qualities of his forebears, and whose only flaw and misfortune was to have carried all those qualities to excess".[2] Countless writers, both before Voltaire and since, have taken up the pen to create a wide range of characterisations. By the nineteenth and early twentieth centuries, these perspectives congealed into the so-called "old" and "new" schools of Carolean historiography. While the duelling schools have strengthened research and placed new attention on the primary source material, assessments of the King remain clouded by centuries of second-hand accounts, propaganda, and myth. As a result, the narrative extremes are now easier to identify and support: is he the doomed hero who fought valiantly until his empire's inevitable collapse, or the villain who sacrificed Sweden's position of power to satiate his war-lust? Did his campaigns have logical reasoning behind them or was he simply charging at windmills? Was he educated and cultured or a simpleton in all but the art of war? Charles never felt the need to defend himself. He brushed aside any judgement of his character, fully convinced of his God-given right and justification of his cause. Ultimately, he wrote very little compared to his contemporaries and the largest cache of material covering Swedish military movements up to Poltava were sunk in the Dnieper River in the battle's immediate aftermath. Besides the written testimony from those closest to Charles, the King's own actions – ranging from magnanimity to utter single-mindedness – provide the greatest insight into his mindset.

Charles ascended the Swedish throne in 1697 at a critical juncture in European history, one that would set the stage for the wars and expansions of the following century. The intrigues of Louis XIV of France led to war over the Spanish succession, England established itself as a Continental power and set the Royal Navy on a course for dominion of the world's seas, and Prussia began the process of transitioning from electorate to kingdom. Most importantly, a foil to Charles emerged in the east as Peter Alexeyevich seized power in Russia, dragged his people through modernisation efforts, and would soon challenge Swedish hegemony along the Baltic coast.

---

2 Francois-Marie Arouet de Voltaire, *The History of Charles XII King of Sweden*, trans. Antonia White (New York: Barnes & Nobel, 1976), p.35.

INTRODUCTION

The Swedish Empire, firmly established by the trials and ruin of the Thirty Years' War and the indifference of its neighbours, was by 1700 isolated on the European stage and deemed a soft target by conspiring states that wanted to grasp at the kingdom's valuable Baltic and North German territories. Sweden's imperial destiny was perhaps always fated to fail – the kingdom lacked sufficient resources in population, industry, and capital. For the duration of its 100-year existence, the empire was sustained by war and the sheer personal will of the monarchy. The Herculean efforts of Gustav II Adolf, Charles X, Charles XI, and Charles XII extended the empire's life but ultimately could not create a stable base. Of all the warrior kings, Charles XII faced the largest concentration of enemies and endured war the longest. In the words of his biographer Eveline Godley: "It may be added that no sovereign, of any time, would have faced the verdict of posterity more unflinchingly or, if responsibility for the future of nations were to be called in question, would more fearlessly have accepted his share."[3]

As Helion's "Century of the Soldier" series continues its laudatory dive into more specialised studies of the Great Northern War, there remains a need to connect these strands to the overarching themes and personalities of the conflict. The King's last major biographical treatment in Swedish came from Bengt Liljegren in 2000 which ended a nearly 70-year historiographical absence. For the English language, Ragnhild Hatton's magisterial work from 1969 has not been challenged or surpassed. In recent years, broad studies of the life of Charles XII have been sidelined in favour of writing about the King within the tight parameters of an editorial theme or an author's specialisation. Such treatments, while extremely useful and necessary, do not always have the scope to cover the King's past experiences in detail. In many cases, these experiences influenced Charles to act or respond in a particular way and without that context, the actions are seen in a vacuum which can lead to incorrect generalisations about the King's behaviour. Understanding Charles's devotion to his father and promises made at his deathbed may shed light on his own approach to war and how he waged it. Regarding Charles famously eschewing peace, a look at the duplicity of Augustus of Saxony reveals why Charles had to seek peace terms with the highest degrees of security and reject anything deemed lighter or less enforceable.

This book, then, seeks to take a fresh look at Sweden's last warrior king via a traditional biographical account. The first chapter is dedicated to the rise of the Swedish Empire and explains how a series of socio-political factors, both internal and external, led to the unique circumstances that Charles had to face in 1700. Childhood and adolescence are vital times for physical and mental maturation and space is dedicated to covering family life and loss during the King's developmental years. Given the title of the book, it is meant to be a biography first and a study of the Great Northern War second, but as a full half of Charles's life was spent in the field, a discussion of the conflict is naturally merited. The focus is on the campaigns and actions in which the King was involved. Unfortunately, this limits the coverage of particular

---

3   Eveline Godley, *Charles XII of Sweden – A Study in Kingship* (London: W. Collins Sons & Co, 1928), p.7.

theatres such as the naval actions in the Baltic or the Polish and Lithuanian civil wars. However, occasional tangents are employed to explain certain events taking place away from the King's person, especially if they impact him at a later point. Appendix I at the rear of the book will look at several other aspects of the King's life that did not necessarily fit into the linear storyline. Finally, the last chapter will explore the narrative of the King's reputation post-mortem and how literature and propaganda have shaped public perception from the 1700s to modernity.

Names and Dates

Regarding fore- and surnames, the most commonly published naming convention, often anglicised, is used. Slight alterations are made in the instance of two or more figures having the same name to help the reader keep track: for example, Frederick IV of Holstein-Gottorp and Frederik IV of Denmark. With monarchs of the same name and no spelling alterations (Charles), their regnal number is used to initially identify them within the text. Once that is established, the regnal number is dropped.

At the turn of the eighteenth century, three distinct calendars were in play: the Julian, Gregorian, and Swedish. The Julian calendar is considered the *old style* whereas the Gregorian, a full 10 days ahead of the Julian, is the *new style*.[4] By 1700 most states switched to the Gregorian calendar but England, Sweden, and Russia retained the Julian. To further complicate matters, the Swedes adopted their own calendar which was 10 days behind the Gregorian and one day ahead of the Julian. Charles XII dropped the Swedish calendar in 1712 and reverted to the Julian. An effort was made to utilise the *old style* dating throughout the work. When there was doubt, the most commonly accepted date was used. Any errors are my own.

---

4 This would increase to 11 days after 1700.

Chapter 1

Stormaktstiden: the Swedish Empire up to 1682

"After the King's arrival at Altranstädt, this Prince, being desirous of seeing the field of battle near Lützen, where Gustavus Adolphus so gloriously lost his life for the liberty of Germany, went to the place … he likewise recollected all that he had read thereof in history …"

Gustaf Adlerfeld describing Charles XII's visit to the battlefield of Lützen, upon the latter's entry into Saxony in 1706.[1]

The 126-year existence of the Kalmar Union came to an end in 1523 when a disaffected nobleman named Gustav Vasa led a rebellion against Danish rule and was subsequently elected to the throne of Sweden. Gustav and his three sons all had an opportunity to rule the fledgling kingdom with varying degrees of success. As part of Sweden's growing pains in the sixteenth century, the Vasa kings struggled with the limits of the constitution, the inherent power of the nobility, and the absence of revenue streams filling the royal coffers. Sweden's reclusive economy, disproportionately scaled to the kingdom's supremacy even in the next imperial century, is considered by one historian to have been on the same developmental level as that of Carolingian France from 500 years earlier.[2] When attention turned to foreign policy, there were mixed results that had, by the year 1600 during the reign of Charles IX, culminated in a complete deterioration of relations with neighbouring states.

Gustav II Adolf, Latinized to Gustavus Adolphus and later known as the *Lion of the North*, ascended the throne in 1611. He inherited from his father a kingdom that was a second-rate power engulfed in constitutional turmoil at home and surrounded by powerful foes abroad – Sweden was involved in no less than three wars with Denmark, Poland, and Russia. With time, Gustavus proved to be a learned administrator and an even greater military commander. His coronation year is oftentimes used to mark the beginning of Sweden's rise to European prominence.

---

1   Gustavus Adlerfeld, *The Genuine History of Charles XII, King of Sweden*, trans. James Ford (London: Booksellers, 1742), p.320.
2   Michael Roberts, *Essays in Swedish History* (London: Weidenfeld and Nicolson, 1967), p.3.

Gustav II Adolf. (Willem Jakobsz Delff, Engraving of Gustav II Adolf, public domain)

The new king was quick to rely on his privy council and the *Riksdag*, Sweden's governing body. He also formed a close relationship with his Lord Chancellor, Axel Oxenstierna. Together they were able to execute a series of domestic reforms and navigate complex foreign affairs to Sweden's advantage. Due to the poor financial state of the kingdom, Gustavus was forced to sell off Crown lands in payment of debts. He was able to eventually compensate for these losses via the export of copper and the establishment of shipping tolls along the Brandenburg coast. These, however, would be temporary solutions and the loss of Crown lands would have severe financial ramifications for his successors until the *reduktion* of Charles XI clawed them back in 1680.

With finances momentarily stabilised, Gustavus then set about modernising the military. He redefined the administrative and tactical unit sizes, reduced the depth of his line formations to bring more firepower to bear, provided updated weapons in the form of the matchlock musket and pike, conducted extensive trainings and manoeuvres, returned the cavalry to an offensive role, and reimagined the use of artillery. He is arguably best known for the latter where he established regimental guns that were light enough to be drawn by one horse and could therefore be repositioned during battle – a significant tactical advantage. While Gustavus is considered to be one of the fathers of modern warfare and a great general, there is a tendency to credit him with too much. In some cases he was not the innovator but rather modified what already existed, especially concepts from the Dutch, and Maurice of Nassau.

By 1617 Sweden was able to conclude the war with Russia by signing the Treaty of Stolbova. This resulted in Sweden gaining Ingria and Kexholm just off the Gulf of Finland which brought major ports under its control and thus allowed for the potential monopolisation of trade between Russia and the West. More importantly, the treaty cut off Russia from the Baltic Sea which provided the raison d'être for Czar Peter I's attack on Sweden some 83 years later. The war with Poland ended with the Truce of Altmark in 1629. Sweden retained the province of Livonia on the Baltic's eastern shores and the capture of the prosperous town of Riga in 1621 is seen as another fateful event that marks the start of the Swedish Empire. Having also concluded the war with Denmark earlier in his reign, Gustavus was then free to intervene in the Thirty Years' War which had been raging in the Holy Roman Empire since 1618. It was in this conflict that the King's reforms and military genius became evident. The Swedes smashed aside the Imperial forces commanded by Count Tilly and drove deep into the Empire. The victory at Breitenfeld in 1631 proved that the Swedish army was on a par with any mustered in Continental Europe. The death of Gustavus at Lützen a year later was a setback for the Swedish cause but involvement in the war continued with hopes of gaining more territorial and material possessions.

Up until 1629 Denmark was the dominant northern power. Christian IV unsuccessfully intervened in the Thirty Years' War in a vainglorious attempt to become the saviour of Protestantism and increase his kingdom's prestige. The subsequent invasion of Germany by Gustavus launched the "Swedish Phase" of the war and denoted a transition of power in the Baltic region. In 1643 Sweden launched the so-called Torstenson War against a weakened Denmark which resulted in the Treaty of Brömsebro two years later. The islands of Ösel and Gotland as well as two Norwegian provinces were transferred into Swedish hands. The victor's shipping was also exempt from the Sound dues with no restrictions. If Brömsebro signalled the end of the Danish *dominium maris baltici*, the Treaty of Westphalia in 1648 heralded the arrival of Sweden as a first rate power. The kingdom emerged from the smouldering ruins of the Thirty Years' War as a guarantor of the peace, a protector of the Protestant faith, and a respected military power. Territorially, Sweden gained a foothold in northern Germany by acquiring the duchies of Bremen and Verden as well as Pomerania. All three territories would become a source of contention between Sweden and its rivals in the coming decades.

The emergence of a Swedish empire on the shores of the Baltic was somewhat of a surprise; given contemporary statistics, it came from such an unexpected quarter. Sweden's population in 1620 is estimated to have been 1.25 million. Compared to four million in England or 20 million in France, this number is miniscule.[3] Except for Denmark, Sweden would never outnumber its major foes. Financial capital was lacking and the natural resources provided by the northern lands could not be exploited on an industrial level. Sweden simply did not have the manpower or economy to support the rapid growth that was part and parcel of establishing an empire. It was, rather, a series of circumstances made possible in large part by the Thirty Years' War which allowed Sweden to start expanding beyond its means. The weaknesses and division among rival states was the primary factor – Poland was fighting a decline, Denmark's king isolated allies with his erratic foreign policy, England had a growing governmental crisis that culminated in civil war, Spain and the Netherlands were at odds, and France was initially focused on domestic policies. Lastly, the early Romanovs of Russia were spending their energies on economic and military reforms. Both would not be fully addressed until Peter I's relentless pursuit of westernisation at the turn of the eighteenth century. Indifference towards external events was prevalent and Sweden's growth, therefore, was largely unchecked.

Once Sweden obtained territories on the eastern and southern side of the Baltic, it became harder to maintain and defend the empire as European attention finally turned towards the upstart power. Sweden had to rely on strength of arms and tactical innovations. Until its reputation was shattered in the Scanian War, Sweden's military supremacy helped deter rivals and fostered alliances. Nevertheless, the overseas territories needed to be

---

3   Paul Douglas Lockhart, *Sweden in the Seventeenth Century* (New York: Palgrave Macmillan, 2004), p.3.

BY DEFEATING MY ENEMIES

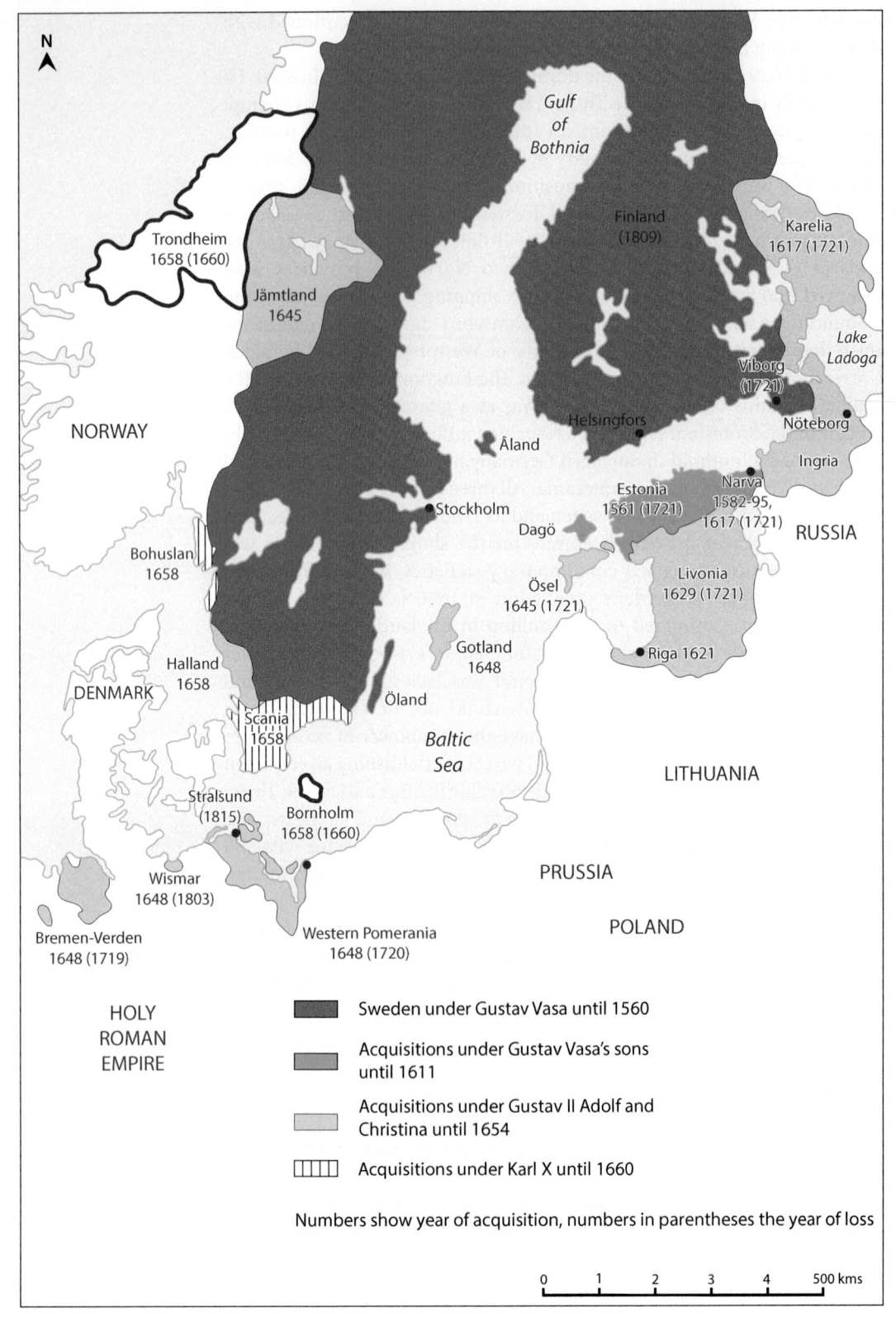

The Swedish Empire.

protected and this required garrisons. Mercenaries were recruited to help with military expansion as they were more affordable than native Swedes. Fighting on foreign soil was also a necessity to help offset the costs of war and put the burden on the occupied rather than the occupier. Historians of the "old school" view on Swedish imperialism suggest that the creation and expansion of the empire stemmed from a need for security. Sweden, being often outnumbered by powerful foes such as Denmark and Poland, needed to launch pre-emptive attacks on foreign soil in order to prevent anything from happening to the homeland. The empire thus came into existence through defensive expansion and could only feasibly exist by continued expansion. To play off the notion that "war feeds war", in Sweden's case "war feeds empire". Gustavus benefited greatly from it and is credited for launching the *Stormaktstid,* the "Great Power Period". Charles X was able to expand the empire even further under the same principle but found conditions much more difficult in the 1650s than his predecessors did in the previous three decades. The completion of the Thirty Years' War removed the temptation to engage in a continuous foreign war to spur financial gain. Peace created stagnation. At the same time, the number of potential enemies had grown: England was coming into its own, Russia was awakening, and northern German electorates, particularly Brandenburg, found a foothold on the European stage. When armed force was necessary, it had to result in victory: "As long as Sweden continued to win victories she could count on winning them at little cost to herself. Retreat and defeat upset the equation. Peace destroyed it."[4]

Assuming the throne after Christina's abdication, Charles X implemented a limited *reduktion* to regain some of the dispossessed Crown lands and help increase funds for the state and military by taxing the occupying farms. Charles sought to safeguard the empire's borders, while simultaneously coveting rich territories like Courland, by launching a war with Poland in 1655. Poland proved difficult to conquer and seeing the

Charles X. (Sebastien Bourdon, Charles X, Nationalmuseum, public domain)

Charles X at the Battle of Iversnaes. (Johan Philipp Lemke, Karl X Gustaf (1622–1660) efter slaget vid Iversnaes, Erik Cornelius, Nationalmuseum)

---

4 Michael Roberts, *The Swedish Imperial Experience 1560–1718* (Cambridge: Cambridge University Press, 1979), p.54.

Charles XII's pocket watch showing the coat of arms of the 49 provinces belonging to Sweden in 1700. (Charles XII's Pocket Watch, 1700, The Royal Armoury)

Swedes struggle emboldened Denmark to attack in 1657. In a daring response, Charles led his army over the frozen Belts separating mainland Denmark from the islands of Fünen and Zealand.

Denmark was unable to resist and forced to sign the Treaty of Roskilde in February 1658 and a follow-up in Copenhagen in 1660. This destroyed Danish hegemony in the Baltic for good, forcing them to give up Scania on the southern coast of the Swedish peninsula, the island of Bornholm, and the Norwegian provinces of Trondheim and Bohuslan (these were returned in 1660). At the same time, the Treaty of Oliva resolved the lingering Vasa dynastic issues with Poland and again secured Livonia for Sweden. By the end of Charles's reign, Sweden had reached its furthest territorial extent and the kingdom's modern borders stem from this time.

Charles X's wars, while successful, created more problems for his son and grandson. He died unexpectedly only six years into his reign and left much unsettled: Sweden had more territory to defend with a drained treasury, Poland was still subject to foreign influence, and the formation of a dynastic–political alliance with the Duchy of Holstein-Gottorp ensured the continuing enmity of Denmark. The dukes of Holstein-Gottorp were vassals to the Danish king and yet maintained autonomy in the governance of their lands. By allying with Sweden, the dukes gained a strong military partner who now had an open door into the vulnerable southern territories of Denmark. This was something the Danish king could not allow. The sudden death of Charles also left the kingdom with another long regency, the third since 1611. With no king directly dictating policy, the nobility overreached itself and there was excessive spending, declining revenues, and a reduction of military readiness. The empire was proving costly to maintain and seemed to be rotting away from within.

In an attempt to offset some of the costs, Sweden agreed to an alliance with France in 1672. In return for an annual subsidy of 400,000 *riksdaler*, Sweden had to maintain an armed force of 16,000 men in Pomerania. By the end of 1674, France demanded a return on their investment via a Swedish invasion of Brandenburg. Tied to the alliance and the promise of an even larger subsidy, the authorities in Stockholm acquiesced. The army was unprepared and quickly ran into problems after entering Brandenburg territory. Near the town of Fehrbellin the Swedes were hemmed in by the terrain as they worked to repair a broken bridge. The forces of Brandenburg set up their artillery on the surrounding hills which caused high casualties and forced the Swedes to attack the position several times. Brandenburg countered and the Swedes conducted a fighting retreat. While the battle was little more than a skirmish and casualties shared almost equally on both sides, Brandenburg capitalised on the propaganda – a larger Swedish force was beaten by a Germanic army. Sweden's military reputation plummeted and Denmark again used the opportunity to invade Scania and reclaim the lost province.

STORMAKTSTIDEN: THE SWEDISH EMPIRE UP TO 1682

The invasion began with the capture of Helsingborg in June 1676. With a mere 5,000 Swedes facing 15,000 Danes, progress through Scania was swift with Malmö being the only town in the south to hold out. By October, the young Charles XI led a 12,000 strong force into Scania and engaged the Danes at Lund on 4 December. At the start of the battle, the King was down to 7,500 men with a three to one ratio of cavalry to infantry. The Danes held a numerical advantage at 11,500 with a more balanced split between foot and horse. In a feat similar to that accomplished by his father, Charles marched his army across a frozen body of water to surprise the Danes. The next morning the battle was joined. Charles and his cavalry succeeded in breaking the Danish left and pursued them off the battlefield. The pursuit was so extensive that the King would not be heard from for hours. The Swedish left was just as unsuccessful and dispersed leaving the Danes with a numerical superiority against the dwindling Swedish centre. The Danish commander then made a startling decision. Instead of pressing his advantage, he paused to reorganise his lines which gave the exhausted Swedes valuable time. Charles XI reappeared on the battlefield from the north and the Danes turned to meet the new threat. This exposed their rear to the remains of the Swedish centre who, reinvigorated by the King's appearance, launched an attack. Caught from both sides, the Danish army scattered. It was a victory for the Swedes but both armies suffered tremendous casualties when viewed as a percentage of their starting numbers – the Swedes at 62 percent and the Danes at 69 percent.[5]

The war continued and ground into a stalemate with the Swedish army and the Danish navy proving too strong for their counterparts. By 1679 Louis XIV of France stepped in to negotiate on behalf of Sweden. He wanted to preserve his northern ally but did not consult with Swedish authorities when negotiating the treaties of Fontainebleau and Saint-Germain. Denmark and Brandenburg had to return any gains made with the exception of eastern Pomerania which the latter got to keep. For Sweden the losses were reversed but: "…it was without doubt the most humiliating and unrewarding series of campaigns in which Sweden had been involved since the Livonian War at the beginning of the century".[6] In addition, the Duke of Holstein-Gottorp was returned to his holdings and his *jus armorum*

The Battle of Lund. (Johan Philipp Lemke, Battle of Lund, Nationalmuseum (Erik Cornelius), public domain)

---

5   For an in-depth review of the Scanian War, refer to Michael Fredholm Von Essen, *Charles XI's War* (Warwick: Helion & Company, 2019).
6   Lockhart, *Sweden in the Seventeenth Century*, p.120.

eventually guaranteed by the English and Dutch via the Treaty of Altona in 1689. The "Holstein-Gottorp Question" lingered and proved to be a thorny issue for Charles XII in the first years of his reign.

Charles XI's education was not a priority for the regency and he therefore did not have the well-rounded schooling befitting a monarch of the late seventeenth century. He was dominated at court by his headstrong mother and even when declared of age he allowed the regency to continue the governing of the kingdom. It was the Scanian War that awakened him to the desperate situation Sweden found itself in and he thereafter resolved to fix the problems himself. Sweden "lost" the Scanian War because it could not sustain its army in northern Germany and suffered a string of naval defeats in the Baltic. While it managed to claw back its territories on the Scandinavian Peninsula, it had lost all German possessions to a combination of mismanagement and united enemies: "It had taken Sweden twenty years to acquire their German lands, they were lost in under three."[7] It was only thanks to high-handed French negotiations that the lost territories were returned. Despite the support, Charles XI developed a loathing of the French, a hesitancy to get too involved in alliances, and an understanding that the governing power of the monarch had to change. All three points were acted upon and would have a profound effect on Sweden and subsequently the reign of his son.

The introduction of absolutism, that is, the consolidation of all governing power with the monarchy, was in direct response to Sweden's crises of the 1670s. The high nobility, in their positions of power, had led Sweden into foreign and domestic fiascos that affected all classes of the population. The lower estates of the *Riksdag* determined that governance was best placed in the hands of the monarch since he, unlike the high nobility, would have their best interests in mind per his sworn coronation oath. The unified support of the lower estates allowed the *Riksdag* to approve the first stages of absolutism in 1680 and firmly set it in stone 13 years later by declaring: "Charles XI is by God, Nature, and the Crown's high hereditary right ... an absolute sovereign king, whose commands are binding upon all, and who is responsible to no one on earth for his actions, but has power and might at his pleasure, as a Christian king, to rule and govern his kingdom."[8] The *Riksdag* and the smaller, more private council were still part of the government but the King held overriding power which he insisted they remember: "You do not have the smallest share in my power. You are my council, which I can consult or not at my will."[9] When questioned about the plan to marry Ulrika Eleonora of Denmark, Charles angrily retorted: "We do not remember having committed the matter to you to discuss."[10]

It is noteworthy that Charles never abused the absolute powers given to him. He considered himself bound by the constitution and governing law. His

---

7   Robert I. Frost, *The Northern Wars 1558–1721* (Harlow: Longman, 2000), p.212.
8   Roberts, *Essays*, p.244.
9   Lockhart, *Sweden in the Seventeenth Century*, p.130.
10 Andrew F. Upton, *Charles XI and Swedish Absolutism* (Cambridge: Cambridge University Press, 1998), p.29.

commitment was further motivated by a deep religious desire to do right by his subjects. His steady hand, combined with the effects of the *reduktion*, resulted in financial stability for the kingdom – the opposite of what occurred in Denmark after the introduction of absolutism in 1660. At his death, Charles reduced the debt by 33 million silver *daler* and created a two million *daler* emergency fund.[11]

The regency government was retroactively found to have mismanaged affairs and was ordered to repay the losses. This burden fell on the wealthy high nobility, the De la Gardies of the Swedish world. The income was not sufficient and it was understood that the Crown did not have the funds to implement effective reforms. The solution was expanding upon the *reduktion* first launched by Charles X. As with the granting of absolute power, an alliance of the lower nobility and the lower estates (the clergy, burghers, and peasantry) in the *Riksdag* allowed Charles to push forward his *reduktion* plans. Eventually, 80 percent of alienated lands were returned to the Crown which broke the power of the nobility and returned vast sums to the state coffers.[12] The *reduktion* ultimately proved successful but it did foster resentment among those affected. There were no widespread uprisings in Sweden, however the policy was seen as particularly harsh in some of the Baltic provinces. Livonia was especially hard hit; where the Crown owned 1.25 percent of land in 1680, it had 72.3 percent by 1697.[13] This led to some disaffected nobles voicing their concerns, one Johann Reinhold Patkul in particular. While he was able to air his grievance to the King, it was dismissed outright by Charles. Smarting from the rebuke, Patkul began to secretly conspire with the old enemies of Sweden in the false hope of establishing an independent Livonia. It can be argued that he was one of the driving forces behind the creation of the anti-Swedish coalition and the start of the Great Northern War.

The Treaty of Lund in 1679, besides formally ending the Scanian War, saw a rare alliance between Denmark and Sweden against foreign interference in the Baltic. While the unity was short lived, the treaty is significant for finalising the betrothal of Princess Ulrika Eleonora, sister of the King of Denmark, to Charles XI of Sweden. Despite her Danish lineage, she quickly endeared herself to her husband and his kingdom. In his *An Account of Sweden*, English diplomat John Robinson describes Ulrika as: "a lady as eminent to piety, virtue, wisdom and all other qualities truly great and noble, as for her

Charles XI. (David Klocker Ehrenstrahl, Charles XI on Horse, 1676, Nationalmuseum (Erik Cornelius), public domain)

---

11 Roberts, *Essays*, p.250.
12 Jill Lisk, *The Struggle for Supremacy in the Baltic 1600–1725* (London: University of London Press, 1967), p.129.
13 Lockhart, *Sweden in the Seventeenth Century*, p.132.

birth and extraction. These, with her great charity to the poor, and liberality to all, have gained her the hearts of the whole nation, and surmounted the aversion they naturally have to those of her country."[14] Her compassion and support of Swedish prisoners during the Scanian War earned her the respect of the public. Charles grew quite fond of Ulrika and although he did reproach her when she challenged one of his policies, he remained devoted and loyal. He had no known mistresses, something that was later emulated by his son. Upon his own deathbed, Charles told his mother that he had not had a single happy day since his wife's passing.

Per historians of the old school view on Swedish imperialism, the aggressive wars of Gustavus and Charles X were meant for protection. Charles XI, and even Charles XII initially, tried to invert the state of affairs and forgo conflict altogether instead relying solely on existing treaties and favourable alliances. It was a delicate balance between commitment and reward; the alliance with France before the outbreak of the Scanian War served as a cautionary reminder. Staying uncommitted was hard to achieve in late seventeenth century Europe and Charles XI's firm resolution towards peace left Sweden politically isolated at the outbreak of the Great Northern War. Robinson again observes: "In relation to foreign affairs, it is apparently the interest of Sweden, to avoid all offensive war, as already being in the quiet possessions of as many conquered provinces on all sides as it can defend."[15] Sweden's lack of involvement on the Continent is partly responsible for Charles XII waging almost the entirety of the Great Northern War without longstanding allies.

Charles had enjoyed hunting and riding from an early age and in later years this translated to an interest in the military. His actions at Lund placed him among the ranks of Sweden's "warrior kings" yet his primary focus was military reform in peacetime. His restructuring of the recruitment of soldiers, known as the *indelningsverk* (allotment system) is, alongside the *reduktion*, his greatest achievement – remaining serviceable with only slight variations until the twentieth century.

Out of the 1682 *Riksdag* came the desire to abolish the *utskrivning* recruitment system which was in place since the days of Gustavus. The power for recruiting was placed in the hands of the nobility and put a higher burden on the lower classes. The *indelningsverk* introduced a contract based system where groups of farms were responsible for the upkeep of a professional soldier in return for service exemption and tax relief. This system will be discussed in further detail in Chapter 5. Charles recognised that Sweden could not afford the large military force it needed to defend its Baltic provinces and north German enclaves. The conditions of the Thirty Years' War were never replicated and foreign subsidies, notably from France, were not sustainable either. The *indelningsverk* reversed the monetary burden and allowed a standing army to be effectively housed and trained on home soil at minimal cost.

---

14   John Robinson, *An Account of Sweden,* 3rd edition (London: Tim Goodwin, 1717), p.33.
15   *Ibid.*, p.70.

Michael Roberts wrote that Charles XI was "ill equipped for the representative side of royalty" and based on the monarch's shyness, lack of public bravado, and love of plain clothing, he is correct. Charles displayed kingship through action. He toured his kingdom extensively to observe the growth of industry and root out any mismanagement of Crown initiatives. His domestic reforms focused on provincial administration, proper taxation, and the consolidation of the Church of Sweden. The province of Scania provides an example of his efforts, having implemented a series of pro-Swedish ordinances after the Scanian War. His work was so thorough that there was no desire from the local populace to support the Danes when they returned to Swedish shores after the disaster at Poltava.

Sweden in 1700

Throughout its imperial existence, Sweden defied the norms of being a great power in that it was a poor and under populated kingdom. This was true since the days of Gustavus Adolphus although the war booty transferred to Stockholm from the Continent, especially from Prague, helped in the attempt of making the capital the "Athens of the North". Stockholm would never obtain the glamour of Versailles or be as cosmopolitan as London; the home of the sovereign, Tre Kronor Castle, was still in its medieval iteration. At the turn of the eighteenth century, Stockholm was the largest city in the kingdom with a population around 60,000. For perspective, both London and Paris had populations over 500,000. Sweden and Finland combined totalled around 1.4 million people. If the Baltic provinces and northern German possessions are added in, the number grows to somewhere between 2.5 and 3 million. When again compared with the populations of other states, Sweden is dwarfed – France had nearly 21 million, Russia had 16 million, and England/Wales had 5.2 million. Of the three primary enemies, only Denmark-Norway was smaller with 1.5 million people. Territorially, peninsular Sweden was a large land mass and heavily forested. It had a very low population density and a reliance on individual farms and small communities to provide for themselves.

As previously mentioned, Sweden's economy was not particularly strong and relied heavily on the exploitation of raw natural resources. The primary

Stockholm, circa 1693. (Erik Dahlberg, Stockholm, 1693, Suecia Antiqua et Hodierna, public domain)

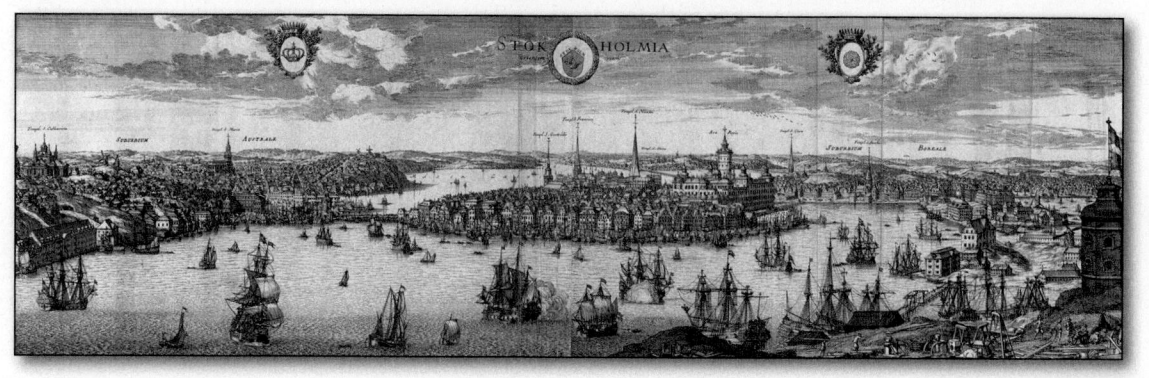

Tre Kronor Castle (Three Crowns) in 1661. By 1695 the castle's northern wing was redeveloped by Nicodemus Tessin the Younger and would serve as the template for today's existing palace. All but the north wing burned down in May, 1697. (Govert Dircksz Camphuysen, Tre Kronor Castle, 1661, Uppsala Art Museum, public domain)

exports were iron, tar, pitch and timber – all important materials required by seafaring states for the building of their navies. Copper and silver, in addition to iron, were heavily mined and the three metals constituted 80 percent of all exports in 1685. These goods would have been shipped out from ports along the Baltic coast via a growing mercantile fleet to Russia in the east or the French, English, or Dutch in the west. Sweden proper had to rely on the import of foodstuffs from its overseas territories which had more temperate climates and fertile soil. Livonia in particular functioned as the granary of the Empire by providing rye, malt, oat, and wheat.

The expanse of the empire across different ethnic areas of the European continent ensured that there were numerous spoken languages. German, not Swedish, proved to be the common tongue. The territories varied culturally as well: the Baltic provinces reflected their past existence as part of a de facto crusader state while the town houses of the German ports had richly ornamented facades that betrayed a link to the old Hanseatic League. There was little else in the way of pulling all the lands together under one aegis unlike what England/Great Britain would go on to achieve. The only factor that unified the entirety of the Swedish Empire was the Crown, and the personality of the wearer.

Chapter 2

Childhood: 1682–1697

Instructor Nordenhielm: "Let the prince share one of his dearest wishes."
Charles: "I wish that I would be fortunate enough to accompany my father into the field."[1]

On the morning of 17 June, 1682, Charles, future warrior king of Sweden, was born at the castle of Tre Kronor in Stockholm. Although the second child of the union between Charles XI and Ulrika Eleonora of Denmark, he was the first son and longed-for heir to the Swedish throne. The King was overjoyed and he recorded the momentous event with administrative care in his journal: "The 17th, which was on Saturday morning at a quarter to seven, My Wife was delivered and bore a son, God be eternally thanked and praised, he who helped her, may he soon restore her to her former health. My son Carel was born in the morning at a quarter to seven."[2]

The royal family into which Charles was born was a caring and mostly close-knit one. While the King was dour and prone to fits of Vasa rage, he maintained a strong sense of duty and devotion to his family and ensured that his children were afforded the best possible upbringing and education. The matriarch was not the Queen but rather the Dowager Queen, the King's mother, Hedvig Eleonora. She was the consort to Charles X and provided a continuous, stabilising presence at court having outlived her husband, son, and nearly grandson. The King always held her in deference and in courtly processions his mother came before his wife. This was widely commented upon, with John Robinson noting: "His respect to his

Charles XII, aged 2. (Anna Maria Ehrenstrahl, Karl XII, 1684, Nationalmuseum (Cecilia Heisser), public domain)

---
1   Ernst Carlson, *Die Eigenhändigen Briefe König Karls XII* (Berlin: Georg Reimer, 1894), p.440. A notation in Prince Charles's exercise book from 10 June 1689, aged nearly seven.
2   Ragnhild M. Hatton, *Charles XII of Sweden* (New York: Weybright and Talley, 1969), p.28.

The Royal Family (Charles XII in the centre, aged 11). (David Klocker Ehrenstrahl, Charles XI King of Sweden and Family, circa 1693, Nationalmuseum, public domain)

Charles XII with his mother and siblings. Note his four deceased brothers depicted as cherubs in the top left of the image. (David Klocker Ehrenstrahl, Queen Ulrika Eleonora and her Children, 1689, Nationalmuseum, public domain)

Charles XII with Hedvig Sophia and Ulrika Eleonora the Younger. (David Klocker Ehrenstrahl, Three Children of Charles XI, circa 1690, Nationalmuseum, public domain)

mother seems to equal if not exceed his kindness to his consort."[3] The young Charles, too, greatly respected his grandmother but as he aged he eventually wanted to separate himself from her designs and this may be one of the reasons for the hasty end of his minority under her watch.

Charles had six siblings in total although his four brothers all came and went in infancy. He had wished for a brother so that he could travel the world while his sibling ruled Sweden in his stead.[4] He was very fond of his elder sister Hedvig Sophia with whom he maintained a close relationship as they grew older. As playmates, they were the subject of several court paintings and many of Charles's early letters from the war were addressed to her as his most private confidant. Besides the deaths of his parents, that of Hedvig in 1708 affected him more than any other. As a result of her loss, his closeness with his younger sister and only remaining sibling, Ulrika Eleonora (the Younger), increased.[5]

3   Robinson, *An Account*, p.35.
4   Hatton, *Charles XII*, p.28.
5   Since the daughter was named after the mother, she is often styled as Ulrika Eleonora the Younger.

CHILDHOOD: 1682-1697

Charles XII with his beloved elder sister Hedvig Sophia. (David Klocker Ehrenstrahl, Charles XII and Hedvig Sophia, 1687, Nationalmuseum, public domain)

Toy whistles used by the prince. (Toy Whistles, Royal Armouries, public domain)

Charles was the pride of both of his parents. His mother, Ulrika Eleonora, was gentle and kind with a penchant for morality and religious observance. Within the royal family she served as a foil to the King's introverted nature and coldness. It was in her care that Charles began his education, learning prayers and studying the Bible – he was later on observed to kneel in prayer before and after making critical decisions and he maintained a Bible at his bedside in the field. Her maxims were duly passed on to him and he would honour these throughout his life: be generous to your subjects, be cautious of false tales, hear both sides of an argument, keep your word.[6] On the latter, we have a recollection from his younger sister: the prince was placed on a chair by his nursemaid and made to promise that he would not move from the spot until she returned. When the Queen arrived earlier than expected to take Charles to prayers, she became flustered by the boy's unwillingness to move. It was only when the nursemaid returned that he got up and left with his family. This anecdote is but one small example of Charles's commitment to the teachings of his parents and the promises he made to them. Voltaire used the King as a shining example of noble virtues and Charles's "commendable firmness of purpose"[7] is indeed praiseworthy, but the inflexible logic had an easy way of slipping into obstinacy much to the detriment, however unintentional, of the army and Sweden in later years.

---

6   Hatton, *Charles XII*, p.52.
7   Robert N. Bain, *Charles XII and the Collapse of the Swedish Empire 1682-1719* (New York: G.P. Putnam's Sons, 1902), p.21.

Unlike the child-rearing protocols of other European monarchies, the young prince stayed close to his family. He was not immediately removed and shipped off to a separate power base with a household and governor and educated separately. Instead, his early years were spent in the company of women – his mother, grandmother, and sisters.[8] He ate with his family and learned and played with them as well. By all accounts, it was a happy childhood. As he grew older, circumstances saw to it that he would spend more time with his father and male tutors and he eventually received his own staff, rooms, and tasks by 1689.

When the time came to begin the formal education of the prince, Ulrika Eleonora had a say in the selection of his first tutor. She chose a professor from Uppsala University, Andreas Narcopensis, who was then ennobled to Nordenhielm to be symbolically fit for the task. He would be at the prince's side from 1686 until his own death in 1694. His first responsibility was teaching Charles how to read and write and he found a willing and responsive pupil. One of the oldest surviving letters from the prince is addressed to Admiral Hans Wachtmeister, thanking him for the gift of a toy ship. A side note indicated that the prince himself, aged seven, thought up and wrote the letter.[9]

History and languages were also emphasised early. The lives of Caesar and Alexander were favourite readings as were the exploits of the prince's immediate predecessors. Charles became fluent in German and well versed in Latin and French although he spoke the latter less frequently owing to his father's own aversion.[10] During his time in exile in the Ottoman Empire he even picked up some Italian and Turkish, thus further showing a propensity for languages. Philosophy was also planned but these studies had to be abandoned when kingship was thrust upon him earlier than expected. Only some downtime at Lund in 1717 allowed him to indulge in the subject. Ultimately, Charles is not Erik Geijer's "illiterate warrior king" and the myth that the King was only knowledgeable in the art of war can be debunked. Rather, his education was well rounded and typical for a European monarch of the time.

Charles also possessed a strong memory that he displayed on several occasions. While in Saxony Charles visited the battlefield of Lützen, and just like Napoleon in 1813 could recall in detail the events of the battle and the units that took part. After his victory at Pultusk in April 1703, Charles received a coded letter from General Carl Gustaf Rehnskiöld but had forgotten his cypher key. In spite of this, Charles was able to read the letter and then replied flawlessly.

As the instructions advanced, Carl Magnus Stuart was appointed to assist in the teaching of mathematics and the art of fortifications. He was a Scottish descendant who entered the service of Sweden, and with Charles XI's support spent time studying Marshal Vauban's defensive designs.[11] His lessons quickly captured the attention of the young prince who came to enjoy

---

8 This may, in part, explain the formation of his attitudes towards women, love, marriage etc.
9 Carlson, *Eigenhändigen Briefe*, p.349.
10 Robinson, *An Account*, p.32.
11 George A. Sinclair, 'The Scottish Officers of Charles XII', *The Scottish Historical Review* 21:83 (1924), p.180.

CHILDHOOD: 1682–1697

Drawing by Charles XII, aged 7. (Charles XII, Fighting Around a Tent, 1689, Nationalmuseum (Erik Cornelius), public domain)

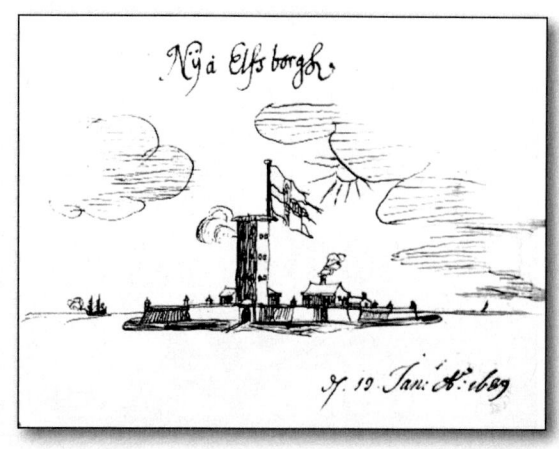

Sketch of Elfsborg. (Drawings by Prince Carl, 1689, Riksarkivet)

them more than any other topic in his weekly studies. Charles's surviving exercise books are full of pencil sketches depicting firing mortars, angled fortifications, and cannon batteries. Charles dove further into mathematics, considering anyone not inclined to the subject as but "half a person".

The first tragedy to impact the prince's life was the death of his beloved mother. Perhaps due to the strain of seven pregnancies in quick succession, the Queen died in the summer of 1693 when Charles was 12 years old. The prince was devastated and took to his bed with a fever. Her maxims and memories remained with Charles and she would continue to be mentioned in his letters:

Sketch of mortar firing. (Drawings by Prince Carl, 1689, Riksarkivet)

> In these sad times, due to the all too hasty and deplorable death of her blessed Majesty, I can only think of one great consolation – that with such luck, on the 24th of November, Sweden became whole with the birth of so great a king. I wish to see this day appear many more times, as it already has, and that the circumstances of the day be better than they are now.[12]

Even at one of the last meetings with his sister in 1716, Charles could not hold back tears when he referred to his mother.

Due to the Queen's death, Charles became even closer to his father and would accompany the King on a variety of tours and inspections as part of his regular duties. While not an academic himself, the King decided to teach his son through actions. Charles XI shouldered the burden of monarchy and worked tirelessly for the benefit of his subjects. He would rise daily around three to four in the morning to begin his tasks. It was a routine he maintained with no exception, even after his

Sketch of a pikeman. (Drawings by Prince Carl, 1689, Riksarkivet)

---

12 Carlson, *Eigenhändigen Briefe*, p.1.

A young Charles XII on horseback. (David Klocker Ehrenstrahl, Charles on Horseback, Nationalmuseum, public domain)

wedding night. This dedication had an impact on the prince who adopted a similar work ethic both at home and in the field.

Like his father, Charles was most comfortable on horseback. His first public appearance on a horse was at the age of four albeit with support at the reins. He quickly learned to hold his own and enjoyed any outing that required riding. The act of hard riding was also a self-devised remedy used to cure any illness. Similarly, it offered a means of escape and councillors would often have to wait on Charles as he rode away from Stockholm until fatigue forced him to return. During the war, ambassadors and diplomats would place themselves along the King's riding routes in an effort to obtain an audience as that offered the best chance of success.

Hunting was another enjoyment shared between father and son and an obvious start to martial practice. The paternal pride with which the King describes his son's exploits is plainly visible in his journal entries. Charles shot three deer in 1690, a wolf in 1692, and a bear in 1694 when he was only 12. Later on, Charles eschewed the musket and would go on bear hunts with sticks, prods, and nets in an effort to capture the bear alive – it was thought to be more of a challenge.

As part of his military reforms, Charles XI would review his regiments on a regular basis as they moved out to muster and train. At Djurgården in Stockholm, the King and prince reviewed the Lifeguard, testing everything from weapons to the cloth of the uniform to ensure the unit was fit to deploy should a war break out. They also toured cannon foundries and watched ships be launched in the harbour of Stockholm until the navy relocated to its newly completed base at Karlskrona.

As prince Charles grew older, and in his initial years as king, he began to participate in staged military drills with the Drabants. The Drabants were an offshoot of the Lifeguard, an elite hand-selected cavalry unit of about 200 men where the lowest rank was the equivalent of a captain. This unit provided a strong corps of officers who would eventually take on command positions in other regiments. They served as a bodyguard to the monarch and would be found close to Charles in the thick of the fighting during the Great Northern War. The regular trainings were meant to establish rapport and discipline as well as test strategy and competency. Because of this, the scenarios were quite varied and intense given the number of injuries that occurred. A report to the King of Denmark during the reign of Charles XI mentioned the dangers of these wargames: "… the king had a horse shot dead under him, a boat blew up with twenty men … a bridge collapsed with some cavalry on it and several of them were injured".[13] Cavalry actions had the men ride without saddles

---

13 Upton, *Charles* XI, p.20.

Karlberg Palace, Stockholm. This palace was a childhood favourite of Charles XII and his family. (Author's collection)

and attempt to de-horse the "enemy" using branches and twigs as swords. Mock naval battles were conducted on small ships outfitted with hoses and pumps to serve as the cannons. Winter provided the cheapest training ground as the snow was plentiful and used in the construction of forts and as "ammunition". Charles was a quick learner and came to respect the opinions of his mentors, Arvid Horn and Rehnskiöld.

Charles's education and training would come to an abrupt halt with the death of his father. In his last years, the King had complained of terrible stomach pains which grew worse with the passing months. The autopsy after his death revealed a stomach cancer that spread throughout his torso. Still, the King pressed on with his duties to the last to ensure the stability of the kingdom for his underage son. The prince spent two hours at the King's deathbed to heed advice and counsel one last time. The exchange between the two is unknown as no papers survive nor did Charles ever speak directly of it. It is probable that Charles made several promises to his dying father which may explain certain decisions he made later on in life. One of the best inferences is on the topic of war: with Charles XI having the Scanian War thrust upon him and having seen the bloodshed at the Battle of Lund, he urged Charles to avoid war "unless dragged in by the hair". Those with a negative view of Charles XII would be quick to note that this advice fell upon deaf ears, but it lends credence to the first half of the King's most famous quote attributed by Voltaire: "I have resolved never to start an unjust war, but only to end a legitimate one by defeating my enemies."[14] Given the flurry of

---

14 Voltaire, *History*, p.51.

Charles XII, aged 4. (Elias Brenner, Charles XII at Four Years of Age, 1686, Erik Cornelius, Nationalmuseum)

Charles XII. (Elias Brenner, Charles XII as the Crown Prince, Erik Cornelius, Nationalmuseum)

diplomacy and the hesitancy to sign defensive treaties until the last possible moment at the outbreak of the Great Northern War, it appears that Charles attempted to follow the form of his father.

At the age of 15 Charles was an orphan. He inherited his father's councillors and advisors and had an overbearing grandmother ready to guide him through his minority. Thanks to Charles XI's tireless work, he bestowed upon his son a kingdom in an advantageous state of peace – the Crown was solvent and had a stronger centralised authority, local government was stabilised and corruption reduced, there were no signs of a discontented population and the treasury was full. More importantly, the late King ensured that Charles was raised on the concepts of absolutism and impressed upon him his work ethic, policies of government, and thoughts on war. Charles XII would need to draw upon everything as he was about to assume control of an empire that had made many enemies during its ascendancy.

Chapter 3

A King Without Concern: 1697–1700

"It pleases me … that my dogs, during my absence, are able to defend the palace. The day before yesterday we were on a bear hunt and managed to kill a bear whose paws I have sent along. Otherwise we amuse ourselves with all sorts of things and tomorrow I hope to shoot another bear…"

Charles XII writing to his sister, Ulrika Eleonora, 1699[1]

Charles XII, aged 15. (David Klocker Ehrenstrahl, Charles XII at the Age of Fifteen, 1697, Nationalmuseum, public domain)

As the kingdom prepared to bury another of its warrior kings, Charles and his advisors had to grapple with the concept of absolutism first introduced in 1680 and the requirements of the Swedish constitution. The latter outlined the appropriate age for a monarch's accession. A monarch was no longer considered a minor once they reached the age of 18, however the legal age was technically 15. Charles was right at the minimum age. In terms of precedent, every previous monarch waited until the age of 17 or 18 to be crowned and rule independently.[2] Having had his own experience with a long minority, Charles XI laid out a plan to ensure his son would be properly supported for the remainder of his.

According to his father's will, the prince was assigned a regency council of six members, with his grandmother, Hedvig Eleonora, at the head. She was the only member to possess two votes and thus break any ties and affect critical decisions with the royal family's best interests in mind. The other members were learned administrators and councillors including Bengt Oxenstierna, a relative of the famous minister who worked hand in hand with Gustavus Adolphus

---
1 Carlson, *Eigenhändigen Briefe*, p. 33.
2 Hatton, *Charles XII*, p.69.

Charles XII in royal regalia, 1697. (David Klocker Ehrenstrahl, Charles XII, 1697, Nationalmuseum, public domain)

when Sweden first rose to international prominence. The council was tasked with assisting Charles on matters of state and guiding him through the quagmire of European foreign policy. Charles carried on in the same vein as his father, rising daily around five in the morning to attend to the needs of his kingdom. On some decisions he could be decisive but on other matters of less importance, or those where he lacked experience, he remained silent much to the dismay of his council who could not act without his word. The topic simply had to be tabled until a later point. The council struggled internally as well with members splitting into different factions based on self-interests. On international relations, there were questions of Sweden retaining its older alliance with France or siding with the Maritime Powers of England and the Netherlands. Continuing support for the small duchy of Holstein-Gottorp also came up with the two most prominent members, the Dowager Queen and Oxenstierna, being in favour.

For all of its good intentions, the regency would barely last eight months. Internal squabbles and a desire to remove Hedvig Eleonora's scheming, perhaps expressed by Charles himself, were contributing factors. The question of absolutism proved to be the most pressing. The councillors did not want to be held responsible for their actions once Charles came of age and could retroactively call them to account – there are earlier examples of Charles threatening his tutors with punishments once he became king.[3] There was also a worry that members of the nobility, still smarting from the harsh *reduktion* policies of Charles XI, would try to undermine the royal prerogative. Some nobles figured that Charles could be more easily manipulated when he was ruling for himself, away from the authority figures put in place by his father. Conversely, members of the other Estates thought that Charles could counter the overmighty nobility by being declared of age and enforcing his will. The push to declare Charles of age therefore came from multiple directions and culminated at a meeting of the *Riksdag* on 8 November, 1697. The first estate pressed the other three to acknowledge Charles's majority and this was agreed upon en masse with only small resistance. The regency would stay in place until the funeral of Charles XI on the 24th.

With Charles XI laid to rest in the Carolean vault of the church on Riddarholmen, thoughts turned to the coronation of the son. Absolutism once again proved to be a topic of contention as Charles was the first Swedish king born to absolutism and this needed to be adequately conveyed in the ceremony. There was, however, no precedent in Sweden and the changes made to the resulting coronation were a complete break from tradition. Given that Charles was not crowned, it was not a coronation at all and was instead

---

[3] Which could also be seen as a precocious boy aware of his princely status.

Courtyard of Wrangels Palace. (Jacques Foucquet the Younger, Charles XII's Coronation, 1697, Nationalmuseum, public domain)

classified as an "anointment". On 13 December members of the Estates huddled in the cold courtyard of Wrangels Palace to individually swear their oaths of fealty.[4] This was notably done before the King was to swear his oath in return. The next day, the royal procession wound its way from the palace to the *Storkyrkan*, Stockholm's cathedral. Charles, still in mourning black, was mounted on his horse with a canopy carried above him and a train of dignitaries following behind. Most shockingly, he had emerged from Wrangels with the crown already on his head. At the cathedral, he would remove and replace the crown himself during the anointment ceremony. The *kungsorsakran*, king's oath, was also omitted. Everyone present could not miss the intended message – Charles XII, as absolute king of Sweden, was crowned by God and therefore answerable to God alone.[5]

Those who thought Charles would stray from the policies of his father were to be disappointed though the King did show some differentiation on two minor matters. He was not parsimonious at all – he enjoyed discreetly slipping small bags of coins into courtier's pockets. In the field, soldiers were sumptuously rewarded for acts of kindness and bravery. His willingness to spend coincided with an increase in royal patronage of the arts. New plays and music were commissioned and Charles displayed a keen interest in architectural design with grandiose plans for modernising Stockholm that were revisited later in life whenever he had a moment to spare.

---

4   Wrangels palace served as the royal residence due to the Tre Kronor palace burning down in May – an ominous sign to those of a superstitious persuasion.
5   Sebastian Olden-Jørgensen, 'Ceremonial Interaction across the Baltic around 1700', *Scandinavian Journal of History*, 28 (2003), p.246. The regnal number XII did not indicate that Charles was the twelfth of that name. He was actually the sixth. The incorrect numbering dates back to Charles IX who adopted his regnal number based on a reading of Swedish mythology.

Wrangels Palace today. (Author's collection)

Decorated interior of Storkyrkan for the coronation of Gustav III. It would have been similarly dressed for Charles XII. ((Decoration of Storkyrkan, Stockholm, for the Coronation of Gustav III, Olof Fridsberg, Nationalmuseum, public domain)

Amid his work on domestic reforms, which he came to enjoy above all else, Charles put an emphasis on strengthening Sweden's defences. Under his watch, the naval base at Karlskrona was finished, thus completing a move begun by his father to remove the Royal Navy from its home port in Stockholm and place it further south in a better strategic position. Fortresses in the Baltic provinces were surveyed, updated, and reinforced including those at Riga and Narva – a fortuitous move given where the first blows of the Great Northern War were to land.

The decision was made to continue the alliance with Holstein-Gottorp and this was strengthened with the marriage of Charles's beloved sister Hedvig Sophia to Duke Frederick IV. Talk of marriage also fell upon Charles and numerous partners were suggested. The primary candidate was Princess Sophia of Denmark, an option that emulated the union of his parents. In the political realm, this was also a way to placate rival Denmark and offset the Holstein-Gottorp marriage. Despite a lot of well-intentioned diplomacy, the marriage never came to fruition

A KING WITHOUT CONCERN: 1697–1700

and Charles would remain a bachelor for the rest of his life despite the pleading of his advisors and grandmother.[6]

Perhaps the most notable, or at least most talked about event in Charles's first years as king was the "Gottorp Fury" or "Mad Period". When Duke Frederick IV arrived in Stockholm ahead of his marriage to Hedvig Sophia, Charles was drawn to the Duke's cavalier attitude and lost himself in amusements that were considered scandalous by the court. The young king and duke would conduct noisy, late night rides through the streets of Stockholm, snatched wigs from courtier's heads, engaged in dangerous sports, and took turns shooting out windows of the palace. A captured bear was also brought into the palace and made drunk on wine before it stumbled out of a window and plummeted to its death. Even with the latter example, there is little evidence to support some of the more extreme reports that were being passed around. It must be remembered that Charles at this point was still an adolescent complete with an as of yet untapped rebelliousness which in lesser instances manifested as condescending behaviour towards certain members of the nobility and elder ministers. After the Duke's marriage and the couple's departure for Holstein-Gottorp, Charles's conduct reverted to its more taciturn state.

Foreshadowing his risk-taking on campaign, Charles willingly exposed himself to greater dangers while hunting. He grew tired of shooting bears from a distance and instead attempted to capture the animals alive with little more than wooden clubs and pitchforks. One such hunt is recalled by Adlerfeld:

Frederick IV, Duke of Holstein-Gottorp. (David von Coln, Frederick IV of Holstein-Gottorp, 1734, Nationalmuseum, public domain)

Grave of Pompe, the first of several dogs owned by Charles XII with that name. The burial is located in the park behind Karlberg Palace. (Author's collection)

> The king feared not to attack one of a prodigious size with only a stick in his hand; the bear had already torn off his peruke, and was going to trample on him, when he found means to escape from his clutches and convey himself out of danger ... but with the help of the hunters who accompanied him, he overcame the bear and himself assisted in binding him.[7]

War would bring an end to the outings.

---

6   See Appendix I.
7   Adlerfeld, *Genuine History*, p.17

The Anti-Swedish Coalition

Sweden gained its Baltic empire through foreign intervention but the aggressive wars fought by Charles X revealed weaknesses in the foundation.[8] Charles XI recognised the need for reform at home and focused on consolidation after decades of expansion. He succeeded in keeping the kingdom out of the squabbles plaguing late seventeenth century Europe: "Sweden attempted, therefore, to pursue a policy of maintaining the balance between the Habsburg and Bourbon blocs. But in the long run this was not a policy calculated to inspire respect."[9] Enemies and prospective allies alike begrudged Sweden's position. The former rued the loss of territories to Sweden and constantly schemed to see them returned while the latter wished for more definitive commitment in conflicts such as the Nine Years' War. Isolationism gave Sweden 20 years of peace but left it devoid of allies and saddled with a military system that was designed for the defence of home soil and not the lengthy overseas campaigns of decades past.

The end of the 1690s saw a series of deaths and accessions among some of the important monarchies of Europe.[10] Most notably for the Baltic region, Christian V of Denmark gave way to Frederik IV in 1699, Augustus of Saxony was elected King of Poland in 1697, and Peter I became sole ruler of Russia in 1696 with the death of his half-brother Ivan V. These rulers inherited their predecessor's enmities and conflicts with Sweden and quickly found common ground for a joint venture against a young, inexperienced king who just assumed the crown himself.

Denmark was Sweden's oldest enemy and primary antagonist until Russia superseded it as the bogeyman in Swedish consciousness. The latest blows fell in the bitterly contested Scanian War from 1675–1679 which resulted in Sweden retaining the province of Scania and continuing its exemption from the Sound Dues. For the Danes, the recovery of Scania was a long held desire but the larger aggravation was Sweden's continued support for the Duchy of Holstein-Gottorp located on Denmark's southern border. The Duke and Danish king had a complicated history over the jurisdiction of interspersed lands in Schleswig and Holstein which belonged to either the King, the Duke, or both. Sweden became involved via the marriage of Charles X to Hedvig Eleonora in 1654 and from then on support for Holstein-Gottorp was a cornerstone of Swedish foreign policy. Denmark was uncomfortable with having an enemy ally in such proximity and wanted to reassert its rights on the duchy. Duke Frederick IV, meanwhile, was engaged in the building of fortresses on ducal territory which further provoked Copenhagen. Immediately after the death of Charles XI, the Danes invaded the duchy and razed several of these border forts. Sweden responded by sending troops to help rebuild them and Charles XII made the Duke commander in chief of Swedish forces in Northern Germany. The aforementioned marriage of

---

8 Roberts, *Essays*, p.228.
9 Sven Lundkvist, 'The Experience of Empire: Sweden as a Great Power', in Michael Roberts (ed.), *Sweden's Age of Greatness* (New York: St. Martin's Press, 1973), p.34.
10 Frost, *Northern* Wars, pp.226–227.

Princess Hedvig Sophia to the Duke further strengthened the alliance between Sweden and the duchy. It was hoped, however, that the crisis would peter out like it had done before.

Running concurrently to mounting Danish tension was an effort to sign a treaty between Sweden and the Maritime Powers of England and the Netherlands. Not only could their combined navies keep that of the Danes in check, but the two nations were also guarantors of the Altona Agreement which supported Holstein-Gottorp's *jus armorum*. England and the Netherlands also maintained trade interests in the Baltic and did not want a war to interfere with imports amid growing tensions with France over the Spanish succession. Charles tried to adhere to the policy of his father – that is to remain aloof of obligations to alliances that required direct involvement on the Continent. It was only after Denmark marched 20,000 men into Holstein-Gottorp to launch the Great Northern War in 1700 that Charles ratified the treaty with the Maritime Powers.

Frederick Augustus (1670–1733), Elector of Saxony, was elected King of the Polish-Lithuanian Commonwealth in 1697 and assumed the name of Augustus II. A vain and pompous man, Augustus was known for his physical strength, patronage of the arts, and his many mistresses. He was not much of a soldier, but always sought opportunities to expand his power base. Augustus wanted to make his newly won Polish crown hereditary and believed that reconquering Swedish Livonia would give him the political capital to deal with rivals among the nobility and gain support from the Polish population at large. Goading him on was Johann Reinhold Patkul, the exiled Swedish subject and Livonian noble who wanted to free Livonian territory from Swedish rule and sought to use the anti-Swedish coalition as the means to do so. Through diplomacy, backroom dealings, and some false reporting, he mediated between Frederik IV, Augustus, and Peter I.

Initial communications between Augustus and Sweden were cordial given that Augustus and Charles were cousins via their mothers – both princesses of Denmark. The Swedish government suspected duplicity from the Danes and Russians but the resulting actions of Augustus deeply

Frederik IV of Denmark. (Hyacinthe Rigaud, Frederik IV of Denmark, 1693, National Gallery of Denmark, public domain)

Augustus "the Strong" of Saxony. (Louis de Silvestre, Augustus II, National Museum Poznan, public domain)

Peter the Great (1672-1725), Czar of Russia. (Anonymous, Rijksmuseum, public domain)

troubled Charles who placed a very high value on honour and keeping one's word. The surprise invasion of Livonia and creation of a third front greatly vexed Charles who from then on was driven by a sense of righteousness against the Saxons and demanded justice from his misguided cousin. This desire may be a factor to consider, however small, when explaining Sweden's immediate push into the Polish-Lithuanian Commonwealth following the winter of 1700. Augustus was not highly regarded in Charles's letters. Only after he was deposed and honour satisfied did Charles extend courtesy and pleasantries with his relative. Nevertheless, distrust lingered and Charles slowed his exit from Saxony as he waited on further guarantees via the Treaty of Altranstädt to ensure that the Elector would be kept in his place.

Czar Peter I (1672–1725) was able to claim sole governance of Russia for himself at the age of 24. He was possessed with his efforts to modernise Russia and over the course of his reign implemented a series of sweeping economic and social reforms. These did not go uncontested and Peter dealt ruthlessly with detractors and the resulting rebellions. He had concluded that a strong navy and access to ports along key trade routes were critical to his goals. Unfortunately for him, Swedish victories in the late sixteenth and early seventeenth centuries cut Russia off from the Baltic Sea. The lands of Ingria, Karelia, and Kexholm were all current Swedish holdings. To the south, the Black Sea ports were controlled by the Ottoman Empire. The Russo-Turkish War was an ongoing conflict and despite earlier defeats in the Crimean theatre, Peter launched his Azov campaign in 1695. His truce with the Ottomans in 1700 allowed him to retain the captured fortress of Azov and transfer his forces to the north. Animosity between the two powers was stoked anew after 1709 when the machinations of Charles, by that point a refugee king, sought to utilise the Ottoman army as a replacement for the one he lost at Poltava.

In 1697 Peter began his 18-month excursion across Western Europe which became known as the *Great Embassy*. His primary objective, though ultimately unsuccessful, was to drum up support for an alliance against the Ottoman Empire. Secondly, Peter wanted to immerse himself in western culture and learn about art, architecture, and industry. He served as an apprentice in a Dutch shipyard and toured armouries in England. He returned home with maps, blueprints, and new customs which were used in his modernisation efforts. The orders to don western (French) clothing at court and to cut off long beards proved to be particularly distressing to the traditionalists.

On his return to Russia to deal with a rebellion of the Streltsy, Peter met with Augustus to discuss plans for their invasion of Swedish territories. The two monarchs would remain in frequent communication as the war progressed though they never fully trusted one another. During the first nine years of the war, they would leverage their fleeting advantageous positions on one another to extract commitments of men and money.

Through the efforts of Patkul, multiple defensive pacts were signed between the three powers. However, it was not until September 1699 that an offensive treaty (Preobrazhenskoe) was signed between Saxony and Russia. Denmark, with its new king Frederik IV, joined the following January. After a year and a half of secret meetings and mediation, the anti-Swedish states had congealed into a unified coalition although the aforementioned mistrust seemingly lingered under the surface. Saxony was to invade Livonia while Denmark was to move into Holstein-Gottorp and then Scania on the Swedish mainland. Russia was to occupy Ingria and thus open three fronts which Sweden could not cover at once. Swedish diplomats, though concerned for a potential breakout of conflict, had remained cautiously optimistic that at least Saxony would remain peaceful.

True to the agreement, Saxon troops marched into Livonia in February and captured Dünamünde in March while Riga defiantly held out. Danish troops moved into ducal territory by 11 March. Russia remained motionless for the time being as a key provision of the treaty required Peter to first have peace with the Ottomans before committing his forces to Ingria. Russia would eventually declare war in August, with Peter citing mistreatment at Riga while incognito on his *Great Embassy* as a flimsy pretext for the attack. The goal was for all three states to strike at the same time but this did not occur. The staggered attacks gave Sweden a small opportunity to quickly eliminate at least one foe and then fight the remainder of the war on two fronts.

Charles was out on a bear hunt when he was first told of the breakout of hostilities. As noted by the accompanying French ambassador, the King seemed resigned but determined: "We shall soon oblige them to return back the same way they came."[11] At this point, only Denmark and Saxony had launched their attacks and the latter must have come as a shock to Charles although he did not show it. Sweden had already placed itself on a war footing since the end of 1699 when reports of an impending Russian invasion circulated. Upon his return to the capital, Charles ordered the mustering of the provincial regiments and started preparations for war. He would take with him a "Chancery in the Field" composed of diplomats and administrators to help him govern Sweden from afar. These men also served as a sounding board for future military plans and from time to time acted as voices of reason. By 1706, the chancery experienced severe turnover due to deaths or reassignments and Charles appointed military men such as Magnus Stenbock and Arvid Horn to fill the vacancies. With his affairs set in order, Charles left Stockholm in April of 1700. He could not have realised that the war would occupy the remainder of his life and that he would never see the capital again.

---

11 Adlerfeld, *Genuine History*, p.17

Chapter 4

The Carolean Army under Charles XII

"His army is his family. He cares for it, loves it, derives his pleasure from it. The soldier, the officer, for his part, devoted through duty and veneration, cherishes the prince, follows him, imitates him, and spills his blood with ardour and valour, convinced that whenever the conqueror wishes to strike he must vanquish."

Jean-Léonor Grimarest on Charles XII, 1706[1]

The prestige of Swedish arms reached tremendous heights and desperate lows during the *Stormaktstiden*. The reforms and tactical innovations of Gustavus Adolphus in the Thirty Years' War created a force to be feared. Marching from Wolgast in the north to Ingolstadt in the south and to Prague in the east, the armies of Sweden were occasionally checked but never so wholly defeated that they relinquished their reputation. Years later, Charles X secured further victories by embroiling the army in the Polish *Deluge* and famously crossed the frozen Belts against the Danes in the Second Northern War. These successes allowed the Swedish Empire to reach its greatest territorial extent by 1660.

And yet, the very size and success of the empire also threatened its collapse. In the brief times of peace, Sweden's slow economy could not support the cost of the large army now required by its first rate power position. War on foreign soil was the only way to pay for such debts: "The 1650s might have shown that Sweden could not afford war; it appeared that it could not afford peace either."[2] A lack of funding and maintenance during the regency of Charles XI allowed the army to whither. Over the course of the seventeenth century, the Crown had continuously lost its land holdings to the nobility and at the most extreme, roughly two thirds of former Crown property belonged to noble owners. The lack of Crown lands meant a lack of farms and a lack of farms meant a lack of taxation and soldiers. With the shocking "loss" to Brandenburg at Fehrbellin in 1675, the inability to generate victories in Germany, and struggling to maintain naval supremacy,

---

1   Jean-Léonor de Grimarest, *Les Campagnes de Charles XII, roi de Suede*, vol. 1 (Stockholm, 1707), p.13.
2   Frost, *Northern* Wars, p.209.

the prestige of Swedish arms hit a low after the Scanian War that Charles XI determined to rectify. Outside observers were also aware of the diminished military machine: "

> But this establishment had been in a great measure corrupted ... the standing forces of the kingdom have been augmented, yet not so effectually established as its necessities required ... the regiments were very thin, and recruits extremely difficult; nor were the officer's salaries punctually paid, as to enable them to be in readiness on all occasions.[3]

The successful introduction of absolutism in Denmark in 1660 did not go unnoticed. It allowed for the full weight of the state to be put behind the construction and mobilisation of the army. Charles XI intended to do the same and upon direct questioning at the *Riksdag* held in 1680, he set the foundations for an absolute monarchy in Sweden and the start of the *reduktion*. The *reduktion* allowed for the resumption of Crown lands, in effect wresting them back from the hands of the nobility. By the end of the policy, the nobility only held one third of lands as before. These newly reacquired lands increased the flow of money into state coffers and, in part, allowed for the success of the *indelningsverk*: "As all the common soldiers are thus provided for at the country's charge, so all officers, both the horse and foot, are maintained by the King, who hath appropriated so much of the lands lately reunited or formerly belonging to the Crown, to that purpose."[4]

The *indelningsverk*, or allotment system, was expanded upon that from the time of Gustavus Adolphus.[5] The Scanian War had shown that losses could not be adequately replaced through the previous method of conscription known as *utskivning*. It simply could not guarantee a steady flow of recruits as it relied on periodic – rather than continuous – conscription and since there were no defined quotas, this left the peasantry susceptible to unfair manipulation by government officials. Changes were made in 1682 which implemented a modified conscription system that was already in use in the province of Dalarna. Farmers would now sign a contract obligating them to provide a single soldier for their respective provincial regiment. The strength in manpower had to be maintained at a designated level in peace or war with an infantry regiment comprising around 1,200 men and a cavalry regiment around 1,000. If a soldier died at home or abroad, the farmers were responsible for furnishing the replacement. The allocations were now, at least, predictable. As the Great Northern War progressed, demand sometimes required for more farms to band together to provide an additional soldier and so keep the burden manageable. These men would then serve in the designated *tremmanning*, *fyrmanning*, and *femmanning* regiments.[6] The *indelningsverk* was not used outside of Sweden and Finland. In the Baltic

---

3 Robinson, *An Account*, p.55.
4 *Ibid.*, p.57.
5 Therefore the system introduced by Charles XI is known as the "new" or "later" *indelningsverk*.
6 *Tre* (3) would indicate three farms needing to join together to provide the additional soldier and resources.

Provinces and German territories, mercenary regiments filled the gap and would serve on garrison duty in the many fortresses and towns. The state took a more active involvement in their pay and maintenance.

Per the *indelningsverk* contract, an infantryman was recruited and supported by a file, or rota, of two farms. He was given room and board, his uniform and kit, and a tract of land in exchange for working on the farm when off duty. When the soldier left for training or war, his wife would work in his place. For their part, the farmer and his family were exempt from service. Members of the cavalry were raised in the same way but either the rota was larger to support the additional costs of horse and man or the farm was more affluent. In one further distinction, the farm was exempt from taxation and called a *rusthåll*.[7] As a result of Charles XI's modifications to recruitment, Sweden's soldiers were quartered with the population at large and their cost of upkeep was evenly distributed. Per the contract, the peasant farmers and soldiers all knew what was expected of them and the Crown ensured that no one file carried an undue burden.

The new *indelningsverk* addressed the major issue of maintaining and paying for a standing army in times of peace. It was, however, meant to be a deterrent and functioned best if the war was defensive and fought on home soil. With the Great Northern War lasting 21 years and progressing deeper into the European continent, the Swedes reverted to their old tendency of "war feeding war" and the system was stretched to its very limits: "this in peaceable times will not be so chargeable as it is in times of war; when men will be unwilling to serve and recruits more frequently needed. And as this is part of the project hitherto unexperienced, so most believe it will be found very difficult, if not impracticable."[8] Despite the strains, the system held together and Charles XII was able to form a new army for his Norwegian campaign of 1718.

Justacorps on display in the Swedish Army Museum. Note the vertical pockets, additional buttons, and lack of a collar. (Author's collection)

The provincial regiments would muster annually for drill and inspection and could be assembled within a month of receiving the order.[9] The soldiers would leave their farms and meet at a designated point to form the smallest unit, a *korporalskap*, which consisted of 49 enlisted men and a non-commissioned officer. As it marched, the unit would link up with others and the ranks would swell: three *korporalskap* became a company (150 men), four companies became a battalion (600 men), and two battalions formed

---

7   Alf Åberg, 'The Swedish Army from Lützen to Narva', in Michael Roberts (ed.), *Sweden's Age of Greatness* (New York: St. Martin's Press, 1973), p.270.
8   Robinson, *An Account*, p.57.
9   Hatton, *Charles* XII, p.115.

Uniform of the Seven Years' War on display at the Swedish Army Museum. This uniform was relatively unchanged from the Great Northern War. (Author's collection)

Drabant barracks on Skeppsholmen, Stockholm. (Author's collection)

the regiment for a total of 1,200 men.[10] This was the standard size but in practice the numbers varied. The Life Guard and the Närke-Värmland regiments tended to be larger while many regiments were undersized in the field due to attrition from battle and disease. For the cavalry, it was 125 horses to a company with eight companies forming a regiment. The tactical unit was the squadron which consisted of 250 horses.

The Swedish army as a whole was never maintained at a set size. In 1632, at the height of Gustavus's achievements, the number was somewhere between 150,000 and 175,000 men with a large number being mercenaries paid via the spoils of war. By 1648 it was down to 40,000. Charles X increased the number for his wars while Charles XI reduced the army again during peacetime. In the last year of peace before the outbreak of the Great Northern War, the army numbered around 40,000 men (23 infantry regiments and 11 cavalry regiments) with an additional 25,000 mercenaries mostly performing garrison duties. By the end of 1700, Charles XII had raised the numbers to 56,837 and 32,052 men respectively.[11]

Since all the conscripted men in a regiment came from the same province – and many from the same villages – it helped foster a strong sense of community and *espirit de corps*. A soldier did not wish to be found wanting in front of his neighbours. In addition to love of home and hearth, a strong religious conviction was unanimously held throughout the ranks. Sweden was "the Lutheran Spain" and most aspects of life fell under religious observation.[12] Both Charles XI and XII held a firm belief that as absolute monarchs they were enacting the will of God. This devotion extended to the men under their command who were expected to fear God and honour the King and who entered battle with the refrain *Med Guds hjalp* (With God's help). A high morale was absolutely vital to the successful employment of the aggressive *Gå På* (go-on, fall-on) tactics favoured by the Swedes which often required execution under withering enemy fire against a numerically superior foe.

The end of the seventeenth century saw an advancement in military technology and a shift in tactical thinking. The cumbersome matchlock musket gave way to the flintlock. It tended to be lighter which eliminated the need for the forked musket rest or the Swedish *schweinfeder*. The drill manual from 1693 prohibited their use entirely.[13] The number of drill

The chalice of Chaplin Nordberg which he recovered from the battlefield of Poltava upon his release from Russian captivity. (Nordberg's chalice, Swedish Army Museum AM.008247)

---

10 C.A. Sapherson, *Forces of the Swedish Crown 1688–1721* (Essex: Partizan Press, undated), p.2.
11 Sven Lundkvist, 'The Experience of Empire: Sweden as a Great Power', in Michael Roberts (ed.), *Sweden's Age of Greatness* (New York: St. Martin's Press, 1973), p.27.
12 Roberts, *Swedish Imperial Existence*, p.64.
13 Lars Ericson Wolke, *The Swedish Army in the Great Northern War 1700–1721* (Warwick: Helion & Company, 2018), p.26.

THE CAROLEAN ARMY UNDER CHARLES XII

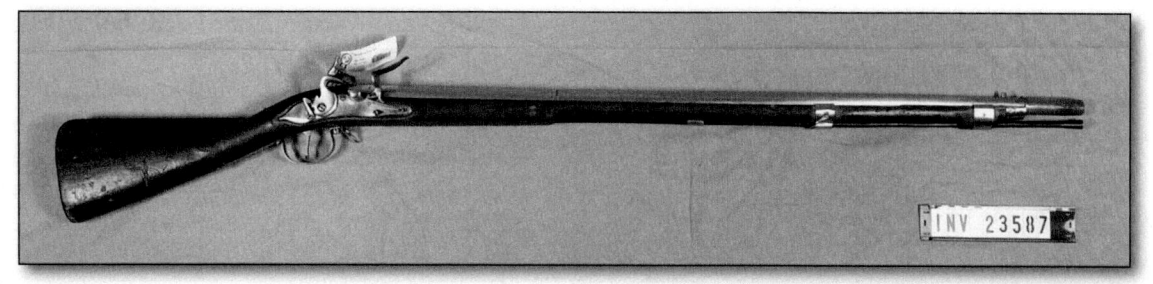

1716 pattern Swedish musket. (Swedish Army Museum AM.023587)

steps going from matchlock to flintlock was therefore significantly reduced which in turn increased the number of shots that could be fired per minute. The flintlock was also more reliable by not requiring a lit cord to be perfectly placed into an open priming pan. This helped make up for the number of misfires although the overall accuracy of smoothbore muskets left much to be desired. Charles XII disliked protracted firefights and preferred volleys at extremely close range to reduce inaccuracy. Adlerfeld recalled the domination of Swedish arms against a unified army of Russians and Poles at the battle of Saladen in 1703:

> Our fire, on the contrary, did great execution, very few shots miscarrying; and our foot, having at last broke through … began to make a dreadful execution in spite of all the vigorous resistance of the Russians who, seeing themselves pressed and lost, fought with the butt-ends of their muskets, halberds, and pikes. The long pikes of our foot were now so extremely useful, that the Russians, seeing themselves unable to make any longer resistance, took to their heels …[14]

Swedish muskets on display at the Swedish Army Museum. (Author's collection)

The pike was a decisive weapon that bridged the transition between the late Middle Ages and early modernity, from the Swiss pike blocks of the Burgundian Wars to the Spanish tercios. At a time when firepower was largely unreliable and not concentrated, the pike provided a defensive picket behind which gunners could reload and avoid opposing cavalry. With the coming of the plug and then socket bayonet, the usage of pike gradually dwindled as the musket could now serve as both the offensive and defensive weapon without a reduction in firepower. In an anachronistic quirk, both the Swedes and Russians continued to field the pike during the Great Northern War although the numbers trailed off towards the end. For the Swedes, the pike suited *Gå På* tactics perfectly as an offensive shock weapon. Up to one third

---
14 Adlerfeld, *Genuine History*, p.114.

Drum. (Drum, Armémuseum)

of each battalion was equipped with the 3.3–5.6 metre-long weapon with the pikemen taking up the centre of the formation. Since a typical musket with mounted bayonet measured to around two metres in length, the pike enjoyed a distinct reach advantage. Following the one or two volleys from the musketeers, the entire battalion would charge with pikes levelled.

Gustavus Adolphus was among the first to reduce the depth of his infantry formations to five or six ranks deep. By widening the frontage, more firepower was brought to bear. The infantry battalion of Charles XII would form up in four ranks with the pikemen in the middle, musketeers on either side and grenadiers on the wings. The order to advance would be given by the sound of drums. At about 40 paces from the enemy, the two front ranks would kneel and the two rear ranks would give fire. The advance would then continue through the cover of the black powder smoke to about 20 paces where the two front ranks would fire. General Stenbock's instructions stressed holding fire until the foe was in bayonet range to maximise the volley's impact. The order was then given to charge, at the double, and if the enemy unit was not already wavering from being shot at point-blank range, they were now assaulted with sword, bayonet, and pike. The aggressive *Gå På* tactic was devastating against low disciplined and ill-trained units but occasionally proved more problematic against a disciplined foe that could weather the onslaught and then bring larger numbers to bear.

The war Charles X fought in Poland in the mid seventeenth century was a "war of movement" and it led to a heavier reliance on cavalry.[15] By the time of Charles XII, the Swedish cavalry tended to make up around 50 percent of the fighting force, one of the highest ratios among the combatants of the Great Northern War. The mounted arm was divided between the traditional cavalry and the dragoons and despite being equipped differently, they acted and fought in the same way. Deployed on the flanks, the Swedish cavalry tended to move quicker than their enemy counterparts and would charge home at full gallop rather than a trot. Per the 1685 regulations, the squadron would advance "knee behind knee" with the cornet at the front and each man slightly behind the next to form an arrow. This wedge shape helped punch holes through infantry and cavalry alike. It was the Swedish cavalry that won the Battle of Lund where Charles XI used the aggressive doctrines to great effect. In addition, he allowed his front ranks to fire their pistols before charging into the foe. Charles XII, favouring speed, decreed that the firing of pistols be avoided. He also had the cuirass removed in an effort to reduce weight and cost.

---

15 Alf Åberg, 'The Swedish Army from Lützen to Narva', in Michael Roberts (ed.), *Sweden's Age of Greatness* (New York: St. Martin's Press, 1973), p.280.

THE CAROLEAN ARMY UNDER CHARLES XII

Battle of Gadebusch. (Public domain)

3 pounder gun in Carolean livery. (Swedish Army Museum, author's collection)

Charles XII's predecessors all valued the artillery. Standardising calibres and introducing light, mobile regimental guns is arguably one of Gustavus's greatest tactical innovations. Charles, however, eschewed artillery much to the dismay of his officers. General Carl Cronstedt, head of the artillery, reflected: "At the beginning of the war His Majesty had a sort of contempt for the artillery; but later bitter experience taught him how valuable a weapon it could be."[16] In the majority of his campaigns, Charles relied on deployment and speed and, more often than not, battle would commence with the attacking Swedes being outnumbered. This meant a traditional artillery duel would be unsustainable. Deploying cannons could be a time-consuming process and the Swedes often had a disadvantage in terms of terrain. To maintain the initiative and use the *Gå På* tactics to full effect, the larger artillery pieces simply had to be left out. In an ironic twist, Charles's demand for mobile artillery spurred Cronstedt, also an engineer, to invent several new devices that helped with the mobility and loading of cannon. His systems were then implemented by several major European powers in the decades after the war. The King therefore had an indirect influence over the future of his least-liked medium of war.

Over the course of the seventeenth century, the army's demographic composition shifted from non-native to native. During the Thirty Years' War the majority of native Swedes were concentrated in the cavalry. Mercenaries, mostly German, formed the bulk of the infantry regiments. By the time of the Great Northern War some 70 years later, mercenaries typically served on garrison duty while the majority of the army, composed largely of the provincial regiments, was in the field. The *Karoliner* were not just the peasants of Gustavus's time but came from other ranks of society as well. The nobility too saw a shift in their role. In previous decades, noblemen were entitled to serve as officers per their societal status but by 1700 they were transformed into professional military men.[17] Due to the extended peacetime of the 1680s and 90s, Charles XI allowed many officers, including two thirds of his lifeguard officers, to serve abroad and assimilate tactics from the armies of Europe.[18] Just like the men under their command, officers were expected to do their duty above all: "When struggle is at hand, the officers in charge must encourage and convince their subordinates to valiant courage for their king, their fatherland and their own immortal fame, being as it is better to die than to fight poorly."[19]

Despite entering professional service, nobles expected to immediately be granted high positions in the officer corps. Charles XII managed to ruffle many feathers by valuing talent over title. The Table of Ranks from 1680 dictated that civil and military posts should be based on merit and length of service rather than inheritance or paid commission. Charles echoed this

---

16 Ibid., p.284.
17 Ibid., p.272.
18 Ibid., p.281.
19 Stenbock's *Instructions*. Quoted in Andreas Marklund, 'The Manly Sacrifice: Martial Manliness and Patriotic Martyrdom in Nordic Propaganda during the Great Northern War', *Gender & History*, 25:1 (2013), p.163.

Hall of Generals, Drottningholm Palace. (Author's collection)

in regards to the promotion of his officers: "Rank, answered Charles, had nothing to do with merit; if the young man was any good, he would become a better officer by sharing for a time the lot of the common soldier … then he would learn to know the problems of his men and be able to care for them when promoted."[20] As with many aspects of his life, Charles led by example and endured the hardships of campaigning alongside his men despite the comforts granted by the Crown. Most famously, he eschewed the wig and courtly finery for a bland cavalry uniform and kept spartan sleeping quarters to the point that many of his officers had nicer clothing and living conditions in the field than their king.

At the start of the Great Northern War, Charles had inherited a well-trained and well-equipped army from his father. They were expected to know and do their duty and they had competent officers to lead them. Morale was high, bolstered by a strong Protestant belief. The strategic approach to fighting a war changed little from Gustavus to Charles. Offensively, the Swedes utilised their bridgeheads on the other sides of the Baltic to launch quick assaults to drive the foe back, claim territory, and then use the occupied land to sustain themselves on campaign. In the case of a foreign invasion, Sweden relied on

---

20 Hatton, *Charles XII*, p.84.

its string of fortresses to stall the foe while the regiments mobilised and could then be transported across the sea. A strong navy was thus a key supporting component. This defensive strategy proved successful in the early stages of the war as the Swedes were able to mobilise and subsequently relieve the Russian siege at Narva and the Saxon siege at Riga without losing either location.

Charles would go on to shape the army in his image. Alongside General Stenbock, he issued updated regulations over the course of the war as he gained bitter and costly experience on the fields of Poland, Russia, and the Ukraine. His army would retain the pike at a time when many armies had disposed of it and he applied the aggressive *l'armes blanche* tactics of the cavalry to his infantry.

Firepower was secondary to cold steel and thus closing in on the foe was preferred to long range firefights. It was often for the best as the Swedish armies tended to be outnumbered two to one and in some cases three to one. As monarchs began to leave the battlefield and let their generals conduct the fighting, Charles led from the front and endured the same hardship as his men which fostered loyalty, obedience, and a spirit of invincibility:

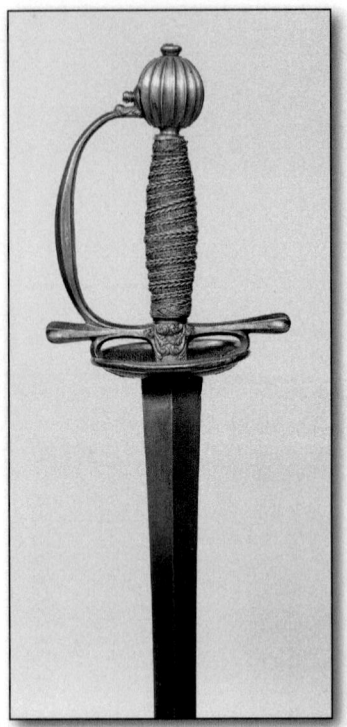

Charles XII's sword. (Charles XII's Sword, 1718, The Royal Armoury)

> The Swedes were not particularly warlike by temperament … and since they went to war only to protect their country, it was necessary for him to take an active part in the actual fighting. He had to show that he was ready to risk as much as they did, their lives, to achieve cohesion and thrust in the attack… but this way, he argued, was essential for a Swedish king in his circumstances.[21]

As a student of history, Charles knew it was the lot of a Swedish king to lead his army from the front and endeavoured to set a better example than that of his father and grandfather, whom he held in high regard.

---

21 *Ibid.*, p.164.

Chapter 5

First Battles, 1700–1702

"In short, a position so advantageously situated for defence and so difficult to be attacked would have disconcerted anyone but Charles XII. His Majesty seeing the absolute impossibility of attacking the enemy, as they stood in Battalia at the head of their camp, making a very smart fire on us from their artillery, performed the part of a great general and ordered the army to wheel a little to the left to gain the rising ground and disengage themselves from the morass which absolutely hindered them from acting."

Gustaf Adlerfeld recalling the critical manoeuvre performed
at Kliszów in 1702[1]

Sweden's initial approach to the Danish invasion of Holstein-Gottorp was to wait for assistance from the other guarantors of the Altona agreement – specifically the Maritime Powers and to a lesser extent the German states of Hanover and Lüneburg. By utilising their combined navies, Sweden hoped to keep the Danes occupied and take over control of the Sound. Given the ongoing animosity between the Netherlands, England, and France over the Spanish succession, Frederik IV of Denmark did not think the Maritime Powers would be bothered to intervene and planned for an invasion of the Swedish mainland through Scania and several focal points on the Norwegian border. His confidence was misplaced. Once it became obvious that the Maritime Powers were mustering a fleet and placed themselves on the side of Sweden, Frederik hastened his plans to besiege the fortress of Tönning in Holstein. A storming of the fortress set for 19 May was called off in order to meet the new threat of a joint Dutch–German army that was marching to intercept the Danes.

Charles and Admiral Hans Wachtmeister moved the Swedish fleet into the channel of the Sound to connect with that of the Maritime Powers. They quickly found their allies to be hesitant to come to blows with Denmark. Instead, the English and Dutch urged caution and wanted to exert pressure on Frederik only as much as was required to maintain the status quo. They preferred that neither the Danes nor the Swedes gain an advantage and upset

---
1 Adlerfeld, *Genuine History*, p.83.

Carl Gustaf Rehnskiöld. (David von Krafft, Carl Gustaf Rehnskiöld, Erik Cornelius, Nationalmuseum)

the balance of power in the Baltic against their own commercial interests.

Having realised that the treaty he ratified was not all he expected it to be, Charles decided to break off on his own and force the issue – to him, patience was not always a virtue and he believed in taking risks while luck was on his side. He ordered Wachtmeister to manoeuvre the Swedish fleet through the narrow *Flintrannan* (Flatts). Despite the shallow depth and high risk of loss to beaching, all but four ships made it through. The Danish navy was caught off guard by the manoeuvre and retreated to safe harbour near Copenhagen. Even with several fireships sent into the harbour, the Danes were able to avoid a direct engagement with the Swedish fleet and stayed under the protection of their coastal artillery. If the situation could not be resolved at sea, it had to be forced on land.

The decision was made to land troops on Zealand and then march to Copenhagen, the capital. Generals Rehnskiöld and Stuart were responsible for formulating the landing plans but they allowed Charles to be involved despite his inexperience. Both Stuart and John Robinson found the young King pacing about the ship anxious for battle and kept him occupied with tasks during the landing preparations. The Maritime Powers, having agreed to the plan, kept the Danish navy from supporting the 5,000 troops stationed in the vicinity of Humlebaek. A feint further south near Rungsted drew a large portion of Danish forces away from the main landing point as the Swedes began to wade ashore on 24 July. For his own safety, Charles was kept in the second wave and placed on the flank that had the least expected resistance. Nevertheless anxious to come to grips with the enemy, Charles jumped out of his transport boat before it reached the shore which forced his men to follow suit:

> His Royal Majesty himself animated and spoke to the soldiers with an incomparable charm, showed also an exceptionally great conduct in correcting everything which he noticed getting into disorder, and wanted later always to be among the first, wherefore also His Majesty jumped in the water before the shallop touched bottom, and then all the others followed him.[2]

An oft-quoted passage from Voltaire has the King surprised by the noise of bullets flying past him and stating that the peculiar sound would become his music.[3] The landing, while not uncontested, went as planned and with minimal casualties as the Danish troops were mostly militia and insufficiently trained. With the beachhead secured, a redoubt was built to

---

2   Hatton, *Charles XII*, p.136.
3   Voltaire, *History*, p.55; Adlerfeld, *Genuine History*, p.25

protect subsequent landings. The army was 10,000 strong by early August and ready to march on Copenhagen. Charles comported himself well in his first military action but his entire involvement was controlled by his veteran commanders.

The successful landing on Zealand forced the Danes to pull back behind the defensive walls of their capital. A blockade was already underway. The looming bombardment of Copenhagen, combined with military pressure in the south, forced Frederik IV to come to terms with Duke Frederick of Holstein-Gottorp. Charles was still on the march when he was notified of the Treaty of Travendal. He insisted the march continue until the terms and signatories were verified although the Maritime Powers and some Swedish officials urged patience. Charles would be satisfied by the final results: Denmark was to withdraw from Holstein-Gottorp territories and respect the *jus armorum*. They also had to pay compensation for damages and made to promise that they would not support Saxony in any way. Thus, by early August, Denmark was knocked out of the war before Augustus achieved any major victories in Livonia and before Peter had even declared himself.

The Maritime Powers considered their obligations fulfilled and offered to escort Swedish forces back home. Given the presence of hostile Saxons in Livonia and the high risk of a Russian invasion further north into Ingria, the Swedes regrouped and set sail for Estonia. Charles and the first wave of his army landed at Pernau on 6 October and found that Augustus had already retreated from his siege at Riga. Upon learning of the Danish defeat, Augustus was quick to approach Louis XIV and have him mediate for peace with the Swedes while simultaneously requesting further military support from Czar Peter. Augustus then pulled back even further to Warsaw and put his army into winter quarters, effectively giving up his part of the fight for the time being. The Chancery in Stockholm wanted to listen to the offers of an armistice but Charles refused. Not for the first time, he sought to achieve a better military position that in turn could translate to a stronger hand in peace negotiations. Despite having a Chancery-in-the-Field, Charles would grow more and more remote from the men in Stockholm. Their influence began to wane especially once he became more politically and militarily adroit himself. While the Chancery had power to govern domestically while he was away from the

Treaty of Travendal. (Public domain)

Charles XII. (David von Krafft, Charles XII on Horse, Skokloster Castle (Samuel Uhrdin), public domain)

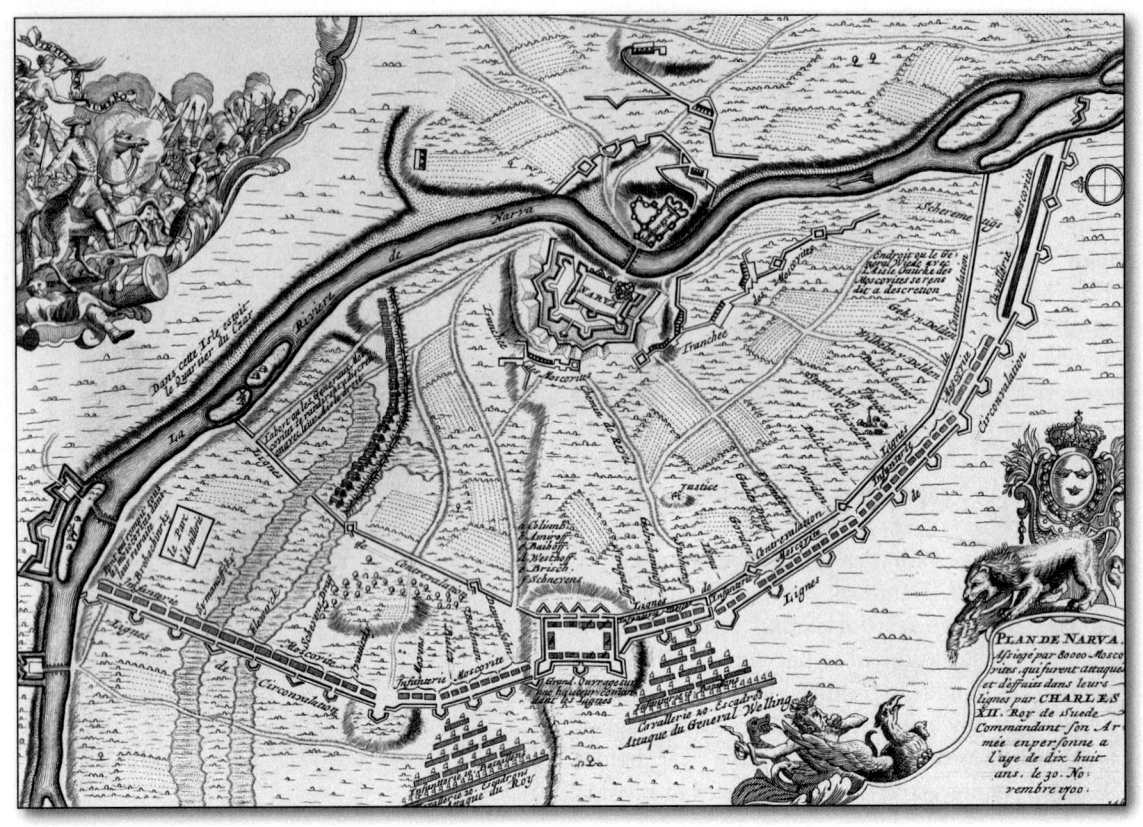

The Swedish attack on Narva, 1700. (Plan of Attack Narva, 1702–03, Rijksmuseum Amsterdam, public domain)

capital, Charles made sure that any decisions on foreign policy would go through him alone.[4]

Thanks to the withdrawal of Augustus and his Saxon army from Riga, Charles could safely turn his attention northwards towards Ingria and the recently besieged fortress town of Narva. Czar Peter, having achieved his desired truce with the Ottomans on 1 July, declared war on Sweden on 20 August becoming the only member of the coalition to formally do so. Narva, lying on the western border of Ingria, was of strategic importance given its close proximity to the Gulf of Finland and the Baltic. For the Russians, it could also be a stronghold from which they could spill into Estonia and Livonia, much to Augustus's chagrin. Heavy siege guns were brought up by November to hasten the capitulation of the garrison which numbered less than 2,000 men under the command of Henning Rudolf Horn. At the same time, the Russians built defensive earthworks around the perimeter of their siege lines to ward off any attack from a relief force.

Charles took the risk of advancing on Narva despite it being late in the fall season. It was the first but certainly not the last time he ignored the accepted conventions of seasonal campaigning. The roads were in terrible shape, neither dry nor frozen, and Russian cavalry detachments did their best to burn and destroy anything that could be of use to the Swedes. The

---

4   Hatton, *Charles XII*, p.131.

King attempted to bolster morale by maintaining a continuous presence at the head of his army regardless of the conditions. The situation became quite dire as the hungry, tired, and cold Swedes marched on, leading Rehnskiöld to comment: "If the King succeeds, there never was any one who had to triumph over such obstacles."[5]

On 17 November Charles and a small reconnaissance force stumbled upon 5,000 Russian cavalrymen under Boris Sheremetev at Pyhajoggi Pass. After some skirmishing, the Russians pulled back leaving the field to the Swedes. The retreat is now known to have been premeditated – Sheremetev was ordered by Peter to not engage the Swedes in a protracted fight. Nevertheless, the Swedes inflated their victory to help boost morale. More importantly, it was the King's first military action where he led alone without the guiding support of his mentors. His courage was praised and the news of his success, however minor it may have been in the grand scheme, was quickly spread.

Sheremetev returned to Narva with news of the Swedish advance but no action was taken. Given the prevalence of siege warfare at the time, the Russian command assumed any pitched battle would take much longer to materialise. For now, they had a three to one advantage in manpower (37,000 to 11,000), a rested force, and a strong defensive position replete with nine-foot high walls and a dry ditch. It was thought that the Swedes would halt before the Russian earthworks and wait for reinforcements. Czar Peter thought similarly and left his army a day before the battle under the guise of attempting to gather additional men. Swedish propaganda was quick to portray the Czar as a fleeing coward who saw the battle as lost before it even began. The departure of the Czar likely had a further negative effect on Russian morale which was already declining due to food shortages and the pervasive diseases spreading through the camp. Before Peter left, overall command was given to Imperial Field Marshal Eugène De Croÿ, a veteran of the battles of Vienna and Lund.

On 19 November, shortly after the arrival of the Swedish army on the outskirts of Narva, Charles and Rehnskiöld made the decision to attack. The Russian forces, while numerically superior, were spread out over a six kilometre semi-circular line. Instead of approaching in linear formation, the Swedes organised two columns of infantry that would concentrate on specific points of the Russian line, penetrate the defences, and then round up the foe within their own camp with the cavalry following behind. The right wing was commanded by General Otto Vellingk while Rehnskiöld led the left wing which included Charles and his crack Drabants. Fortuitously, a snowstorm manifested in the early afternoon and blew directly into the face of the Russians, resulting in their shots flying harmlessly over the Swedes as they advanced. A return volley from the Swedish infantry just before the earthworks resulted in the foe "falling like grass", a testament to the shattering effect black powder can have at close range. Pre-made fascines were flung into the dry ditch by the grenadiers and the Swedes quickly traversed the *chevaux de frise* and scaled the defensive walls: "The attack on the entrenchment

---

5   *Ibid.*, p.151.

BY DEFEATING MY ENEMIES

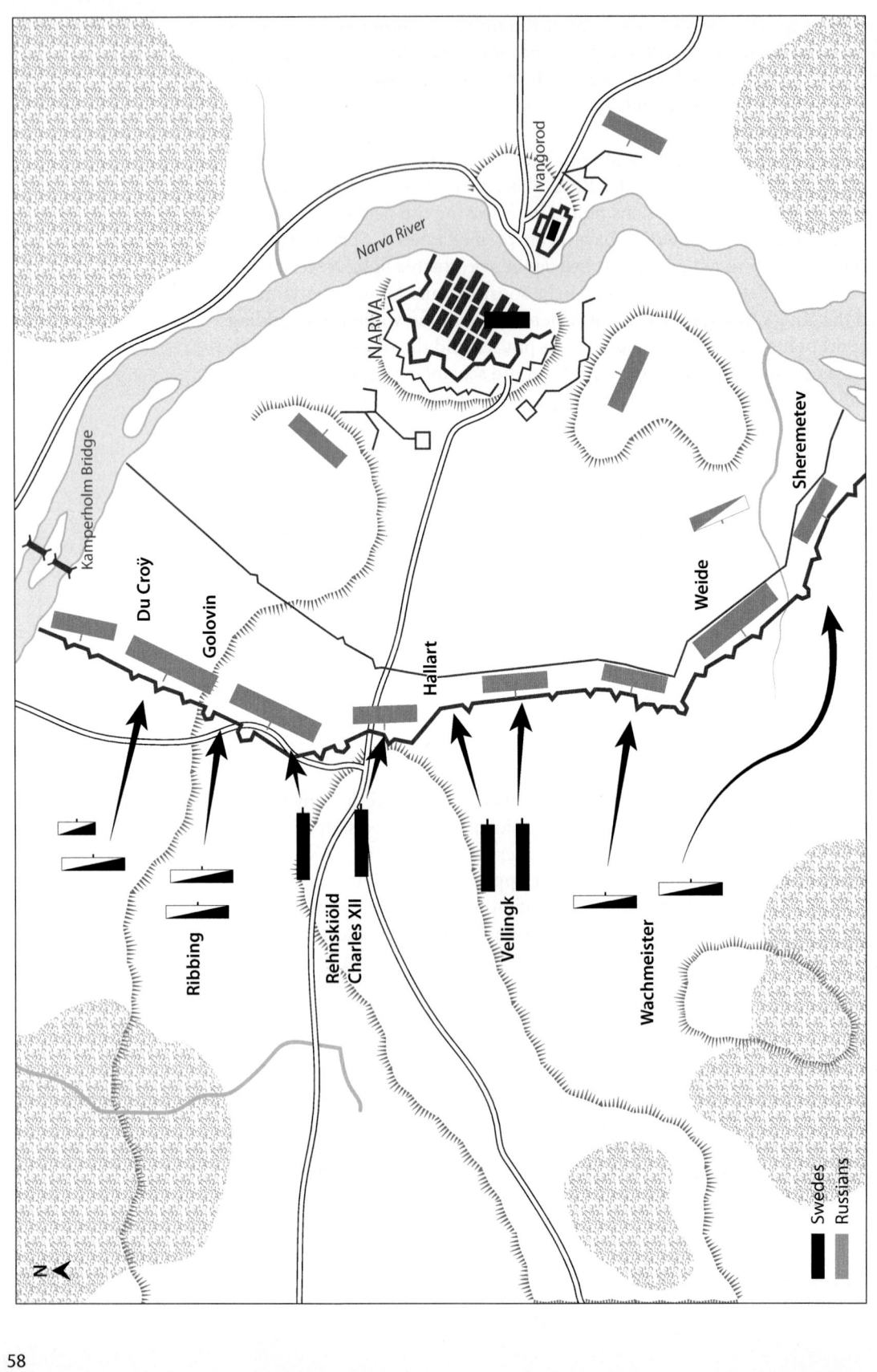

The Battle of Narva, phase 1.

FIRST BATTLES, 1700–1702

The Battle of Narva, phase 2.

BY DEFEATING MY ENEMIES

The spent projectile that hit Charles XII at Narva. (Projectile that hit Charles at Narva, 1700, The Royal Armoury)

was made with so much bravery and followed everywhere with so happy a success, that the foot made a lodgement in less than a quarter of an hour, and prepared a way for the horse to enter."[6] A vicious close combat ensued within the Russian lines. That the fighting was intense is evidenced by Charles who had a horse shot out from under him and lost a shoe in the mud and chaos. Two of his bodyguards in close proximity were cut down by musket fire. At the end of the battle, a spent musket ball fell out of the King's cravat, the first of five bullets to hit him in his life.'

Once inside the Russian camp, the Swedes were quick to turn on the flanks. Any order among the Russians collapsed due to a combination of poor training, low morale, and a lack of cohesion between native Russian soldiers and some of their foreign superior officers. General Ludwig von Hallart, a Saxon siege specialist assisting the Russians, observed: "They ran around like a herd of cattle, one regiment mixed up with the other, so that hardly twenty men could be got into line."[7] The Preobrazhensky and Semyonovsky guard regiments managed to rally and put up a stiff resistance behind makeshift barricades as hundreds of soldiers ran past them. After three hours De Croÿ surrendered, but fighting continued sporadically. Many Russians fled across the Kamperholm Bridge but it could not sustain the weight and collapsed resulting in many men drowning in the River Narva. As the firing eventually ceased, the staggering result became clear. For 667 Swedish dead, the Russian casualties numbered anywhere between 6,000 and 12,000. Due to the sheer number of prisoners taken, Charles was forced to release the lower ranks and let them return to Russian territory. All of Peter's artillery was included in the spoils, forcing the Czar to famously confiscate bronze church bells in an effort to rebuild his depleted train. The captured colours and standards were carried through Stockholm amid great thanksgiving and the jubilant firing of cannons.

---

6   Adlerfeld, *Genuine History*, p.33.
7   Ludwig Nicolaus von Hallart, *Das Tagebuch des Generals von Hallart uber die Belagerung und Schlacht von Narva 1700*, ed. Friedrich Bienemann (F. Kluge, 1894), p.17.

FIRST BATTLES, 1700-1702

The victory of 11,000 Swedes over 37,000 Russians astonished many in Europe. Newspapers commented on the King's "signal victory"[8] and developed an infatuation with following the King's exploits. The broadsides in Sweden were also quick to mark the string of battlefield successes under their young and noble king. In one printed example, the poem and song *Göta Kämpavisa* depicts Charles as the honourable hero who saves the maiden Narva from the rapacious grasp of the Czar.

In his *Histoire de Charles XII*, Voltaire dismissed the Russians as savages, equipped with little more than clubs and bows. Frederick the Great, in his assessment of the Swedish king, makes a similar observation. Modern research dismisses this entirely as Russian forces spent the previous decades fighting the Ottomans and therefore had battlefield experience.[9] Peter's military reforms were already under way by the time of Narva, but it would require a few more years for them to truly take effect. The result was a painful learning curve as the army adapted to new tactics and uniformity and also learned to grow and promote its own officers. Poltava, some nine years later, would prove to be the pinnacle of this transition.

Captured Russian colour. (Russian flag captured at Narva, 1700, Per-Åke Persson, Swedish Army Museum)

Captured Russian colour. (Swedish Army Museum, author's collection)

The Fateful Choice

Having knocked Denmark out of the war and routed the main Russian army, Charles was faced with a critical decision that many historians since have deemed as fatal to his empire. Much has been made of the King's decision to not pursue Peter after Narva and instead march into the Polish-Lithuanian Commonwealth to deal with Augustus. With his enemy reeling, why did Charles not immediately invade Russia and force Peter to terms? Could the disaster of Poltava have been avoided and the Swedish Empire sustained? The benefit of hindsight makes the answer seem obvious but it was not necessarily clear at the time.

An immediate push into Russia at the onset of winter was not possible due to the Swedish

---

8   *London Gazette*, number 3666, December 1700.
9   Frost, *Northern Wars*, pp.231–235.

army being understrength. The Swedes first rested in the camp established by the Russians and then moved into winter quarters to the south and west of Narva with Charles setting up his headquarters at Lais Castle near Dorpat. Camp illnesses ravaged the army and forced them to wait until spring for reinforcements to arrive and supplement their depleted ranks. Charles was shaken by the unnecessary loss of his men and resolved to never again keep an enclosed camp in an effort to stave off the spread of diseases. Money needed for provisions was also in short supply and living off of the land was not a possibility.

After Narva, Augustus emerged in a stronger political position having once again pursued secret diplomacy with France and the Holy Roman Empire. As the only undefeated member of the anti-Swedish coalition, Augustus was able to dictate new terms to Peter via the Treaty of Birsen. Russian money and troops were now sent west in support of the Saxon war effort. Militarily, the Saxons remained active and continued to conduct raids into Livonia whereas the Russians stayed within their own territories for the time being. The as yet unbeaten Saxon army was considered a strong, professional, western force and more than a challenge for the Swedes. If Charles pursued the Russians, it would have left the Baltic provinces vulnerable to an attack from the rear. In terms of sustainability, provisions and supplies would be easier to obtain in the south-western lands than in Russian territories where their scorched earth tactics would have destroyed any remaining winter stores. The loss of Lewenhaupt's supply train at Lesnaya and starvation of the Swedish army in the 1708/09 campaign illustrates the risk. An alliance with a friendly Poland-Lithuania could therefore grant Sweden access to supplies on the Russian border – a key necessity for any push towards Moscow. All factors considered, the conditions were more favourable for a Swedish invasion of Russia in 1707/08 than in 1700/01.[10]

Erik Dahlberg. (David Klocker Ehrenstrahl, Erik Dahlberg, Nationalmuseum, public domain)

By the end of May, 1701, reinforcements had arrived and the campaign against Augustus began in earnest with a planned crossing of the River Düna and relief of Riga. A joint Saxon–Russian force under General Adam Heinrich Steinau was responsible for ensuring a defence of the river. The question was where the Swedes would attempt to cross. While it was given to be in the vicinity of Riga and Kokenhausen, Steinau had to split his forces to cover various landing points and conduct reconnaissance. Charles initially moved his army toward Kokenhausen but then wheeled north and hastily marched on Riga where the venerable Erik Dahlberg was in command and had assembled some 200 boats for the crossing attempt.

10　Frost, *Northern Wars*, pp.279–283.

FIRST BATTLES, 1700–1702

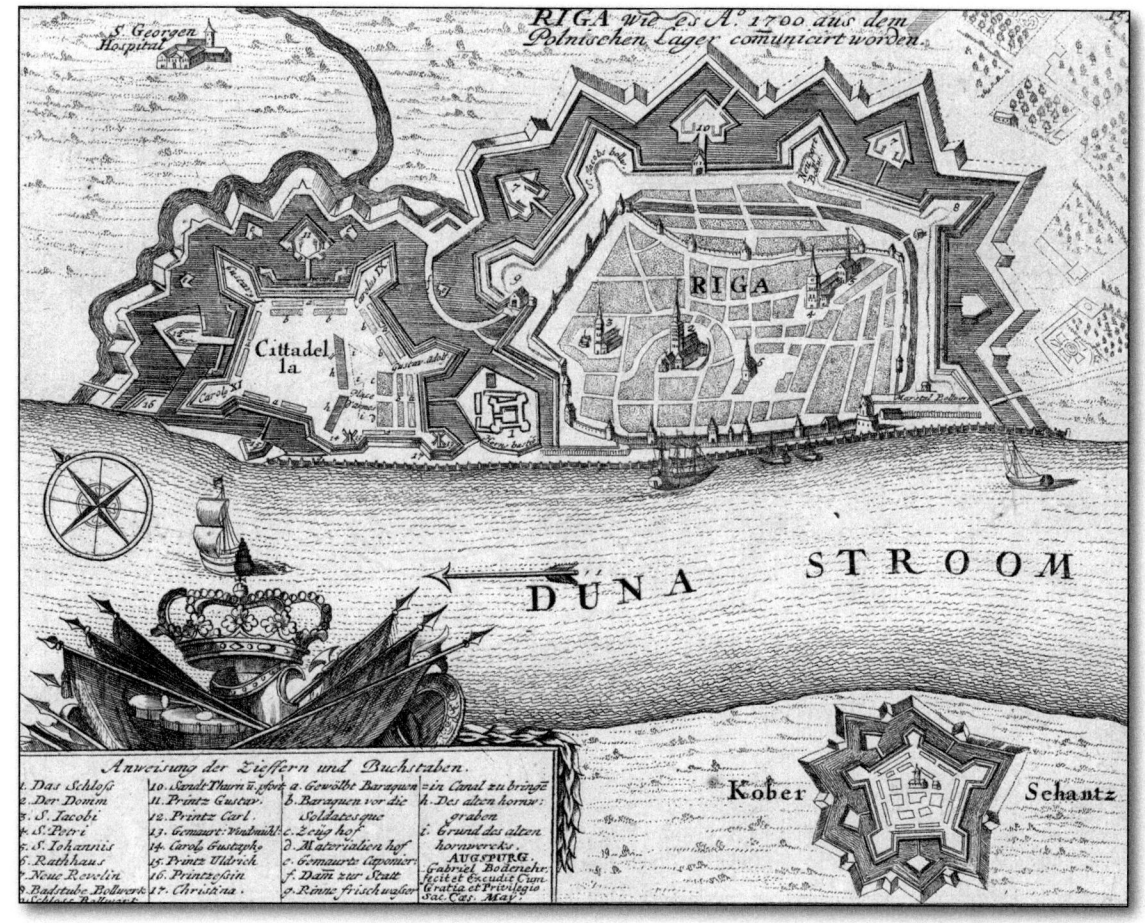

The fortifications of Riga. (Gabriel Bodenehr, Riga in 1700, Latvian National Library, public domain)

Charles had a hand in planning the river crossing but the true logistics were again left to Rehnskiöld, Stuart, and Dahlberg. The Swedes began to assemble along the shoreline during the night and early morning of 8/9 July. A series of feints helped divert Saxon forces along the southern shore to prevent the true landing site from being overwhelmed. A smokescreen was sent across the water followed by boats loaded high with hay bales to block or slow incoming fire. The transport boats then rowed swiftly behind under the cover of friendly artillery fire from several floating batteries and the cannons of Riga. Unlike at Humlebaek, Charles was now in the first wave with around 3,000 men who were tasked with securing a beachhead so the second wave of 4,000 men could land and defend the construction of a pontoon bridge that was slowly being pushed across the water from the north. Having left his mentors behind, Charles remained calm under fire, organising his infantry on the beach and diverting the few cavalry units he had to strengthen the flanks when needed. The majority of the landed Swedish troops were infantry although Charles did have a small number of Drabants and Lifeguard cavalry who managed to cross over the Düna with him. After taking the beach redoubts, the Swedes stubbornly repelled three consecutive Saxon attacks. With the third attack failing to push the Swedes back to the river bank, General Steinau decided to retreat his men and was

BY DEFEATING MY ENEMIES

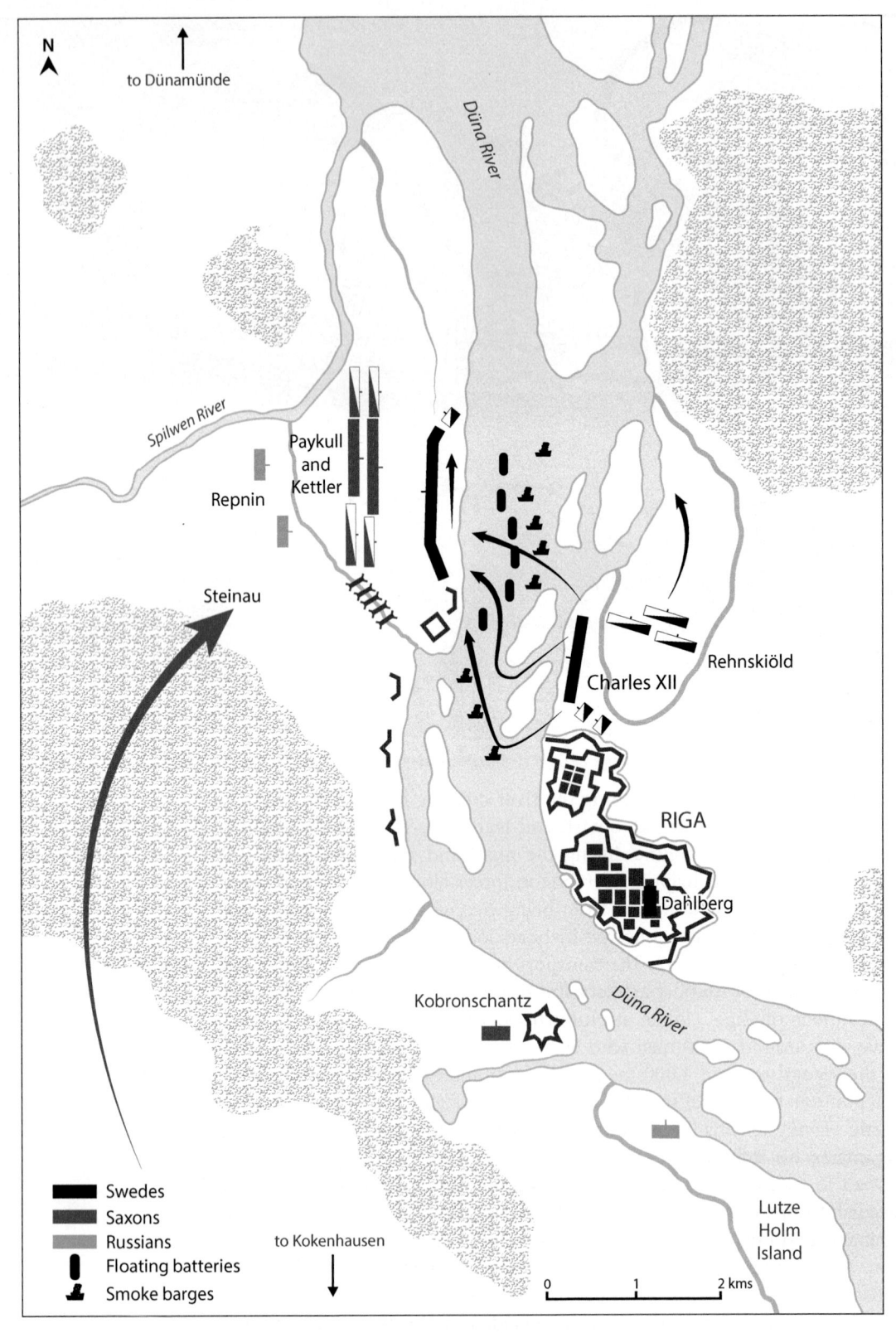

The Crossing of the Düna.

Crossing the Düna. (Johan Philipp Lemke, Crossing the Düna, 1701, public domain)

Medal commemorating the Crossing of the Düna. (Bengt Richter, Commemorating the Crossing of the Düna River, 1701, Jens Mohr, Skokloster Castle)

able to do so in good order. The Swedes were in no position to pursue as their main cavalry force had not yet arrived due to the failed deployment of the pontoon bridge. Adlerfeld concludes:

> Thus ended this glorious action in which the King with an army, at first very inferior, passed a very large rapid river, defeated a formidable enemy, advantageously posted on the river's bank, and rendered himself master in twenty-four hours of five little forts and batteries, of two breastworks, the enemy's camp, thirty-six pieces of their cannon, three standards, one pair of colours, and the greatest part of their baggage.[11]

Since the Saxon army was not broken or even severely damaged, the campaign had to continue with Swedish forces leaving their own territory and moving into the Duchy of Courland. They secured *Dünamünde*, Mitau, and Kokenhausen but the move into Courland caused agitation on many sides. The Maritime Powers saw this as a challenge to their shipping interests in the Baltic as more ports would fall under Swedish control. The Poles and Lithuanians, neutrals in the current conflict but subjects of Augustus, did not want to provide for a Swedish army on their home soil. Poland was riven by factionalism both for and against Augustus but

---
11 Adlerfeld, *Genuine History*, p.47.

Cannon captured by the Swedish army at Neumünde, 1701. (Swedish Army Museum, author's collection)

Charles's eventual decision to pursue the deposition of Augustus challenged the dearly held laws of the Commonwealth. Charles compounded his error by supporting hated noble families such as the Sapiehas which drove the Lithuanians especially further into the arms of Augustus and Peter. The Swedes pushed deeper into the Duchy of Lithuania and occupied the capital, Vilnius, in April of 1702. Just a month later on 14 May, Warsaw fell in the west.

Augustus spent the early part of 1702 secluded in Saxony. Upon hearing that loyalist Prince Hieronim Lubomirski was on the march with nearly 7,000 men of the Polish Crown Army, Augustus moved towards Cracow to merge their forces. Charles too was expecting reinforcements of a similar size. The Battle of Kliszów was thus preceded by a game of movement and anticipation as each side tried to meet their reinforcements and force a battle before the opponent met theirs. The Swedes were worried that the merging of the Polish army with that of the Saxons would supplement the ranks with additional cavalry in the form of dragoons, *pancerni*, and the famous hussars. Secondly, the Crown Army's involvement could force the Swedes to fire upon Polish troops which could make their delicate position in Polish opinions untenable.

The two armies nearly stumbled into each other, with the Swedes emerging near the village of Borczyn some two and a half kilometres north of Augustus' headquarters at Kliszów. Rumours of an impending Saxon attack forced Charles to keep his army in battle formation for two hours. By nine in the morning, no attack had materialised. The King grew impatient, and fearing that the initiative could be lost decided to launch his own attack without having reconnoitred the enemy position.

The Swedes formed their right wing with a mix of cavalry and dragoons under the reliable Rehnskiöld. In the coming battle, the general would be

FIRST BATTLES, 1700–1702

isolated and forced to fight without infantry support. His command and initiative solidified the flank which gave Charles the ability to execute his daring manoeuvre on the left without the risk of being rolled up from behind. Most of the 8,000 infantrymen were concentrated in the centre of the formation while the left flank had the remaining horse in the first line and the remaining infantry following behind. They were under the command of the King's brother-in-law, Frederick, Duke of Holstein-Gottorp. Artillery support was negligible with only four light guns brought forward in support. In total, the Swedes numbered around 12,000 men.

Shortly after Charles gave the order to advance, the Swedes came into view of the Saxon position. The army was led by Augustus himself alongside Generals Steinau, Johann Matthias Schulenburg, and Jakob Heinrich Flemming. Together they had created a strong defensive position and utilised the surrounding terrain to full effect. In the centre, on a large hill, were 46 artillery pieces. A smaller hill, protected by a stream and marshland, was in front of the artillery and the majority of the infantry, some 7,500 men, were stretched along the slopes behind a wall of *chevaux de frise*. It was Steinau who would line up against Rehnskiöld which left Flemming with his half of nearly 9,000 total cavalry on the right. Lubomirski's newly arrived Polish Crown Army, consisting of hussars and *pancerni* along with elements of lighter cavalry, would add further numbers to this flank. Overall, the combined Saxon–Polish army numbered 24,000 men which gave them a distinct advantage in manpower (two to one), artillery, and deployment.

Instead of immediately assaulting the well-fortified Saxon centre, Charles moved left in hopes of finding the enemy in a position more advantageous for his men to attack. The Saxon infantry on the lower hill, hemmed in by the

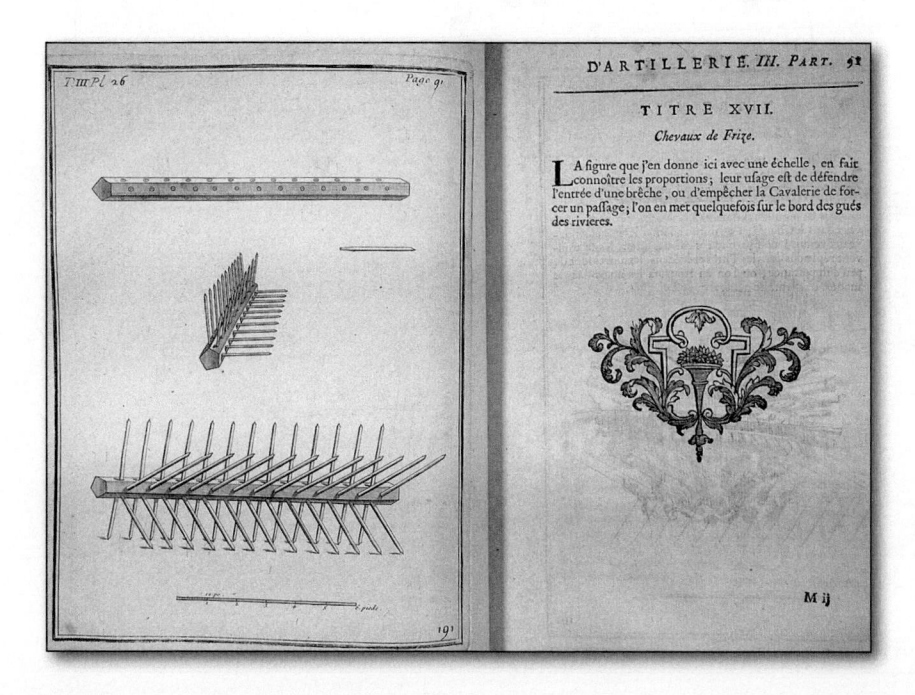

Chevaux de fries, also known as *Spanish Riders*. (Pierre Surirey de Saint-Remy, *Memoires d'artillerie*, 1745, Bibliotheque Carnegie (Reims), public domain)

BY DEFEATING MY ENEMIES

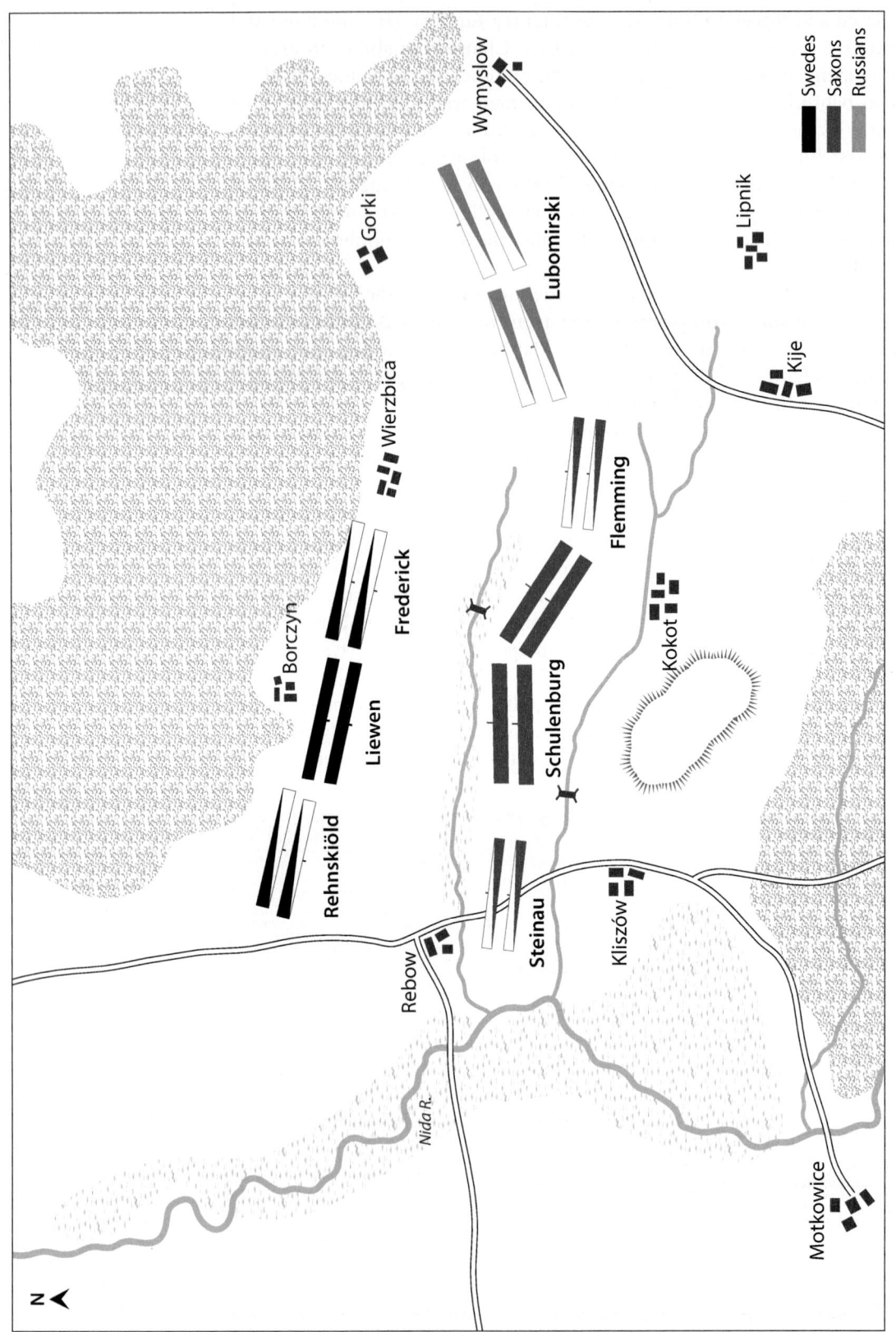

The Battle of Klissow, phase 1.

FIRST BATTLES, 1700–1702

The Battle of Klissow, phase 2.

69

very terrain that gave them security, watched as their artillery opened fire on the Swedes. The 12-pounders were able to hit their targets at range and inflict some casualties. An early victim of the battle was Duke Frederick, who was mortally wounded by a falconet ball.

Lubomirski thought the time had come for the Crown Army to catch the Swedes unprepared. As the Poles galloped towards the Swedish left, they cut in front of Flemming's own cavalry effectively denying themselves Saxon support. Charles saw the attack build and hastily shifted some infantry regiments from the centre to intercept the charge. The pike proved its worth at Kliszów and helped stall the Polish charge as two close range musket volleys shattered the cavalry. The Crown Army suffered enough casualties to lose cohesion and flee from the battlefield. General Flemming followed up with his own cavalry but suffered the same result.

The Saxon cavalry on the other side of the battle met with initial success. The surrounding marshland prevented the Swedes from launching their favoured 'knee behind knee' charge at the gallop. As they mulled about, they were surprised by a Saxon assault that had navigated the marsh via pre-emptively placed wooden planks and bridges. However, any momentum was lost when the Saxon cavalry halted and began to caracole. The outdated technique of firing pistols at short range and wheeling to the rear of the column to reload gave the initiative to the disciplined Swedes who regrouped under fire and countercharged. The Saxons could not withstand the weight of the charge and fled, which now left both flanks open to the Swedes. Here then is an example of the decisiveness of cold steel over firepower, which is why by 1710 Swedish drill instructions for the cavalry forbade the use of pistols on the move.

With both flanks secured, all resources were devoted to swarming the central Saxon position. In typical *Gå På* fashion, the Swedish infantry rushed through terrain and defences with abandon to reach the Saxon line. Realising the situation was lost, General Schulenburg had the army launch a fighting retreat which allowed the majority of the army to escape and fight another day. There was no time to organise the baggage train and its contents fell into Swedish hands. One notable capture was the tent of Augustus, itself a trophy taken from the Ottomans at Vienna. It is now on display at the Army Museum in Stockholm.

German historian Otto Haintz wrote a three volume military biography of Charles XII in the 1930s and 50s and saw the Battle of Kliszów as the "glittering victory" of Charles's career. In terms of the results, he could make a valid argument. The Swedes had just over 1,000 casualties (300 killed, 800 wounded) while the Saxons had 4,400 killed, wounded, or captured and they lost all of their artillery and their baggage train. Augustus could only watch as the Swedes continued to march through Poland in an attempt to undermine his authority. The loss of a significant war chest did not help matters either. Charles secured another victory but it was not the decisive one he needed. Any relief and happiness was also tempered by the loss of his brother-in-law. His relationship with the Duke was cordial but he felt the loss more for his beloved sister Hedvig Sophia, to whom he wrote after the battle: "I do not dare try to console *Mon coeur* in this painful subject but rather wish that the

Ottoman tent of Augustus. (Swedish Army Museum, author's collection)

Lord, the all-powerful God, will console, strengthen, protect, and help you. This is my consolation on which I rely."[12]

With the victory at Kliszów, Charles and his Swedes completed the opening phase of the Great Northern War with astonishing success. Denmark was knocked out of the conflict in a matter of months, the main Russian army was repulsed, and the Saxons suffered two straight defeats although they were able to avoid disaster by retreating in good order on both occasions. Charles had a whirlwind of victories to his name, each accomplished in a different fashion and underlined by his growing confidence and abilities as a military commander: the amphibious landing at Humlebaek, the column assault on fortified siegeworks at Narva, the screened river crossing near Riga, and the tactical repositioning at Kliszów. The Swedish General Staff, writing in the shadow of World War I, held Charles in very high regard and credited him with eschewing linear tactics and developing new ways of waging war. This is an overexaggeration – while columns were employed at Narva (1700) and Holowczyn (1708), Charles fully utilised linear deployment. It was, rather, his ability to identify enemy weak points and his emphasis of aggressive infantry assaults to exploit them which led to success. Over time, the King

---

12 Carlson, *Eigenhändigen Briefe*, p.13.

moulded the army in his own image as he further encouraged the use of cold steel over firepower due to its efficiency and shock value.

It would of course be wrong to give Charles all of the credit for his early victories. He inherited a well-trained and disciplined army that had an established identity for fighting aggressively at close range. Charles was also surrounded by veteran commanders, many of whom would rise to even higher ranks as the war progressed. The early tutelage and leadership of Dahlberg, Stuart, and Rehnskiöld, the latter in particular, gave Charles time to gain valuable experience while simultaneously granting him increasing responsibilities. As his career progressed, the King's reliance on his mentors diminished and while Charles sought council among his officers, his decision was final. From a purely military perspective, Charles was in the right more often than not and he would showcase his firm grasp of command during the Grodno campaign and at the Battle of Holowczyn.

When looking at the major battles in which Charles was involved between 1700 and 1702, there is a clear progression of his leadership skills and tactical decision-making ability. At Humlebaek, Charles deferred the planning of the attack to his mentors and was content to lead his men in the second wave of landings. It was his first test under fire. The brief skirmish at Pyhajoggi Pass was the first action of the King away from his mentors. Charles maintained control of his cavalry and did not commit any errors either in engaging or attempting to pursue the Russians. On the southern bank of the Düna, Charles was busy repositioning his infantry and limited cavalry along the beachhead to repulse the Saxon waves all the while encouraging his men to press on. At Kliszów Charles made the decision to attack and took command of the left flank after Duke Frederick fell, and made a crucial decision in the heat of battle to bolster said flank. In doing so he first routed the Polish Crown Army under Lubomirski and then the Saxon cavalry under Flemming. It was also the first display of his ability to immediately understand the surrounding terrain and use it to his advantage. Having seen that the Saxon artillery and infantry positioned on the hills were limited in their movements due to a flowing stream and marshland, Charles manoeuvred his infantry before them with impunity. General Vellingk recalls the phases of Kliszów in which the King had a hand: "It was a battle which began with firm resolution, was continued with due caution and ended in the highest glory."[13] Within the first two years of the conflict Charles had already progressed to such a firm command in the art of war. He was only 20 years old.

---

13 Hatton, *Charles XII*, p.185.

Chapter 6

The Venture Into Poland and Saxony, 1701–1707

"We shall be fighting this side of the water for many a year to come."
Charles XII to Josias Cederhielm, 1701.[1]

The Polish-Lithuanian Commonwealth had remained formally neutral in the quarrel between Sweden and Saxony but the actions of Augustus, in his capacity as King of Poland and Duke of Lithuania, forced the Swedes to advance inland to bring him to heel. Their involvement in the Commonwealth was, at least initially, never intended to be lengthy but early projections from officers and chancery staff were not optimistic. The Swedes wanted to march directly on Saxony and effect a quick capitulation similar to the result of the Danish campaign the year before. However, the volatile political situation in Western Europe prevented this from happening in 1701. Augustus had to be forced out of the war in a different way and the idea of removing him from his Polish throne was floated to Charles. He approved but with the caveat that the action would have to come from the populace and not a Swedish military coup. As was typical of Charles, once he committed to the plan, it was adamantly pursued with full force until achieved. The King was not completely inflexible but the Elector's dubiousness left Charles with little choice: "Believe that I would give Augustus peace immediately if I could trust his word; but as soon as peace is made and we are on our march towards Muscovy, he would accept Russian money and attack us in the back, and then our task would be even more difficult than it is now."[2]

Efforts towards peace negotiations were first attempted in the aftermath of Kliszów but quickly fell apart when Augustus would not confirm his intentions of accepting a brokered peace. He did not need to. At both Düna and Kliszów, the defeated Saxon forces were able to retreat in good order and regroup with as many as 20,000 men. Augustus also enjoyed the allegiance of the majority of the Polish Crown Army which consisted of German and Hungarian infantry,

---
1   Hatton, *Charles XII*, p.178.
2   Letter to Count Piper in Joran Nordberg, *Konung Carl den XII:s Historia*, 2 vols (Stockholm, 1740), p.284.

light cavalry, mounted *pancerni* and the famous Winged Hussars – just over 18,000 men.[3] With these combined numbers, Augustus was still a major threat despite the losses inflicted upon him. In his eyes, he was far from defeated and decided to press on. He had cause for optimism as his revised treaty with Peter ensured that money and men continued to flow in from the east and Russia was beginning to nip at Swedish held territory in Livonia and Courland. The Poles themselves were no immediate threat either. The ruling nobles had split into factions with support directed towards Augustus, Charles, or a variety of pro-Poland figureheads. At this point in time, Augustus had overwhelming support and Charles could get no serious commitment on deposing Augustus as King of Poland from the population at large. Therefore, a decisive military engagement was needed to sway the opposition. For the next several years the Swedes marched and countermarched throughout the Commonwealth, taking strongholds and towns only to have them recaptured once they moved on. The ghosts of the Second Northern War returned – Poland and Lithuania, with their vast territory, proved hard to conquer.

The War of the Spanish Succession

As previously mentioned, the Swedes were prevented from a direct march on Saxony by the unravelling political situation in Europe and their uneasy alliance with the Maritime Powers. Charles bitterly learned during the brief war with Denmark that the English and Dutch were only willing to provide support as far as their own interests required. As guarantors of Altona and Travendal, the Maritime Powers kept King Frederik IV and Denmark from resuming the war with Sweden and reopening a third front. If Sweden were to agitate the Maritime Powers in any way, the pressure on Denmark could be lifted. Having already drawn rebukes for the invasion of Courland, Sweden had to be cautious. This relationship became even more complex with the sudden change of situation in Spain.

While Charles and Sweden celebrated the victory at Narva in November 1700, the childless Spanish Hapsburg Carlos II died. His death and appointment of Philip of Anjou as his heir sparked a succession crisis that had the shadow of King Louis XIV looming over a united France and Spain. This was something the Maritime Powers and their ally, the Holy Roman Empire, could not allow. The resulting War of the Spanish Succession lasted from 1700 to 1714 and ran concurrently to the events of the Great Northern War in the east. Sweden's manoeuvres in Poland and especially Saxony were as close as the two conflicts came to merging. Any Swedish invasion of Saxony would be an intrusion on the sphere of influence of the Holy Roman Empire. In turn, this could be seen as support for Louis XIV and thus be in direct conflict with the interests of the Maritime Powers. Charles and his government had to tread lightly and bide their time. It was only in 1706, when the War of the Spanish Succession was going well for the allies that

---

3   Michal Paradowski, 'The Once Glorious and Powerful Polish-Lithuanian Commonwealth Army', in Steve Kling (ed.), *The Great Northern War Compendium* (St. Louis: THGC Publishing), p.99.

THE VENTURE INTO POLAND AND SAXONY, 1701–1707

Charles decided to risk the invasion of Saxony. And while there was a flurry of diplomatic activity and the wringing of hands by many an ambassador, the risk paid off and the Treaty of Altranstädt and the removal of Augustus from crown and conflict was quick to follow.

The stunning victory at Kliszów and retreat of Augustus to Sandomierz cleared the way for the Swedes to take Cracow on 31 July, 1702. The Swedes were masters on the battlefield but it was a struggle off it. Polish light cavalry proved to be very successful in harassing Swedish forces and their supply trains as they marched. Charles gained a grudging respect for these units and had a Vallack regiment created from pro-Swedish Poles in 1706. In addition to the cavalry, Polish irregular infantry were mounting a guerrilla campaign and engaged the Swedes with hit-and-run tactics. These actions elicited a harsh response from Charles as is evident in several of his letters to General Rehnskiöld:

> I hear that our men are being attacked. It would be best that those who caused this be destroyed through plundering and burning, even those who, guilty or not, find themselves living at the spot of occurrence. On our end, we have burned down at least three or four villages and a large farmstead.[4]

> From here there are no other matters of importance to mention except that every location where the foe can be found is burnt down. Recently I had a whole town reduced to ashes and the inhabitants hung up.[5]

> I ordered the new dragoon recruits to conduct a mission on the other side of the Drewenz river, to forage and drive in cattle and to burn down villages.[6]

The private letters and journals of officers such as Rehnskiöld and Stenbock reveal more brutal reprisals against the local populace. Even though these are set against the backdrop of an ongoing guerrilla campaign, the harsh actions of the Swedes did nothing to endear them to the Poles and instead united the resistance under Augustus. Much like the German lands in the Thirty Years' War, the Commonwealth became a battleground for warring states and suffered severely from famine, plague, and marauding armies in the coming years.

The rest of 1702 was spent consolidating positions and the battle of Pultusk on 20 April, 1703 was the next major action that Charles experienced in his young military career. Pultusk is important for being the King's first fully independent operation and command. The Swedish army left Warsaw a few days before and began the march north-west to the Saxon held town of Thorn. General Steinau was under orders from Augustus to delay the Swedes by moving to intercept them from the rear. Upon hearing of Steinau's

---
4 Carlson, *Eigenhändigen Briefe*, p.245.
5 *Ibid.*, p.249.
6 *Ibid.*, p.250. In a postscript, Charles moves on to mention that a comedy troupe arrived from Stockholm and were putting on a performance later that night – quite the opposite experience from the day's activities.

diversionary force, Charles countered by peeling off from the march with a mixed detachment of infantry and cavalry.

Both forces met at the prosperous town of Pultusk which was situated on an island in the Narew River. The waterway flowed from Danzig bringing economic prosperity via the valuable trade commodities that were shipped down the river. Due to its location, Pultusk was only accessible by three bridges on either bank and control of these would be vital for any successful attack on the town. Having left his infantry behind after hastily fording a stream, Charles and his remaining 2,000 cavalrymen found nearly 6,000 Saxons arrayed in advantageous positions on the southern bank of the Narew. This strong deployment was relinquished without a fight when Steinau skittishly ordered his men to pull back into the town proper after seeing the Swedes approach. Perhaps he deemed the town as a better defensive position against horse as no infantry were to be seen. Charles used this moment to launch his attack, and before the Saxons could completely cross the bridge, the Swedish cavalry was among them:

> Steinau … surprised at the number of our horse, which were superior to his own, thought of taking the necessary measures for a retreat. With this view he gave his men orders to return to town, which is surrounded with water, intending to defend himself by pulling up the drawbridges on all sides; but the king, who presently suspected his intention, detached the dragoons to cut off his passage, who attacked him so briskly that Colonel Buchwald was with his squadron on the bridge at the same instant as the last Saxons were pressing to pass. Buchwald made himself immediately master of the gates of the town after a very slight resistance.[7]

Order quickly collapsed and a desperate race for the northern bridges leading out of the town ensued. After several Saxon units crossed the bridges, they became severely damaged and trapped the remaining men in Pultusk with no escape routes. Many who tried to swim across the Narew drowned. Some accounts suggest thousands of drownings but given the total casualty count, it is more likely that a few hundred succumbed in the river. Steinau himself barely escaped but managed to rally his men sufficiently enough that Charles chose not to attack again. At the age of 20, Charles had his first independent victory which he quickly announced to his mentor Rehnskiöld: "Our Lord graciously allowed us to knock our foe about and scatter him. I later took part in his pursuit but I was unable to reengage. Our horses were completely weary so that we could not get them back in order."[8] A well-trained horse was capable of several hours of exertion and having completely exhausted beasts speaks to the speed of *Gå På* and the relentless follow-up employed by Charles and his men. Pursuit after victory was not widely practised at the turn of the century but the King used this method with success either pushing the enemy back even further or capturing more of the foe as they exhausted themselves on the run. The King once again demonstrated an

---

7 Adlerfeld, *Genuine History*, p.119.
8 Carlson, *Eigenhändigen Briefe*, p.243.

eye for engaging weak points, having charged his cavalry as soon as the Saxons moved away from their initial positions.

The victory at Pultusk kept the road to Thorn open and the Swedes arrived with no further delays. A large Saxon garrison was barricaded within the fortified town which lay directly south of the vital port city of Danzig. Thorn was also strategically located near the border of the newly elevated Kingdom of Prussia which would allow Charles to keep a watchful eye on the designs of Frederick I. Thorn had to be taken and it would require a siege to do so.

Early eighteenth-century warfare tended to see more sieges than pitched battles as defenders could try their luck and hold out against numerically superior forces in the hope that the besieger would succumb to attrition first. Names like Vauban, Hallart, and Dahlberg, all siege engineers, were just as important in securing victories for their monarchs as Marlborough, Eugene, Villars, and Rehnskiöld. Conducting a siege could take weeks, months, or even years depending on the morale and supplies of the defenders. Attackers had the option of launching a blockade, mining the walls, ordering a bombardment, or staging an assault. While a bombardment was the most commonly used option, and also made for a great stylistic print for the broadsheets, besiegers tended to employ a combination of tactics. In the Great Northern War alone, there were over 70 recorded sieges.[9]

Charles XII (Stanislaus I Leszcynski, Equestrian Portrait of Charles XII, circa 1706, Nationalmuseum, public domain)

Charles would now have to trade a quick strike for seven months of attrition. Thorn was well stocked and defended and the Swedes launched the siege without heavy artillery. It would take time for these to arrive from the northern Baltic ports. As the months passed, the Swedish siege lines drew closer to the city walls and Charles was often seen at the forefront. In what was to become his custom, Charles put himself in harm's way to endure the same experiences as his men and by doing so encourage them to press on. Councillors and officers alike feared for the King's safety but, as noted by an officer at the siege of Fredriksten, trying to dissuade the King would only encourage him to risk further danger. For the standard soldier however, having an absolute monarch, answerable only to God, dig in the same trench or eat the same food fostered extreme loyalty and high morale. Given the Swedes' strict adherence to the Lutheran faith, the actions of Charles also fortified the fatalistic belief that one's death was already set and it was just a matter of when and where it was to occur.[10] It was simply not worth worrying about in the meantime. Some believed that the King enjoyed divine protection, a suggestion that was not far-fetched in contemporary eyes:

---

9   Boris Megorsky, 'Siege Operations in the Great Northern War', in Steve Kling (ed.), *The Great Northern War Compendium* (St. Louis: THGC Publishing, 2015), p.172.
10 It is the equivalent in modern terminology to "having a bullet with your name on it".

> It is astonishing that his Majesty, who with his usual intrepidity visited the posts every day and approached so near the town, that the gunners were obliged to fire several times at his little body of attendants, during the whole siege received no wound ... for the balls flew either over their heads, or between the legs of their horses, or else past them.[11]

There are two further examples that occurred at Thorn. In one instance, an enemy cannonball took out the legs of a subordinate that Charles was speaking to in close proximity. In the other, Charles was helping place gabions on the trench lip and had one shot out from under him. Charles never seemed to be rattled and would brush these occurrences aside with a dismissive wave of the hand or uttering one of his favourite words, *lappri* (rubbish).

The arrival of the heavy artillery forced the matter and Charles noted in a letter that the town hall and many other buildings burnt to the ground due to glowing hot cannon balls.[12] The capitulation of Thorn in October of 1703 and the subsequent surrender of Posen reduced the effective fighting size of the Saxon army in Poland with the loss of some 6,000 men killed or captured. Such was the legacy of the siege that among the spoils of war and captured banners that once adorned the walls above Charles's sarcophagus were the keys to the town of Thorn.

With the loss of Thorn and a growing number of Poles flocking to Cardinal Radziejowski's call for the King's dethronement, Augustus found himself in a tenuous position at the end of 1703 – the complete opposite of where he was in 1701. Augustus was forced to sign another treaty with Russia but the terms were now dictated by Peter given his successes further east. Augustus received additional funds and men from the Czar but was now bound to provide military support for Peter if Russia was invaded. Because the treaty stressed that the war be continued on Polish soil, the movement for the deposition of Augustus grew stronger and allowed the Swedes to capitalise. Charles chose Stanislaus Leszcynski, governor of Posen, as the top candidate for the Polish Crown. The newly formed Warsaw Confederation, which held anti-Saxon views, convened under Swedish protection to vote on the deposition of Augustus. The result was a forgone conclusion. Charles was elated and congratulated Arvid Horn for his statesmanship:

> I am very pleased that through your activities such a good work has been completed and the dethronement, which the Poles found too difficult, came about through your resolute work. I am also impressed that you are already working towards the election of a new king ... all matters hang on this, to bring the Republic to peace and security.[13]

In response, supporters of Augustus and the sovereign laws of the Commonwealth deemed the deposition and subsequent election as illegal and created the Sandomierz Confederation. They formally declared war on

---

11 Adlerfeld, *Genuine History*, p.129.
12 Carlson, *Eigenhändigen Briefe*, p.15.
13 Carlson, *Eigenhändigen Briefe*, p.317.

Sweden, thus ending Polish neutrality. The two rival factions vying for power plunged Poland into civil war from 1704 to 1706.

Despite the political victory, the decisive military engagement had not yet materialised. Augustus meanwhile continued to frustrate Charles with his movements in a proverbial game of cat and mouse. In a letter to his younger sister, Charles described the summer campaign of 1704: "The whole time was spent in the familiar back and forth marching. First past Warsaw then to Sandomierz, past Lublin and then Weingraf, over the Bug river, back to Warsaw and from there finally on the way to Silesia."[14] After recapturing Warsaw, Augustus and General Schulenburg were again approached by Charles and decided to move towards the safety of Saxony. On 27 October, with only four dragoon regiments under his command, Charles managed to catch Schulenburg and his army at Punitz and force a battle. Schulenburg formed up behind the town with 12 infantry battalions arrayed in two lines in the centre and his 14 cavalry squadrons split evenly on the wings. While the units were all understrength, they still maintained a numerical advantage with some 4,100 Saxons facing 2,300 Swedes.[15]

Arvid Horn. (Lorens Pasch, Arvid Horn, Nationalmuseum, public domain)

Charles ignored the advice of his officers to wait for reinforcements and ordered a direct charge of all four regiments at once. The initial volleys from the Saxon infantry combined with that of the nine artillery pieces inflicted casualties but not in sufficient quantities to stop the momentum of the charge. Seeing their Swedish counterparts continue at full gallop through the black powder smoke, the Saxon cavalry pulled back on the flanks and left the infantry dangerously exposed. Charles immediately took advantage of the new situation and concentrated his cavalry on the Saxon centre. To his credit, Schulenburg was able to organise a fighting retreat to save his infantry but had to sacrifice two battalions under General Biron to stall the Swedes for time. He redeployed the remnants of his army in square formation with his remaining cannon protected by the infantry. This time their discipline held firm and the Saxons managed to repulse two further charges by the Swedes. With mounting casualties and daylight running out, Charles called off the attack. His three head-on assaults, devoid of any tactical manoeuvring or artillery support, forced the Saxons to retreat but at a great loss to his own men. Another quick attempt to wholly defeat the Saxons had failed.

With Augustus pushed back to Saxony and a large part of his army retreating into Silesia, efforts to install Stanislaus as king went ahead. The Swedes managed to resist outside interference in July 1705 when General

---

14 *Ibid.*, p.68.
15 Damian Plowy, 'The Battle of Poniec (Punitz) 1704', in Steve Kling (ed.), *The Great Northern War Compendium* (St. Louis: THGC Publishing, 2015), p.174.

BY DEFEATING MY ENEMIES

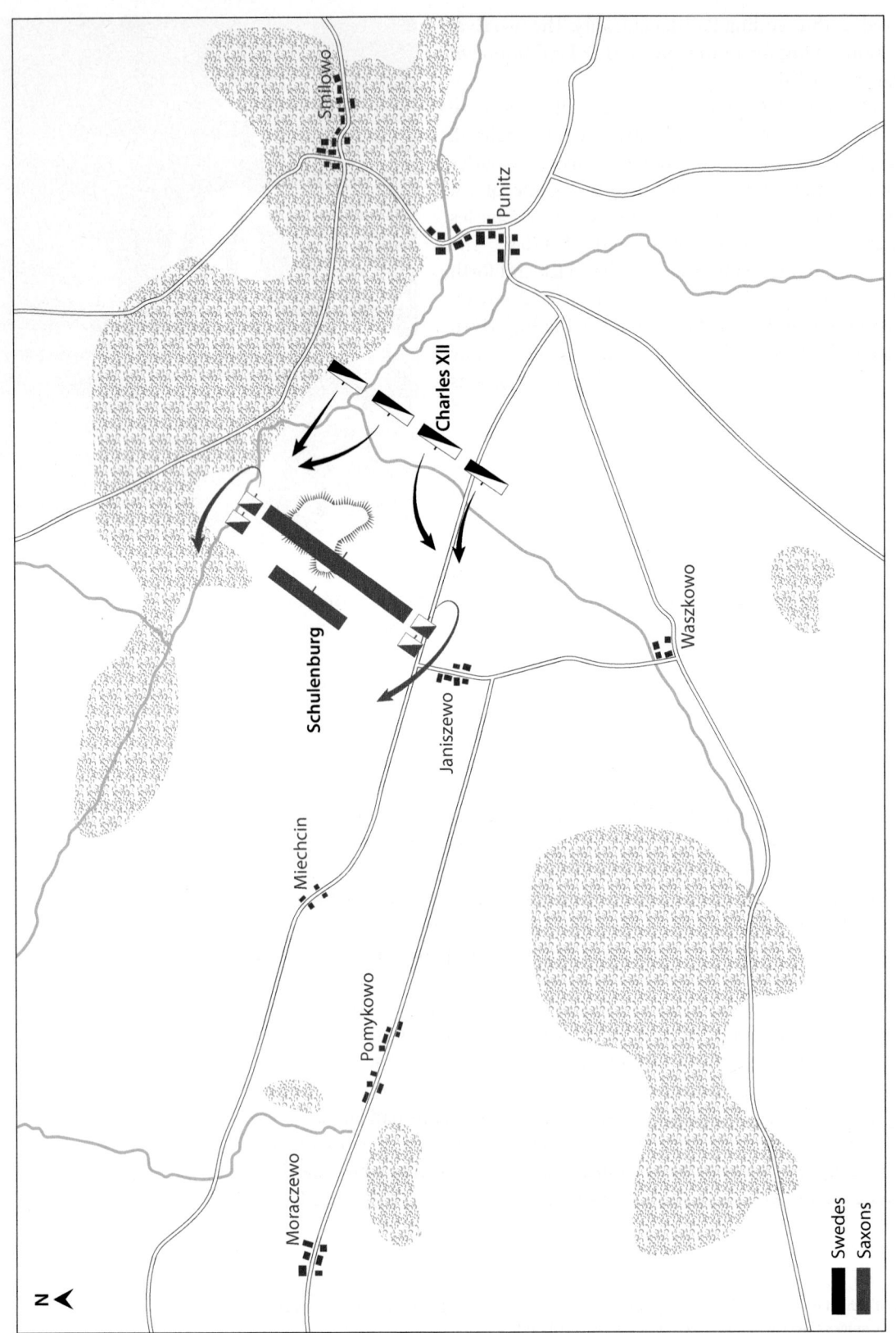

The Battle of Punitz, phase 1.

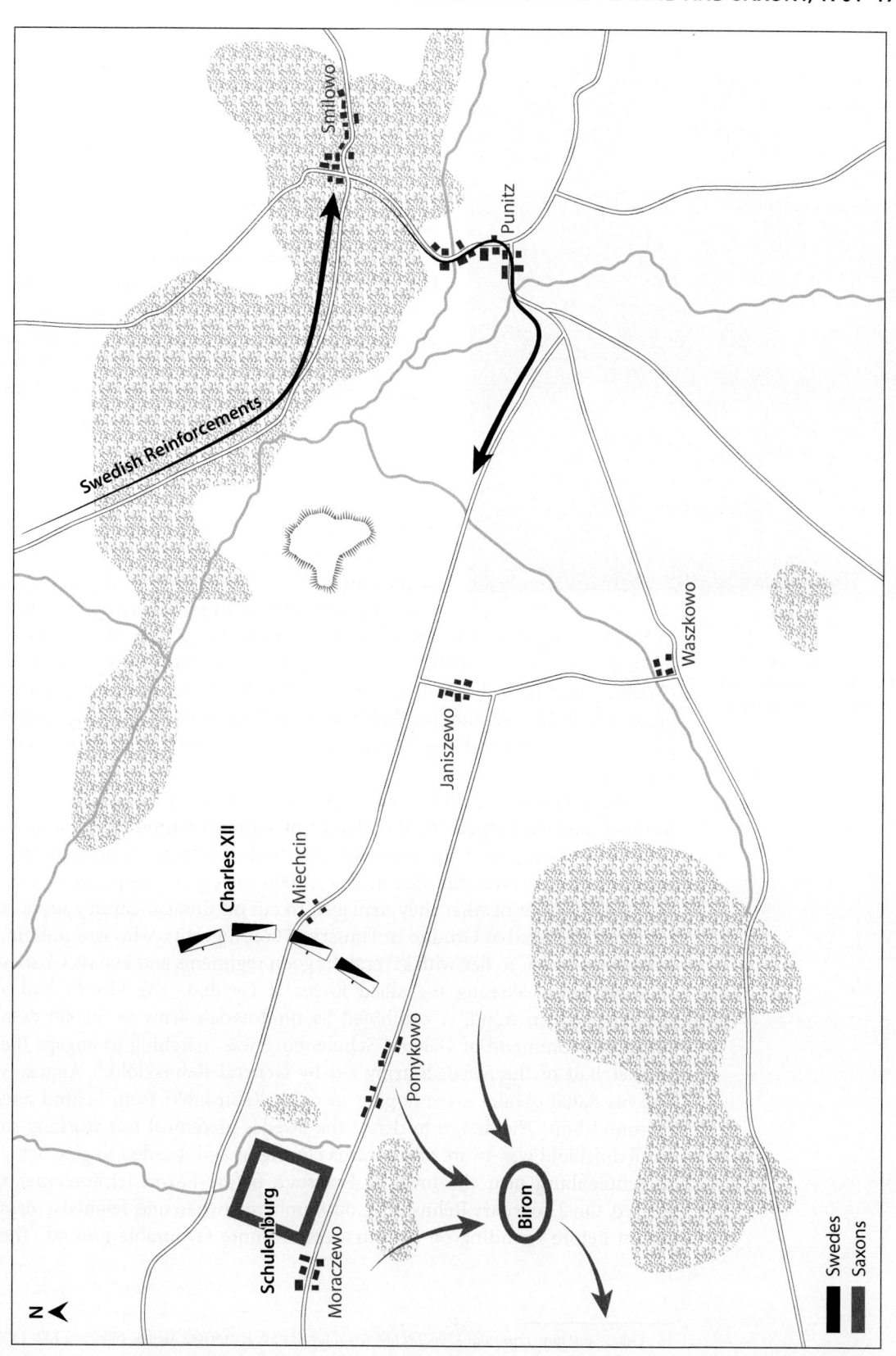

THE VENTURE INTO POLAND AND SAXONY, 1701–1707

The Battle of Punitz, phase 2.

81

BY DEFEATING MY ENEMIES

Stanislaus I Leszcynski. (David von Krafft, *Stanislaus I Leszcynski King of Poland*, Nationalmuseum (Rickard Karlsson), public domain)

Lewenhaupt temporarily halted Russian advances in Courland at the battle of Gemauerthof. Around the same time a small Swedish force stopped an assault on Warsaw. These victories allowed the coronation to proceed and Stanislaus was crowned King of Poland on 14 September. Since Augustus managed to flee with the Polish crown jewels, Charles ensured that a newly minted crown was ready for the occasion. The new Polish king needed to be recognised as such. Only after the Treaty of Altranstädt did a good number of European states acknowledge Stanislaus as the rightful king. Denmark and Russia, to no surprise, did not. Recognising that he owed his crown to Charles, Stanislaus was quick to sign a treaty with Sweden that was heavily weighted in the latter's favour. This served as confirmation for the opposing factions that Poland had now become nothing more than a Swedish puppet state. Charles promised to honour the borders of the Commonwealth and try to help it regain lands formerly lost to Russia. Many opportunists in Sweden hoped that Courland could transfer hands and provide more lucrative ports on the Baltic. With peace made via the Treaty of Warsaw Charles could now move more freely within the Commonwealth, and it granted him the freedom to split his army and counter an emerging "grand plan" between Peter and Augustus who conspired to trap the Swedes between opposing forces.

A large Russian force of about 41,000 men had entered Commonwealth territory and encamped in the vicinity of Grodno within the Duchy of Lithuania. Having split his army, Charles took the larger contingent and marched east to meet the threat. His 21,000 men were supplemented by 10,000 Poles and together they managed to cut off Russian cavalry support for those stationed at Grodno in January 1706. Augustus, who was present, used the moment to flee with several dragoon regiments and bypass Charles thus further weakening the allied forces at Grodno. The Elector had a different goal in mind. A combined Saxon–Russian army of 20,000 men under the command of General Schulenburg was marching to engage the smaller half of the Swedish army led by General Rehnskiöld.[16] Augustus and his 8,000 cavalry were hoping to catch Rehnskiöld from behind and surround him. The design to defeat the Swedes piecemeal was working so far. Rehnskiöld was aware of Augustus closing in and decided to give battle to Schulenburg near the town of Fraustadt before Saxon reinforcements arrived. On 2 February Rehnskiöld, outnumbered two to one, feigned a mass retreat before rounding on his pursuers on more favourable ground. The

---

16 Oskar Sjöström, *Fraustadt 1706. Ett fält färgat rött* (Lund: Historiska Media, 2008), pp.132–133.

THE VENTURE INTO POLAND AND SAXONY, 1701–1707

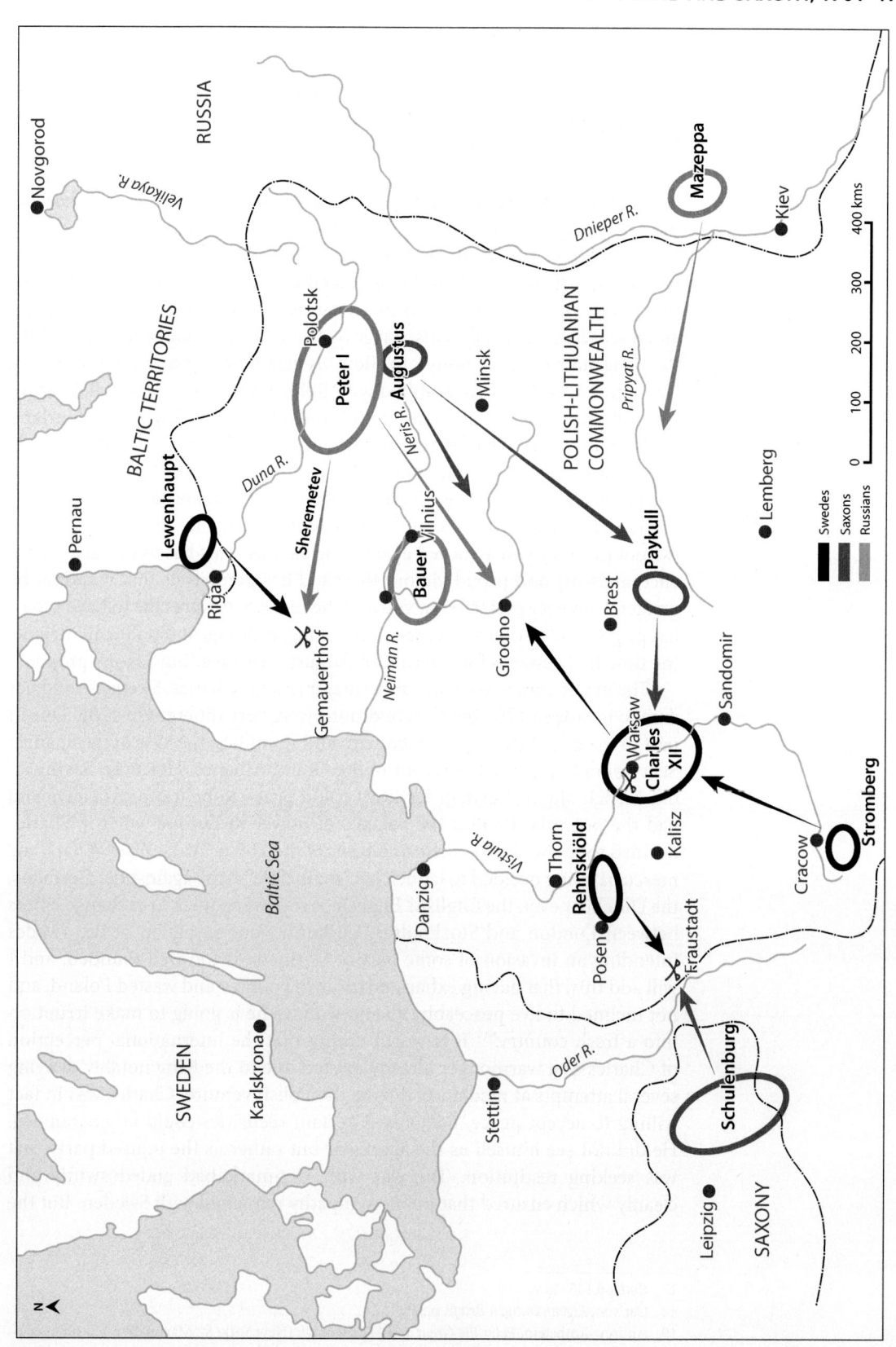

The Grodno Campaign.

83

success of the Swedish cavalry on both flanks led to a pincer manoeuvre that has since been compared to that of the ancient battle of Cannae. The Swedish infantry in their headlong charge on the enemy centre had identified the Russian position as a potential weak point of the line. Such was the speed and ferocity of the *Gå På* charge that several battalions never fired a volley before engaging in close combat. The result was catastrophic – the complete destruction of the Saxon army with some 15,000 casualties.[17] Upon hearing the news, Augustus retreated to Cracow, his plan in tatters.

At Grodno, the weather conditions in April allowed the Russians to retreat towards Kiev without being forced into a battle against Charles. The main body of troops remained intact but was heavily weakened by hunger and disease and ordered to disengage by Peter. Charles doggedly pursued the Russians but halted at Chomsk to allow his men to rest and gather provisions. By August 1706 the King reunited with Rehnskiöld to reform the field army. The full retreat of the Russians from Lithuania and subsequently Courland in the north gave Charles sole possession of the Commonwealth and the decimation of the Saxons at Fraustadt gave him the decisive battle that he had been seeking since 1701. A pleased King ennobled Rehnskiöld to count and promoted him to field marshal: "I cannot delay giving my congratulations for the bold victory you achieved against the Saxons. This has to be such an all-encompassing and proud victory that God has granted us that it cannot be greater. I am very pleased that you and the regiments were able to have such a happy go of it."[18] After five years of marching, fighting, and political intrigue, the time had come to force terms on Augustus by invading Saxony proper.

The march into Saxony was still a major risk for Charles. Sweden could not dare to invade in 1701 but the conditions were very different in 1706. Due in part to the grand victories at Blenheim and Ramillies, the War of the Spanish Succession had turned in favour of the Grand Alliance. However, having an old French ally in German territory could prove to be too provocative and had the potential to alter the balance of power in Europe: what if Charles decided to revive the Swedish ambitions of the Thirty Years' War? What if the mercurial King decided to launch his "invincible" army against the Germans, the Dutch, or even the English? English envoys were quick to exchange letters between London and Stockholm: "Certainly your suspicion of the Swedes intending an invasion of some part of Germany is too well founded; and I will add this, that having exhausted his own country and wasted Poland, and not inclined to live peaceably, it is no wonder he is going to make irruption into a fresh country."[19] It is worth noting that the international perception of Charles as a warmonger already existed due to the King notably denying several attempts at mediation during the Polish venture. Charles was in fact willing to accept peace, but only if certain securities could be guaranteed. He did not see himself as the aggressor but rather as the injured party that was seeking restitution. The war with Denmark had ended swiftly and cleanly which ensured that public sympathy remained with Sweden. But the

---

17 *Ibid*, pp.145–146.
18 Carlson, *Eigenhändigen Briefe*, p.276.
19 Andrew Rothstein, *Peter the Great and Marlborough* (New York: St. Martin's Press, 1986), p.63.

THE VENTURE INTO POLAND AND SAXONY, 1701–1707

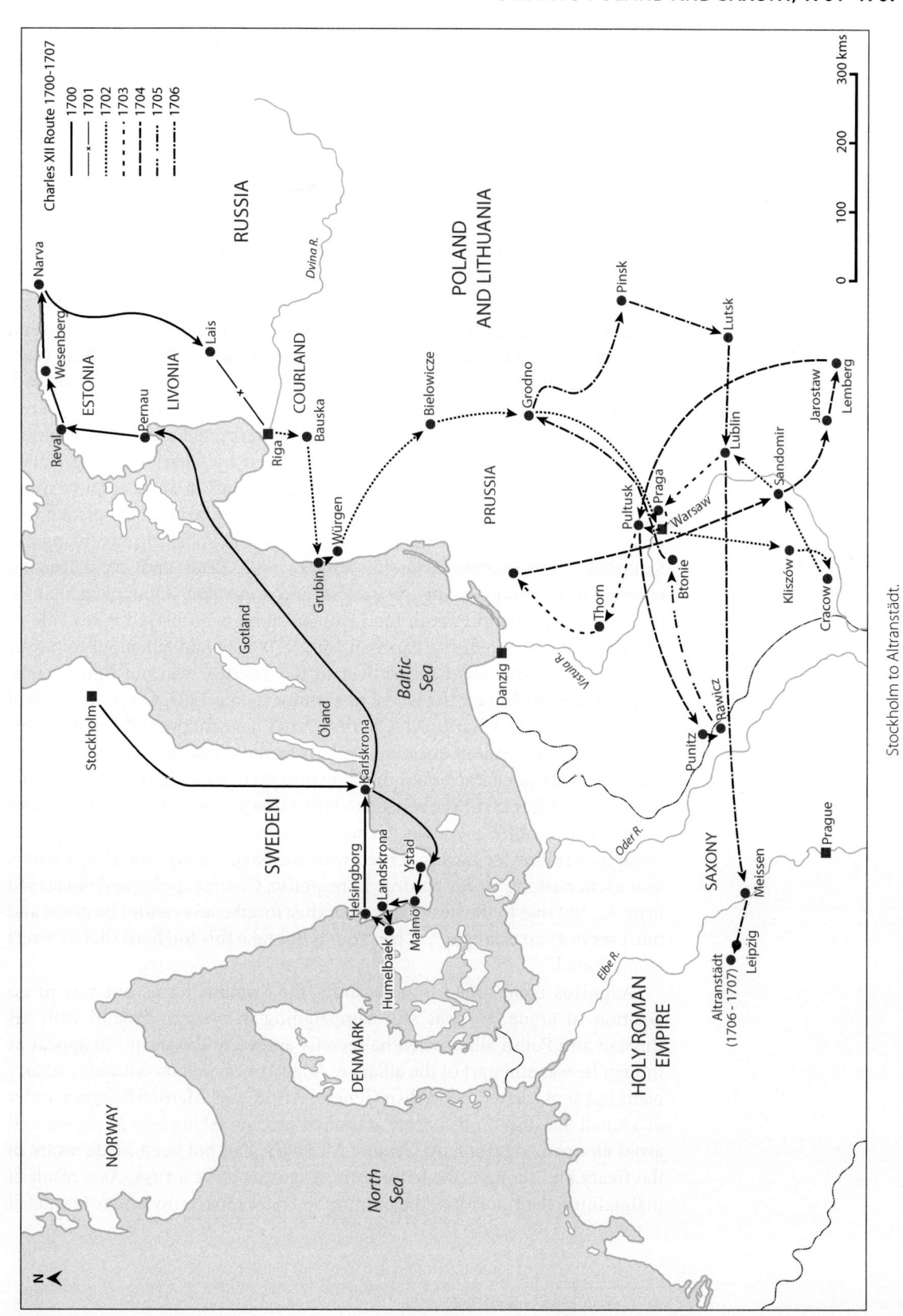

quagmire in Poland, with its political manipulation, subversion of law, and terrorised civilian population removed the veneer. All of the acts perpetrated by the Swedes could not be explained away in the name of defence. Peace may have been achievable earlier in the venture but would the protections for Sweden have been sufficient enough to ensure a lasting peace rather than a mere truce in a longer conflict? The King's decision to persecute the war until the best position for negotiation was achieved ties back to the lessons learned from Charles XI – to "avoid war unless dragged by the hair" but, if engaged, to wage it with all means. Perhaps the deathbed conversation between father and son continued to drive certain decisions.

A mutual fear of what could become of Saxony with the Swedes on the doorstep led Augustus and the Saxon Council, the *Geheimrat*, to send negotiators to Charles on 4 September. Just as he did on Danish soil six years earlier, Charles refused to halt his march while negotiations proceeded. "The sword does not jest" is a quote from the King that is often taken out of context. On its own, the phrase could be interpreted as another example of the King's war-lust. However, it was uttered by Charles during stalled negotiations and is the equivalent to "sabre rattling" in an attempt to make a point. Nine days later, Charles halted outside of Leipzig at Altranstädt and accepted the terms: Augustus would renounce the Polish throne, recognise Stanislaus, immediately cease his alliance with Peter and expel Russian troops, and relinquish any prisoners and deserters. One particular of the latter was Johann Patkul, the Livonian noble who played a key role in forming the anti-Swedish alliance in 1699/1700. He had fallen out of favour with Augustus and was handed over to the Swedes, who put him on trial and had him broken on the wheel as a traitor in late 1707. Given that Patkul was denounced by Charles XI, Charles would have followed through on his father's decision without question. Patkul's brutal execution is often seen as a stain on Charles's character but the King refused to tread lightly when it came to treason for fear of others being encouraged to pursue similar paths. Earlier in the year, another Livonian, General Otto von Paykull was sentenced to death as a traitor for having served with the Saxon army. The King's sisters sent a letter asking for his pardon. In response, Charles apologised but stayed firm: "… but due to the heavy nature of this, forgiveness cannot be given and must serve as an example … I beg you to not take this too hard that he won't be pardoned."[20]

Augustus complained bitterly about the Swedish terms but was in no position to argue. He was still campaigning in western Poland with his Russian and Polish allies when he secretly agreed to the treaty. To appear as though he was still part of the alliance, Augustus carried on with his military plans but sent a letter to Swedish General Arvid Axel Mardefelt, commander of a small Swedish–Polish army stationed nearby, asking him to retreat and avoid an open engagement. General Mardefelt had not been made aware of the treaty and thought the letter from Augustus to be a ruse. As a result of maintaining their position, the outnumbered Swedish army under Mardefelt

---

20 Carlson, *Eigenhändigen Briefe*, p.81.

suffered a defeat at Kalisz which affected the desired peace and threatened to destabilise the tenuous Swedish grip on Poland proper. Exasperated by Augustus's duplicity, Charles revealed the terms of the treaty to the public on 4 November which effectively cancelled out the loss at Kalisz. Swedish prisoners taken after the battle were released and Augustus returned to his electorate to renounce his Polish crown.

The King at Altranstädt

By the end of 1706 two of the three antagonists who started the Great Northern War had been removed. Charles and his ministers now fought on the political battlefield to ensure that the Treaty of Altranstädt was fully recognised and guaranteed as they did not trust Augustus to hold to it. At the same time, Charles worked on strengthening ties with Frederick I of Prussia, a growing power in the region. In return for recognising Stanislaus as the new rightful king of Poland, Frederick gained some territories that the Swedes had previously denied him. Negotiations with the Holy Roman Empire were having less success. Distrust was high as Sweden protested at the lack of religious freedom for Protestants in Silesia, a treatment contrary to the agreements of Westphalia of which Sweden was a guarantor, and the appearance of Russian troops in Saxony under Imperial control. Vienna was worried that the Swedes were acting in French interests and intended to destabilise the ongoing War of the Spanish Succession.

Memorial at Altranstädt. (Memorial at Altranstädt, Martin Geisler)

Whether he sought it or not, Charles was now the arbiter of Europe and garnered all of the attention. The whirlwind successes of the undefeated 24-year-old king – from Copenhagen to Warsaw to Leipzig – saw to this. During his stay at Altranstädt, Charles became somewhat of an attraction. Copies of his portrait were sold like souvenirs while any information about him in the broadsheets was quickly read and commented upon. Even dinners became a spectacle: "Altranstädt was every day filled with an infinite number of people, and the hall where the King dined was often so crowded, that the pages and domestics found it difficult to wait at table; the spectators, for want of room, were forced to stand upon chairs and windows, to get a sight of the King."[21] He was accosted by diplomats from all sides. The French encouraged him to recognise their claimant to the Spanish throne and tried to dissuade him from undertaking a Russian campaign. The Maritime Powers wanted the Swedes out of their theatre of war as quickly as possible and were of the

---

21 Adlerfeld, *Genuine History*, p.336.

Charles XII and Augustus at dinner. Note the older model uniform worn by the Swedish guards at the door. (Dinner with Charles and Augustus, 1706, public domain)

Late nineteenth century depiction of Charles XII and John Churchill, Duke of Marlborough. (Henry Edward Doyle, Charles XII and the Duke of Marlborough, 1886, public domain)

belief that the King intended to press on against Russia no matter what: "… the King of Sweden would pursue war vigorously against the Czar. If this is so and the Czar does not at once make peace, as is reported, we should have nothing to fear from this campaign."[22]

In late April of 1707 John Churchill, the Duke of Marlborough, arrived at the Swedish headquarters to obtain a personal audience with the King. At the negotiating table were two of Europe's finest generals, known for their astonishing victories and firm grasp of command. There were pleasantries and flattery but the meeting had a vital objective: the allies wanted to confirm the intentions of the King's next move. In his acting capacity as a diplomat, Marlborough was given power to negotiate but did his best to prevent any full commitment from the English. It was agreed that the Maritime Powers would keep Frederik IV and Augustus in check and tied to their respective peace treaties. This security would allow Charles free movement against Russia without worrying about

---

22 Rothstein, *Peter and Marlborough*, p.67.

having his back turned to Denmark and Saxony. Additionally, it was agreed that the Treaty at Altranstädt would be guaranteed and Stanislaus recognised as king of Poland. In hindsight, the former never happened while the latter was indeed confirmed by Queen Anne. For Sweden's part, they promised to work with the Maritime Powers in their efforts to end the War of the Spanish Succession. This was not a declaration of war against France but rather the simple promise that they would not intervene against the Grand Alliance. Allied pressure was also put on Vienna to ease tensions. The Holy Roman Emperor eventually consented and signed a second treaty at Altranstädt granting improved rights to Protestants in Silesia and allowing the Swedes free passage through the territory. A direct march on Russia was now possible.

It was also during the stay at Altranstädt that Charles rode to Leipzig to meet his cousin Augustus for the first time. He was the only sovereign that Charles would ever meet in person. The visit was cordial and there was none of the animosity that Charles had displayed towards Augustus during the war. To the King, justice was served and honour satisfied. In a letter home, Charles penned his observations of the Elector: "He is bright and entertaining. He is not very tall but strongly built, he is also a little corpulent. He carries his own hair which is dark in colour."[23] With Charles's own unique body shape of broad shoulders tapering to a narrow waist, the two monarchs were as different physically as they were in personality. A medal struck to commemorate the peace of Altranstädt depicts Charles and Augustus as Mars and Hercules, respectively, in a nod to their attributes.

Medal commemorating the Treaty of Altranstädt. (Muller, Medal commemorating Treaty of Altranstadt, 1706, public domain)

Running parallel to the political enforcement of the peace treaty was the preparation of the army for the Russian campaign. The work went on peacefully as the Swedes in Saxony found themselves among a population more akin to their own. The land, weather, people, and language reminded them of home, much more so than what they experienced in Poland. Strict rules were imposed on the army to ensure that no mistreatment befell the population. Non-Swedes descended on Altranstädt to join the ranks so that several regiments were raised out of mercenaries alone. Combined with new recruits shipped in from Sweden, Charles could field the largest army he had to date. His force in Saxony now numbered around 33,000 men (7,100 cavalry, 9,600 dragoons, 14,200 infantry, 1,500 Vallacks). This number does not include chaplains, *attachés*, and other noncombatants which may explain the size variations in the source material.[24] Swedish forces in the Baltic provinces under Lewenhaupt numbered 11,400 and there were another 14,000 men available in Finland.

It was at this point that many units in the army were outfitted with fresh uniforms. 1706 saw the introduction of the "younger" uniform model where the coat had more fabric due to the addition of pleating but fewer buttons that

---

23 Carlson, *Eigenhändigen Briefe*, p.80.
24 Hatton, *Charles XII*, p.233.

now only went down to the waist.[25] The collar and cuffs remained, as did the underlying camisole and knee-length trousers. The coat turnbacks tended to be yellow folded against the traditional dark blue, but red and white turnbacks were also used by certain regiments.[26] This uniform, combined with the black tricorne hat laced in white, is the lasting image of the Karoliner to modern eyes. In reality, changes came slowly and older uniform models would have still been in use along with variations of headgear and other equipment. Full standardisation had not yet been achieved. Uniforms would only last a few years before being worn down by the elements and battlefield conditions. In one example, the *Södermanland* regiment was described as "well clothed" in January of 1710 but then quite the opposite by the summer of the same year.[27] As the war progressed after Poltava, there are more accounts of units being described as "ragged" as supplies dwindled. For now, the army had reached its high water mark in terms of appearance. Well rested, fed, and supplied, the Swedish army marched eastward out of Saxony and into Silesia on 10 August, 1707.

After six years spent marching across the lands of the Commonwealth, Charles finally achieved the outcome he desired since his invasion of Courland in 1701. His campaign objective from the beginning was the expulsion of Saxon forces from Swedish territories which was then further modified to include the removal of Augustus from his Polish crown when a direct march on Saxony proved too contentious. The modification of his campaign aim led Charles and the Swedish army into the lion's den of Polish-Lithuanian politics where they were less adept. On the battlefield proper, Charles swept all opposition before him with victories at Riga, Kliszów, Pultusk, Thorn, Punitz, and Grodno.[28] He earned a sterling reputation as a military commander with Marlborough going so far as to say, with a healthy dose of diplomatic flattery, "I wish I could serve some campaigns under so great a general as your Majesty, that I might learn what yet I want to know in the art of war."[29] Despite usually being outnumbered, Charles knew how to apply immediate pressure when a weakness was spotted in the enemy's lines. Kliszów, Pultusk, and Punitz are all examples where wavering Saxon units exposed gaps that Charles ordered his cavalry to charge through. During the Polish venture, his military acumen continued to grow as he learned and endured through the experiences of the men under his command. One noteworthy observation came from General Roos who commented on the King's innate ability to distinguish Swedish fire from that of the enemy based solely on the pattern of the musket report; historian David Chandler's comment, therefore, bears credence: "Here was a monarch who was a genuine

---

25   Lars-Eric Höglund and Åke Sallnäs, *The Great Northern War 1700-1721 Colours and Uniforms* (Karlstad: Acedia Press, 2000), p.13. The authors contend that there were three distinct uniform models: Older 1680s–1692, Transitional 1694–1706, Younger 1706 onwards. The spread of each uniform style depended on the unit and its location. See Wolke, *Swedish Army*, pp.23–25.
26   Närke-Värmland, Jönköpping (red), Västerbotten (white)
27   Höglund, *Colours and Uniforms*, p.68.
28   Fraustadt, one of Sweden's greatest victories in the war, was won by Rehnskiöld while Charles was moving to engage the Russians at Grodno.
29   Rothstein, *Peter and Marlborough*, pp.74–75.

warlord in our period whose dedication to the practice of the martial arts and sciences at times bordered on the near insane."[30]

Charles was rash on occasion and quick to commit for fear of losing an opportunity at a swift, decisive victory. His two unimaginative cavalry charges on the Saxon infantry square at Punitz are a prime example of him replacing patience with a dogged belief that his will would be accomplished regardless of outside variables. Nevertheless, the King learned to adjust his tactics in real time, which culminated at Holowczyn in 1708.

Charles was victorious on the battlefield but he allowed himself to be drawn into the factional bickering in both Poland and Lithuania. His harsh dealings with the Lithuanians, the assault on the capital Vilnius, and his support for despised members of the local nobility drove many nationals into the hands of the Russians. His support for Stanislaus Leszcynski was, in the eyes of many Poles, simply for want of creating a Swedish satellite state. So while the move to engage Saxony over Russia may have been the right decision, the excessive time spent pursuing the Saxons and policing the population was not. Johann Patkul gleefully noted at the time: "the chief might of Sweden is kept there [in Poland] for amusement",[31] and according to Robert Frost, the time spent in the Commonwealth arguably set the outcome of the entire war:

Charles XII at the height of his power. (Johan David Swartz, Charles XII, 1706–07, Nationalmuseum, public domain)

> The Great Northern War was largely won and lost in the Commonwealth long before 1709; for, despite the fact that Charles won every battle that mattered until Lesnaya in 1708, he was comprehensively outmanoeuvred by Peter, who showed a far surer grasp of Polish politics than Charles.[32]

Peter was not idle after his loss at Narva. He managed to exert soft power in Poland while simultaneously creating a foothold in the Baltic provinces via military actions. Charles had an army in the region under general Lewenhaupt who managed to repulse the Russians on several occasions, but could ultimately not sustain the string of early victories as numbers worked against him. One by one the strongholds fell and Charles himself could not be bothered to support the regional army – he was too involved in Poland.

---

30 David Chandler, *The Art of Warfare in the Age of Marlborough* (Staplehurst: Spellmount, 1976), p.22.
31 Godley, *Charles XII*, p.92.
32 Frost, *Northern Wars*, p.264.

Chapter 7

The March to Russia, 1707–1709

"Thus ended this day so glorious both to the arms and person of his Majesty, whose valour, supported by the courage and bravery of his troops, gave the Russians to understand, with what ill judgement they had compared their forces to ours."

"… the troops were drawn up to mount the assault … but as the enemy had thrown a quantity of water on the ramparts which was frozen on all sides, and the garrison taking advantage of the difficulty which our men met … defended themselves in the most desperate manner … We lost many brave men at this attack."

Gustaf Adlerfeld recounting the success at Holowczyn and the pyrrhic storming of Verpik.[1]

The Baltic provinces were arguably the lifeblood of the Swedish Empire. Besides filling the coffers via the lucrative trade entering and exiting their ports, Ingria, Estonia, and Livonia also provided valuable and fertile farmland. In particular, Sweden relied heavily on the grains exported from Livonia as it could not produce enough on its own. The dependence was so great that the only article favourable to Sweden in the final peace treaty with Russia in 1721 granted Sweden the right to continue to purchase grains from its former province. Historian Michael Roberts therefore argues that Sweden's final demise as an empire stems from the loss of the Baltic provinces as they were the only overseas possessions that were "still discharging a vital political function".[2] If the region was such a valuable asset to Sweden, why was it not provided with a more solid defence during the war? Charles seemed to put a strong trust in the fortifications that dotted the landscape, but as early as 1681 Erik Dahlberg reported on the decaying state of the region's fortresses. Some of these locations were reinforced prior to the outbreak of war but others were still medieval in construction or simply weakened by dilapidation. An unhealthy lack of respect for the modernising Russian forces may be at fault as well – the sweeping victory at Narva encouraged this. Saxony was

---

1   Adlerfeld, *Genuine History*, pp.383, 413.
2   Roberts, *Swedish Imperial Experience*, pp.148–149. Refuted by Lockhart, *Sweden in the Seventeenth Century*, p.150.

deemed the stronger opponent and the King's attention eventually settled on the Commonwealth since an alliance with a friendly Poland could be quite lucrative and support a Swedish push into Russia at a later time.

The Swedish forces left in the provinces were small and therefore severely outnumbered in the subsequent engagements. As Ingria fell to the Russians, Charles remained confident that the area could be reclaimed despite several attacks on the newly founded St. Petersburg from land and sea being rebuffed. As the main Swedish army marched out of Saxony in 1707, it was argued that the Baltic provinces would make for the best destination. Czar Peter supposed this himself, but Charles had another objective in mind: to march on Moscow and dictate peace on Swedish terms to see all lost territory restored. As with the Saxons, he was looking for a singular, neat and decisive military engagement but the Czar wisely refused to meet Charles on a level playing field. By subjecting his own lands to fire, Peter manipulated the movements of the Swedish army and the unpredictability of the weather coupled with the vagaries of fate finally pushed the Swedes into a decisive engagement they were not prepared for.

The Russian Campaign in the Baltic

The crushing defeat of the Russian army at Narva in 1700 illustrated just how far Peter's military reforms needed to go. There was a distrust between subordinate and officer which led to orders not being carried out effectively. Once the Swedes penetrated the Russian siege lines, discipline failed and units broke and fled en masse with the exception of the guard regiments who had better training. Peter recognised that when he had to face the Swedes again, his men needed to not only have numerical superiority but also maintain the firm discipline and structured organisation required to fight in the evolving art of western warfare. This would be his counter to the *Gå På* tactic. His military reforms had already yielded fruit with victories over the Ottomans and the capture of the fortress at Azov on the Black Sea in 1696. However, the Ottomans and even the Russians, did not conduct war in the same style as that of Western Europe. What Peter needed was time to help with the implementation of his reforms and some victories to generate confidence. Immediately after Narva he had neither, and the days and weeks following the battle were filled with dread as there was nothing standing between the Swedes and a direct march on Moscow.

Due to the approaching winter and brutal attrition from camp diseases, Charles kept his army quartered in and around Narva and Dorpat and waited for reinforcements to arrive in the spring. Peter had retreated to Novgorod and utilised the fortuitous gift of time wisely. He saw the loss at Narva as the motivational force behind his work: "When we had that misfortune, or putting it better great fortune, compulsion then drove away sloth, and forced us to labour day and night."[3] With the notable speed and persistence

---

3   Rothstein, *Peter and Marlborough*, p.35.

he became known for, Peter cobbled together a new force of 23,000 men. The army would learn new musket drills and utilised Major Adam Weide's *The Brief Drill Manual* published in 1699/1700. This manual would be regularly updated afterwards with Peter adding his own instructions over time. Muskets were initially imported until factories could be set up to manufacture them domestically. As with most armies of the time, the flintlock musket became the primary armament for the infantryman. The Russian army also "trailed the pike" but not to the extremes of the Swedes and therefore bridged the divide between their foes and other western powers who had abandoned the pike altogether. Source material from 1700 does not even mention pikes but their successful employment by the Swedes prompted the Russians to outfit some of their regiments with them. Towards the end of the war, the pike was again out of favour and all but dropped. The only type of regular horse in the army were the dragoons. They existed in earlier editions of the Muscovite army but it was Peter who reintroduced them as he valued their mobility, firepower, and flexibility. Whereas Swedish dragoons tended to stay in the saddle and fight as if they were heavy cavalry, the Russian dragoons would fire from horseback and on occasion dismount to engage on foot. Peter's army also retained some eastern flair with the maintenance of irregular horse ridden by Cossacks. These light and loose formations were ideal scouts and were very successful in harassing Swedish foraging parties, supply trains, and even the main army on the march. Such was their effect that the Swedes would form their own units from allied Cossacks loyal to Charles.

It was also around the end of 1701 when Peter began refitting his army in a western-style uniform. Gone were the fur-lined coats, sashes, caps, and knee-high boots, replaced by a coat with large rounded cuffs in the French/Saxon fashion and trousers that were met at the knee by woollen stockings. The ubiquitous dark green lined internally with red was the predominant colour combination that Peter warmed to. By 1712 he made the colours a requirement, although blue and red still made appearances among several regiments. As with the Swedes, the cap known as the *kartuz* gave way to the tricorne although it tended to be worn without the lace trim.[4]

When Charles made the decision to first move south-west and attack Augustus and his Saxons, he took the majority of his field army with him. The smaller force left behind was placed under the command of generals Adam Lewenhaupt and Wolmar Anton von Schlippenbach. Sweden also possessed a good number of garrisons and forts in its Baltic territories such as those at Pernau, Dorpat, and Riga and would rely heavily on these to nullify the Russian advantage in numbers. In practice, however, the Swedish army of the Baltic would be constantly stretched in manpower and could not meet the Russians on equal footing. Just over a year post-Narva, the Russians achieved their first significant victory against the Swedes on 29 December, 1701 at Erastfer in Livonia. Some 18,000 Russians under the command of Peter's trusted general, Boris Sheremetev, pushed back 3,500 Swedes and

---

4   For a much deeper look into the Russian army, refer to Boris Megorsky, *The Russian Army in the Great Northern War 1700–1721* (Warwick: Helion & Company, 2018).

captured their artillery. The victory, however small, was celebrated by Peter back in Moscow. Success was found again at Hummelshof in July of 1702 when the hapless von Schlippenbach was again defeated by the numerically superior Russians. Peter did not want to engage the Swedes in a pitched battle and instead preferred to target smaller parts of the Swedish army and use his superior numbers as the primary advantage. The successes at both Erastfer and Hummelshof confirmed the validity of this strategy and the Czar's military commanders were ordered to comply and above all not risk the loss of the armies under their command. For example, General Repnin was instructed in 1704 to support Augustus in any capacity with the exception of engaging in an open battle. It was only in 1708, starting with the Battle of Lesnaya, that Peter became more aggressive but he still looked for other factors, such as terrain, to be in his favour and bolster his odds of victory.[5]

From the onset of the war the Czar's primary goal was the establishment of a port on the Baltic. The province of Ingria was identified as ideal territory owing to the Neva river flowing 72 kilometres from Lake Lagoda into the Gulf of Finland. Two Swedish forts guarded either end of the river – Nöteborg in the east and Nyenskans in the west. The former became the first target of the Ingrian campaign as trade moving into northern Russia had to pass Nöteborg. The fortress itself hailed from earlier centuries and despite some modifications maintained its medieval character. It was not adapted to combat modern artillery but it still had walls that at certain points were 4.3 metres thick and punctuated by seven defensive towers. It was situated on an island at the confluence of the lake and river which gave it control of the waterways and forced any besieger to row boats across open water to launch an assault. There were over 100 cannon but the Swedish garrison only had a fighting strength of 440 men meaning that not all of the guns were adequately used. The Russians under Peter's direct command deployed 12,500 men. After establishing a blockade to prevent any Swedish relief forces from reaching the fort, the Russians launched a successful amphibious landing although a large number of casualties occurred while reaching the shore and walls. In conjunction with the assault, a bombardment from mortars about 275 metres out on the mainland caused damage to the walls and opened up some gaps that were fiercely contested. The storming of Nöteborg lasted 13 hours but the Swedes managed to repel the attackers. While the Russians suffered more deaths, 538 to 200, the Swedish garrison was down to nearly 50 percent fighting strength and did not have the manpower to withstand further assaults. They opened negotiations for an honourable surrender and were allowed to march out with their banners and arms and the fortress transferred hands. Peter renamed it *Shlisselburg* as it was to be his "key to Ingria".[6] The victory parade in December 1702 honouring the success at Nöteborg gave Peter the perfect opportunity to debut the new western uniforms.[7]

---

5   Megorsky, *The Russian Army*, p.155.
6   Shlissel/Schlüssel is German for key.
7   Megorsky, *The Russian Army*, p.101.

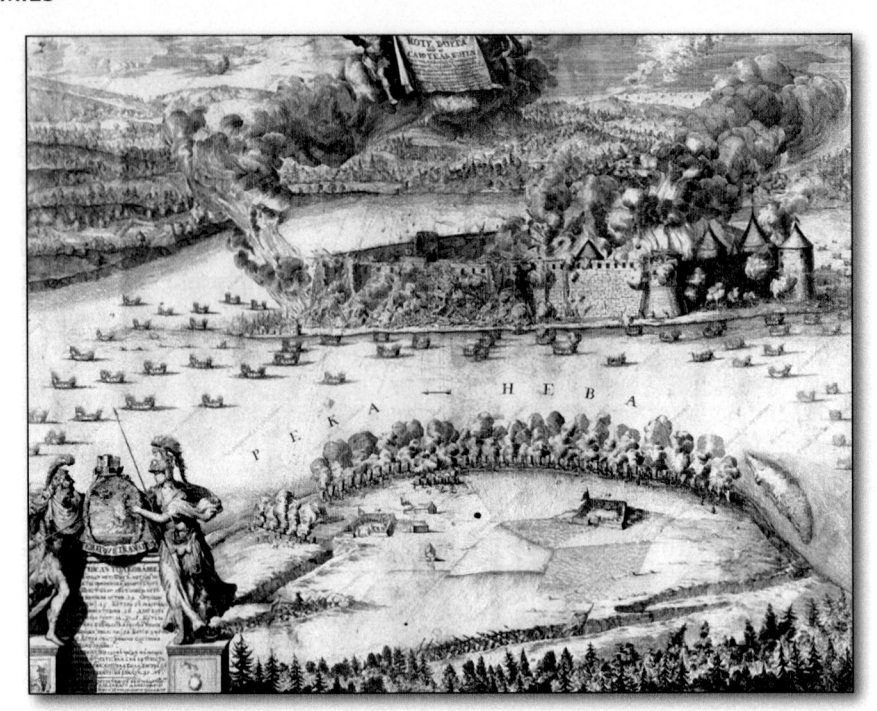

Shonebek (artist), The Siege of Noteborg, 1702. (Public Domain)

On the opposite end of the Neva was the small fortress of Nyenskans. Outdated and undermanned, it was the perfect target and a means to place the whole river under Russian control. The fort fell on 1 May, 1703 after token resistance. Barely two weeks later, Peter laid the foundation stone of what would become the Peter and Paul Fortress which still guards the city of St. Petersburg. His longed-for "window to the west" was achieved and he would go to great lengths to protect his prize as the Great Northern War progressed. Between 1702 and 1704 Sweden lost control of the Neva, and the lakes Lagoda and Peipus. Ingria was effectively cut off from the southern provinces and was never recovered.

As Charles continued his march throughout the Commonwealth, the Swedish army in the Baltic was fighting a losing battle: "Whilst the King was every day thus gathering fresh laurels in Poland, our poor frontiers of Livonia lay exposed to the plunder and barbarity of the Russians."[8] Russian sieges were grinding down the lynchpin fortresses that were meant to hold the enemy's advancement. From the end of June to early August 1704, Narva was besieged a second time and fell to Peter's forces.[9] The subsequent Treaty of Narva renewed the alliance between Peter and Augustus and included agreements with the Sandomierz confederation of Poles loyal to the Elector. Dorpat was also taken in 1704 resulting in territorial losses in Estonia. The gains were not uncontested. Lewenhaupt and his men won at Saladen in 1703 and at Jakobstadt in 1704 despite being outnumbered three to one. The final victory came in July of 1705 at Gemauerthof. The success proved

---

8   Adlerfeld, *Genuine History*, p.123.
9   For more information on the siege, refer to Boris Megorsky, *Peter the Great's Revenge: The Russian Siege of Narva in 1704* (Warwick: Helion & Company, 2018).

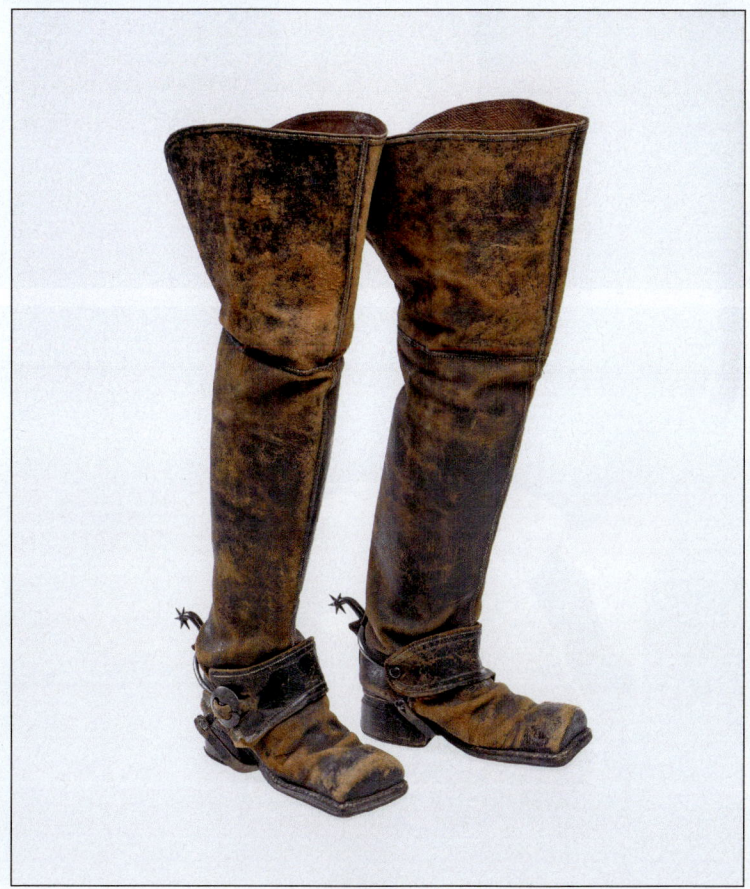

Plate 1
Charles XII's Neckcloth, 1718; Charles XII's Boots, 1718
The Royal Armoury, Stockholm (Livrustkammaren)
See Colour Plate Commentaries for further information

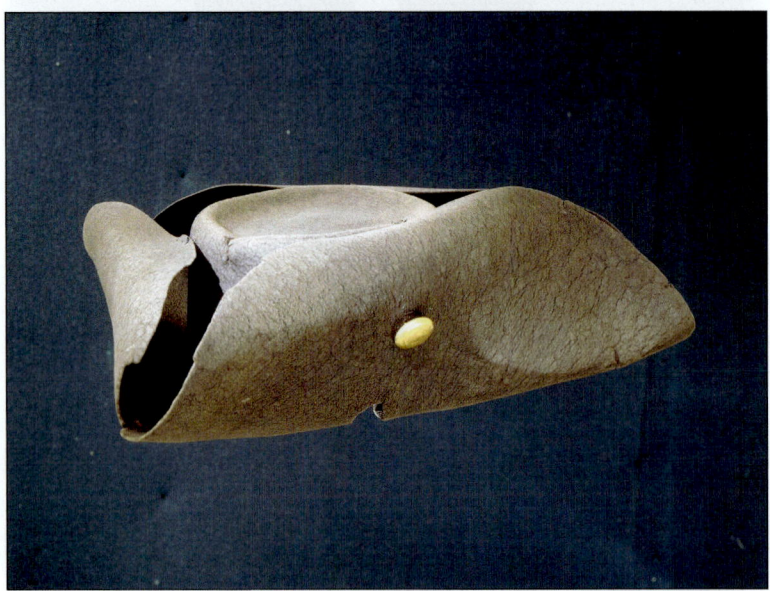

Plate 2
Charles XII's Gloves, 1718; Charles XII's Hat, 1718
The Royal Armoury, Stockholm (Livrustkammaren)
See Colour Plate Commentaries for further information

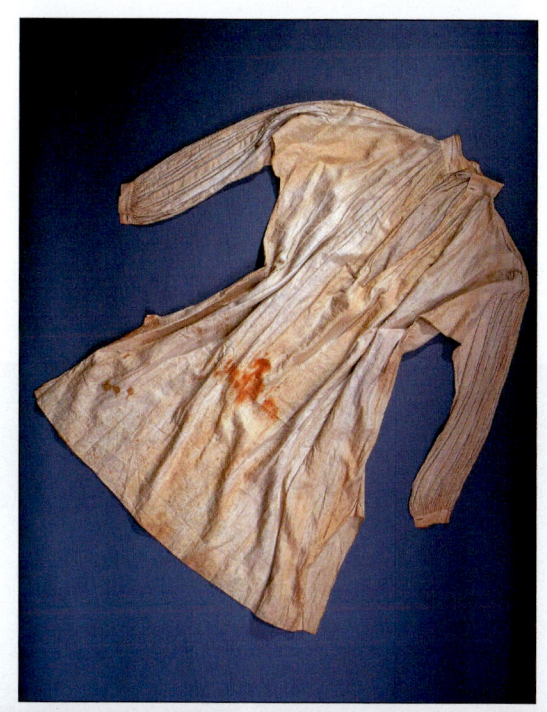

Plate 3
Charles XII's undershirt, 1718; Charles XII's Uniform, 1718
The Royal Armoury, Stockholm (Livrustkammaren)
See Colour Plate Commentaries for further information

Plate 4
Charles XII's Uniform, 1718
The Royal Armoury, Stockholm (Livrustkammaren)
See Colour Plate Commentaries for further information

THE MARCH TO RUSSIA, 1707–1709

to be short-lived. The Russian plans for 1705 were to support the Saxons in the Commonwealth and they pushed an army of 45,000–50,000 men into Lithuania. The Swedes had around 20,000 men split between Livonia and Courland. Despite Lewenhaupt's victories, Sweden did not have the manpower to defend the provinces and following the capture of Mitau, the remaining Swedish forces moved to the security of Riga. Courland was next to fall and by the end of October vast swathes of provincial territory now belonged to the victorious Russians. Sweden made several attempts to blockade St. Petersburg and launch assaults from southern Finland but to no avail. More worryingly for Swedish observers, the Russian army no longer resembled that which the Swedes so easily swept aside in 1700:

> the Swedes are forced to own the Muscovites have learnt their lesson much better and have made great improvements in military affairs since the battle of Narva and Fraustadt, and that they equal if not exceed the Saxons both in discipline and valour ... their infantry stand their ground obstinately and it is a difficult matter to separate them or bring them in a confusion if they be not attacked with sword in hand.[10]

After leaving Saxony and Silesia, Charles referred to his return to Poland as "a walk home". Given the five years spent in the Commonwealth, he had grown accustomed to the land and people but he did not have the opportunity to linger for long at any one location. The Vistula was crossed on 1 January, 1708, and it would prove to be the King's personal Rubicon. To better navigate the rough terrain and want of provisions, Charles split his army into three manageable columns and had them conduct quick marches across territory not deemed passable in a military sense. By the 27th he was back at Grodno, the target of his daring 1706 campaign, and managed to surprise the contingent of Russians quartered there. Unknown to Charles, Peter was also at Grodno but managed to extricate himself along with his men. The Russians would return to fight a brief skirmish but then retreated completely. The speed with which the Swedish army moved eastward kept the Russians on the back foot and their defensive line was pushed back towards the Russian border without a single large-scale battle being fought. Poland was mercifully spared of the ravages it endured from 1701 to 1706 despite Peter wishing to fight on non-Russian soil for as long as possible. It was becoming apparent that Charles picked the most direct route towards Moscow rather than the one more commonly used and thus expected. There were, in fact, four options – via Pskov in the north, via Smolensk, via Briansk, and from the south via the Ukraine and Poltava.

Due to their frenzied pace, the Swedes spent little time in good quarters and were constantly exposed to the ever-changing elements as they trudged along uneven roads and executed several dangerous river crossings. Captain James Jefferyes, an English agent who "volunteered" to join the army, had a

---

10 James Jefferyes, *Captain James Jefferyes's Letters from the Swedish Army*, ed. R.M. Hatton (Stockholm: P.A. Norstedt & Sons, 1954), p.59.

strong admiration for the hardiness of the Swedish soldiers who were asked to endure such adversity:

> I cannot on this occasion pass by the praises due to the Swedish troops, for whether I consider the great hardship they have been obliged to undergo, by forcing their way through places almost impassable, and by wading through morasses up to their middle, or I consider their patience in suffering hunger and thirst, they being for the most part reduced to coarse bread and water, I must conclude they are as good subjects as any Prince in Europe can boast of.[11]

His observations were to become a theme of Swedish movements up to the battle of Poltava. The majority of time was spent on the march with constant corrections caused by setbacks from weather, lack of supplies, and enemy harassment. Illnesses, which included fever and dysentery, spread through the army. Charles and his general staff were not immune and suffered alongside the rank and file to the point that "few of the new recruits which came over from Sweden last harvest but have had either the one or the other".[12]

It was hoped that the main Swedish army would receive reinforcements from the Commonwealth and Finland and be able to exert pressure on the Russians from multiple fronts. Charles kept 8,000 men, mostly German volunteers under General Krassow, in Poland to support Stanislaus's delicate position by suppressing any resistance. Swedish diplomats were still spilling ink seeking further international recognition of Stanislaus as the rightful King of Poland. The need was so pressing that Charles initially slowed his march from Saxony to Poland to wait on English confirmations. If additional guarantees and securities could be negotiated, the 8,000 men and the Poles loyal to Stanislaus could then provide added numbers for the push into Russia.

The Swedish army stationed in Finland was tasked with marching south to capture St. Petersburg since the newly established city meant everything to the Czar. In subsequent attempts for establishing a peace, Peter offered to return all territories taken by Russia with the exception of St. Petersburg and Shlisselburg along the Neva. This rapprochement was denied by Charles who would see all lost territory restored. The denial remains a criticism of the King's inflexibility but it is worth asking the question: would Peter really have been content with this small outlet to the Baltic in light of his attempts to have Russia become a major European power? What if his growing fleet

Charles XII in 1707. (David von Krafft, Charles XII King of Sweden, 1707, Nationalmuseum, public domain)

---

11 *Ibid.*, p.47.
12 *Ibid.*, p.39.

and army were given additional years to build strength – could Sweden afford another war against an even stronger opponent? Carl Piper, an official of the field chancery, echoed the thoughts of his monarch when rebuffing mediation attempts by the Holy Roman Emperor: an honest and lasting peace could only be achieved by destroying the Russian army and thus gain the desired security for Sweden. Russian power had to be weakened to a level that Sweden could adequately handle on its own at a moment's notice.

Despite the Czar's overtures, there were several attempts to blockade St. Petersburg by sea and launch an assault but they never amounted to realistic threats. While General Menshikov believed the Swedish army would push south towards Kiev in what is now the Ukraine, Peter was still convinced that the main thrust would go through the Baltic provinces. He therefore spent more time in the north preparing the defences of his beloved city.

After passing through Minsk, Charles launched a masterful series of feints and the Swedish army managed a successful crossing of the Berezina River nearly uncontested. The passage allowed a Russian contingent under Sheremetev to be outflanked. Adhering to the Czar's standing order that the army should only engage if it had a high chance of victory, Sheremetev pulled back to the Vabich river near a village called Holowczyn. In an effort to not be outflanked again, the Russian army was divided into three sections and stretched along the river bank concentrating heavily around two crossing points. Sheremetev had 23 battalions of infantry, eight dragoon regiments, and an allotment of Cossack light cavalry. Further south along the banks were another 17 infantry battalions under General Repnin and 10 dragoon regiments with more light cavalry under General Goltz.

Charles recognised that the terrain between the three Russian forces would hinder their ability to reinforce one another and decided that Repnin's corps, the central position of the Russian lines, was the most geographically isolated. On the night of 3 July, 1708, the Swedes attacked. Using the cover of darkness and the noise of an artillery barrage from 28 guns, Charles and the first wave of his infantry managed to wade across the river without alerting the Russians of their presence. At dawn they stormed into Repnin's flank, thus circumventing the fortifications that were hastily erected facing the river. Repnin understood that all would be lost if the Swedes sustained the fight at close quarters and he ordered his men to fire and retreat when approached: "the enemy discharged commonly their guns at 30 or 40 paces distance, then run, charged again, rallied and so discharged …"[13] He hoped to stall for time and get support from the other Russian contingents in the area. Charles too appreciated the urgency of the situation and the need to break Repnin's men. The King moved from battalion to battalion urging his men to forgo shooting and charge with sword, bayonet, and pike. He could not afford a musketry stand-off. After hearing the sounds of battle, Goltz brought up his cavalry but was intercepted by that of Rehnskiöld. The Swedes succeeded in pushing the cavalry back and set off a domino effect as subsequent waves of Russian infantry and cavalry emerged from the woods only to become disordered by

---

13 Jefferyes, *Letters*, p.51.

BY DEFEATING MY ENEMIES

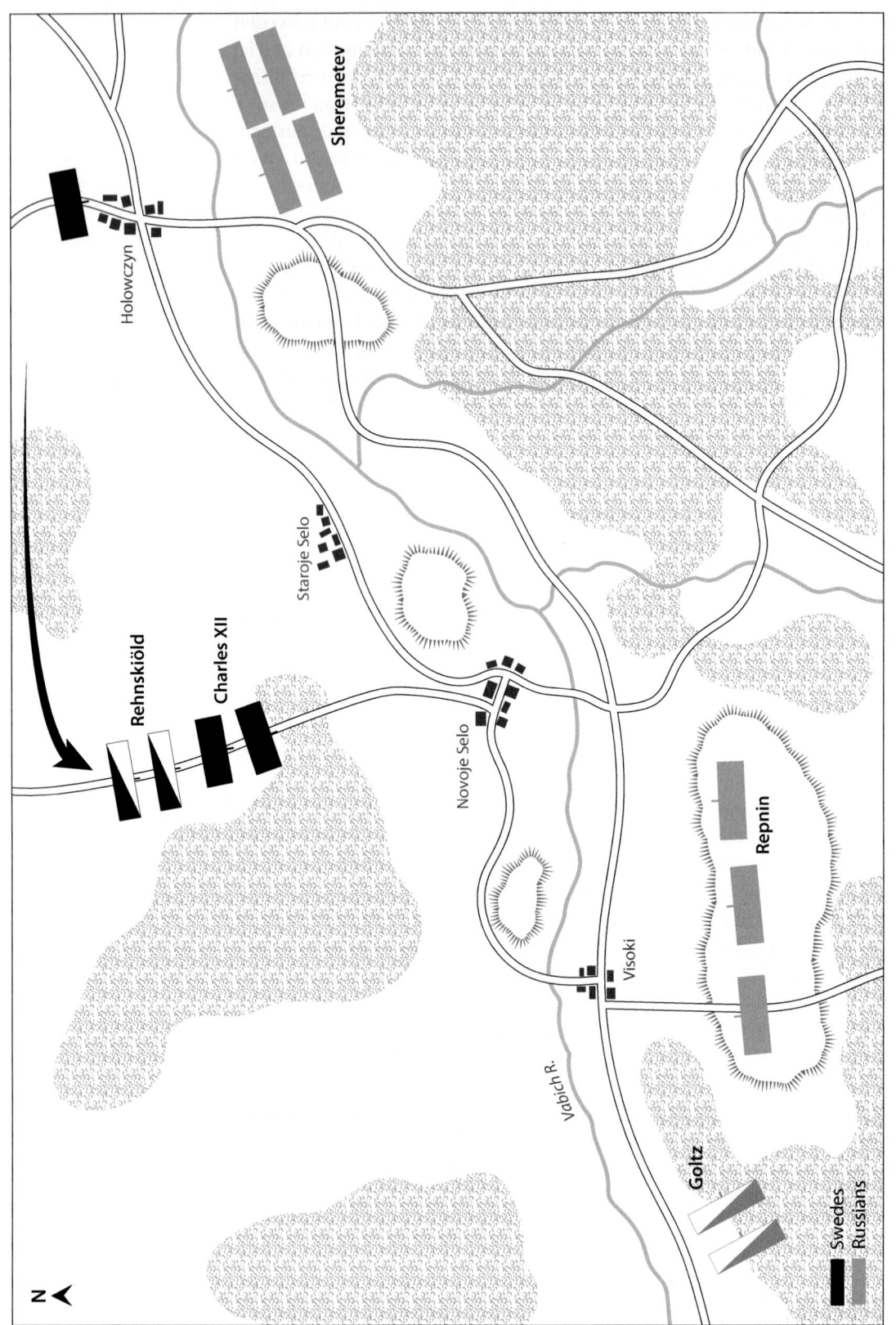

The Battle of Holowczyn, phase 1.

THE MARCH TO RUSSIA, 1707–1709

The Battle of Holowczyn, phase 2.

The order of battle for Holowczyn, 1708. (Order of Battle for Holowczyn, 1708, Krigsarkivet, public domain)

having the retreating units interpenetrate their lines. The result was that 13 Swedish squadrons routed 50 Russian squadrons.[14]

The flight of the Russian cavalry forced Repnin to launch an infantry charge but it was ultimately unsuccessful. Convinced he had no other options, Repnin retreated to keep his forces intact. Sheremetev, who never fully joined the battle from his position further up the river, also retreated to fight another day. The Swedes suffered 260 dead and 1,000 wounded while the Russians sustained casualties anywhere between 1,000 and 5,000 men. Charles succeeded in a surprise night-time river crossing and again used his eye for terrain to identify the best point of attack. Despite being outnumbered 12,500 to 28,000, his attack on the centre put a wedge in the Russian lines so that only 9,000 Russians could actually take part in the fighting. Out of all of his victories, he reputedly considered Holowczyn to be his favourite.

In the aftermath of Holowczyn, Jefferyes observed:

> … that His Majesty has acted at this time with more coldness and circumspection than he used to do on the like occasions, for there being but a little river between us and the enemy, fordable in several places … it is a sign he begins to set a greater value on the lives of his soldiers than he has done in former actions … and shows in him a more than ordinary patience.[15]

---

14 Nicholas Dorrell, 'On the Road to Moscow: the Battle of Holowczyn 1708', in Steve Kling (ed.), *The Great Northern War Compendium* (St. Louis: THGC Publishing, 2015), p.238.
15 Jefferyes, *Letters*, p.49.

THE MARCH TO RUSSIA, 1707–1709

While it was true that the King's usual urgency was abandoned for a well-designed attack, there existed a contemporary opinion that Charles did not care for the lives of his men given how haphazardly he seemed to throw them into combat. An Imperial diplomat, disappointed by his failed negotiations with the Swedes, blurted out: "The greatest evil of all evils is that this prince has no rule or policy and cares nothing for his life or for his states."[16] The *Gå På* tactics employed by the Swedes favoured aggressiveness. By assaulting lines of infantry or fortified defences with *l'armes blanche*, the Swedes could force quick victories but they could be costly in casualties depending on the strength, training, and discipline of the opponent. It was a tactic that matched the King's own style but it simultaneously garnered the impression that men were simply run into the line of fire without being allowed to fire return volleys. However, given the discipline of the Swedes, the tactics could provide lopsided results in their favour. At Narva the Swedes only lost 667 men, at Kliszów 300, and at Fraustadt around 450. The foe, in turn, suffered much higher casualty ratios. Charles did not take the loss of Swedish lives lightly – at one point he even mused about challenging Peter to an individual duel as a means to spare the common soldiers. As the campaign continued he maintained his outward stoicism, but officers close to the King noted how he agonised over decisions and mounting casualties and how he had trouble sleeping, now more than ever before.

On 9 August, the Swedes crossed the final major river, the Dnieper as the hunt for the Russian army continued. The Battle of Malatitze at the end of August saw the Russians attack a few isolated Swedish regiments within their own camp. With usual speed, Charles had his army arrayed for battle but found just the Russian rearguard evacuating the area. A skirmish at Rajowka occurred when Russian dragoons directly targeted Charles, who was at the head of a unit of horse that had become isolated from the main army. Charles had his horse shot from under him and one of his commanders, Prince Maximilian of Württemberg, only escaped by posing as a Russian officer. The Swedish army again assumed battle formation but no further attacks came. The Russians were conducting successful hit and run tactics which forced the Swedes to use ammunition and waste precious time and resources as they searched the vicinity for the larger Russian army. The success of these attacks kept the Swedes on alert "both day and night with one foot in the stirrup", and began to wear on morale.

The situation grew worse over time. As the Russians withdrew, anything that was of potential use to the Swedes was either hidden or destroyed. Stores of grain, flour, and other foodstuffs were buried underground and fields used for the grazing of horse were set alight. Krassow's 8,000 men in the Commonwealth were not able to leave their charge as Stanislaus continued to struggle with insurrections against his authority. Any push from the Finnish troops was also rebuffed by the Russians in Ingria. This left General Lewenhaupt and his army of Livonia. In May of 1708 the general had met with Charles near Minsk and was ordered to gather a three-month supply

---

16 Michael Hochedlinger, 'The Mad Swede: the Habsburg Monarchy and Charles XII', in John B. Hattendorf (ed.), *Charles XII Warrior King* (EU: Karwansaray Publishing, 2018), p.237.

Adam Ludwig Lewenhaupt. (David von Krafft, Adam Ludwig Lewenhaupt, Nationalmuseum, public domain)

of provisions and ammunition for the main army and then march south to link up with Charles. For perspective, the daily rations of a Swedish soldier included 637 grams of bread, 285 grams of meat, 170 grams of lard, two jugs of peas, and several litres of ale and some schnapps. The initial deployment date of the train was surpassed as supplies were difficult to gather in a region that had experienced both famine and a fair share of the conflict over the past eight years. Only in July, a month behind schedule, was the supply column able to set out from Livonia.

The sheer scale of the supply train slowed the march from the beginning. To sustain a field army for three months would require thousands of wagons and horses all moving together with armed support. Historian David Chandler extrapolates the challenging logistics using bread as an example. He cites an estimate that an army of 60,000 men would need 900 quintals of bread per day. To bake such a large amount would require 60 ovens with each oven needing a wagon to transport the bricks alone. To support a single baking session required nearly 200 wagon loads of fuel.[17] Lewenhaupt had the unenviable task of escorting some 4,500 wagons, 18,000 horses, 13,000 cows and sheep, and nearly 20,000 soldiers and civilians through sodden roads all while being shadowed by the Russians.[18]

Charles, who valued speed above all else, was hampered by the need to stay close to Lewenhaupt and the expected rendezvous point. A rainy summer had hindered both Swedish armies and moving cartloads of supplies proved difficult on waterlogged roads. The slow progression of the supply train kept Charles camped in Mogilev for nearly a month and a good portion of the late summer campaigning season was therefore wasted.

The lengthy wait and deteriorating conditions in and around the army forced Charles to make another critical decision at Tatarsk in early September. With the vital supply train bogged down by the roads and still many miles away and the Russians burning everything to the point that the Swedes could see the horizon lit up in flames, a decision had to be made on how to progress. Pskov to Smolensk, a distance of some 400 kilometres, was subjected to Peter's scorched earth policy. Smolensk was Charles's target and Moscow was on a direct route from there. However the supplies were running low: "I fear his Majesty would bring into Russia a parcel of starved beggars", and a growing number of men were beginning to desert the army among the "occasioned murmurings".[19] Charles gathered his top generals and advisors including Rehnskiöld, Piper, and Meijerfelt as part of

---

17 Chandler, *Art of Warfare*, p.15.
18 Einar Lyth, 'The Battle of Lesnaya 1708', in Steve Kling (ed.), *The Great Northern War Compendium* (St. Louis: THGC Publishing, 2015), p.263.
19 Jefferyes, *Letters*, p.61.

THE MARCH TO RUSSIA, 1707-1709

the emergency council. After three days of debate, the decision was made to move south towards Severia where the lands were not devastated. The army could rest, resupply, and then follow the roads from there to Moscow. On paper it would be a slight diversion. Other theories about the decision to move south include planning a south-to-north route in warmer areas for a quicker push on Moscow, utilising Ukrainian territory as an easier way to move back into Poland if needed, and trying to gain support among disaffected Cossacks and the Ottomans. The army split into two columns with Charles commanding one and General Lagerkrona the other. The latter went off route and then neglected to take the region's capital, Starodub, when he fortuitously appeared at its outskirts. Capturing the stronghold would have given the Swedes some longed-for security but it was the Russians who profited instead. The normally reserved Charles angrily lamented over Lagerkrona's "madness" for not taking Starodub. The exhausted Swedes who reached Mglin suffered larger losses in the march from Tatarsk than at any other point of the campaign as Jefferyes astutely noted: "'tis thought we have lost more in this ramble than if we had given the enemy a battle".[20] Hatton believes the march cost more Swedish lives than the battles of Holowczyn, Malatitze, and Rajowka combined.[21]

Lewenhaupt and Charles had been in frequent communication via messenger about a planned conjunction, but the King's ultimate decision to move the main army south surprised the general. Charles wrongly assumed that the supply train had already crossed the Dnieper and was closer than it really was. With the main army pulling away, the supply train was isolated and exposed. As the Swedish army camped at Mglin, there was a report of cannon in the distance: "we heard great firing of guns from a town half a mile from this place in which lies a muscovite garrison. We are since informed it was for a victory the Muscovites have had over Count Lewenhaupt ... I presume that action has not gone according to wish."[22]

On 28 September, Lewenhaupt had his army organised in marching column as they slowly crossed a bridge south-west of the village of Lesnaya towards Propoisk. The Russians used this opportunity to commit to a full attack. For once the Czar had opted to not exercise caution and this caught Lewenhaupt by surprise and his army unprepared. The general managed to rally his men and with efficient use of cavalry was able to repel the first Russian wave. The battle raged for a day with interspersed breaks as men regrouped and reformed. The Swedes were at a disadvantage by having some units already over the bridge, having a lower overall number of available men, and having to protect the vulnerable wagons. The addition of Bauer's Russian dragoons and roving Cossacks meant the Swedes were in danger of being surrounded. Lewenhaupt ordered a retreat during the night but had to leave the wagons and cattle behind. In doing so he managed to save a large portion of his army but had to sacrifice the train. 7,000 men escaped leaving around 3,000 dead, though these numbers are still disputed. When

---

20 Jefferyes, *Letters*, p.63.
21 Hatton, *Charles XII*, p.273.
22 Jefferyes, *Letters*, p.64.

the remnants of the army met up with Charles in early October, Lewenhaupt was not punished as he had comported himself as best he could given the circumstances. For the first time, the Russians beat the Swedes at their own game – they attacked first and maintained that momentum, forcing the Swedes to fight the majority of the battle on the defensive. When the Swedes managed a counter attack, the Russian infantry was properly supported by the cavalry and artillery, something that was not as common in earlier battles. Peter's reforms were taking hold and it is for this reason that the Czar referred to Lesnaya as "the mother of Poltava".

The reliance on the supply train and the subsequent wait for it to arrive was the primary miscalculation of the summer campaign. The decision to move south in search of accessible provisions at once risked the supply train but also reduced the need for it. Since the Swedes tended to go into battle with inferior numbers, the loss of the men accompanying the train was a more severe blow. With the missed opportunity of capturing Starodub, Charles's army moved even further south and it is now known that the King was looking to establish an alliance with the Cossack Hetman Ivan Mazeppa.

Mazeppa had previously fought against the Swedes but circumstances forced him to change sides. Peter had increased the taxes levied on the Cossacks and required all Hetmanate forts to fall under Russian military control. The Czar also neglected to provide military support which violated the old Pereyaslav treaty. Mazeppa sought to leverage the discontent and unify the northern Hetmanate Cossacks with his southern Zaporozhian Cossacks. Just before Mazeppa formally allied with Sweden, Peter sent a Russian force to Batruin in effect setting off a race for the Cossack capital. Charles recognised the opportunity to have a secure location for winter quarters but arrived too late. Menshikov and his dragoons razed the entire town and had the inhabitants subjected to rape and massacred. Charles was only four miles away. The harsh Russian dealing with Batruin gave other Cossacks pause about their allegiances. The resulting split of support was strikingly similar to what had occurred in Poland. The 1708 campaign saw a notable increase in the brutality of war and Batruin was but the most recent example. For his part, Charles disliked unnecessary massacre.[23] The King had previously intervened at Pultusk to save the remaining Saxons that were trapped in the town. After Holowczyn, he refused to have Russian prisoners killed because of an acute food shortage and he angrily rebuked his men for killing a Polish villager who approached with a white shirt to enquire about the Swedish army passing through. Charles was, however, ruthless in countering guerrilla warfare and never suffered from a troubled conscience after killing whomever he deemed the enemy.

With the Swedes now committed in the Hetmanate, Peter began to fortify towns which lay on the southern route to Moscow in order to make the passage as costly in Swedish lives as possible. The pyrrhic assault on Verpik illustrated the brutal effectiveness of the Czar's strategy. Verpik was a Cossack fort occupied by 2,000 Russians and loyal Cossacks. The Swedes sent 3,000

---

23 The King was not present at Fraustadt where 500 Russian prisoners were controversially executed after the battle.

THE MARCH TO RUSSIA, 1707–1709

men against the fortifications on the morning of 7 January but they were repulsed due to a combination of poor, hasty planning and accurate enemy fire that picked off the storming parties and individual officers. The garrison ended up surrendering during the night, but the loss of 400 dead and 600 wounded aggrieved the King who became increasingly desperate. Charles could not afford continued losses, being so far removed from any chance of reinforcement. His immediate goal was to clear Ukrainian territory of Russians so he could adequately prepare for a spring offensive in 1709 and give his men valuable time to rest.

The luck that Charles oftentimes relied on when taking calculated risks began to run out. Having navigated a very wet summer, the Swedes were now subjected to one of the coldest winters in European history. Deaths from exposure spiked throughout Europe and important waterways froze over allowing impromptu "frost faires" to be set up on the ice. Both the Swedes and Russians suffered tremendously as the temperatures dropped, with Charles noting: "The winter was very cold, so much so that it seemed unordinary and many of the foe and our own men froze to death or suffered [frostbite] on their hands, feet, and noses."[24] In the same letter, Charles wrote that despite the cold it was a *joyful* winter because the Swedes were able to conduct small-scale operations against the Russians and achieve success. The King always tended to downplay the severity in his letters home regardless of it being a personal injury, a loss in battle, or some other unfortunate fate. When he broke his femur in a camp accident in 1702, he simply mentioned it as "a little hurt in his leg" and an infected wound in his foot that made officers fear for his life in 1709 was just "a fever". In an extreme understatement, Charles noted Poltava as "an unfortunate setback".

The necessity to reflect on events in a positive light for the sake of maintaining morale at home cannot be neglected when interpreting the King's letters. Similarly, the recipient of the letter lends additional context. The majority of Charles's surviving letters were addressed to his younger sister, Ulrika Eleonora. When she was still considered a child, the King's letters to her tended to be jovial – in one example he goes to great lengths to describe the foreign customs of a peasant wedding – but as she grew older, he began to share some of the harsher realities of campaign life. But perhaps the King really did believe that any setback could be overcome through dedication and faith, regardless of how extreme or costly it was. Even at the Kingdom's darkest points, Charles sought to achieve a complete reversal of fortunes through one overwhelming

The King's femur, which did not set properly and caused a slight limp. (Author's collection, public domain)

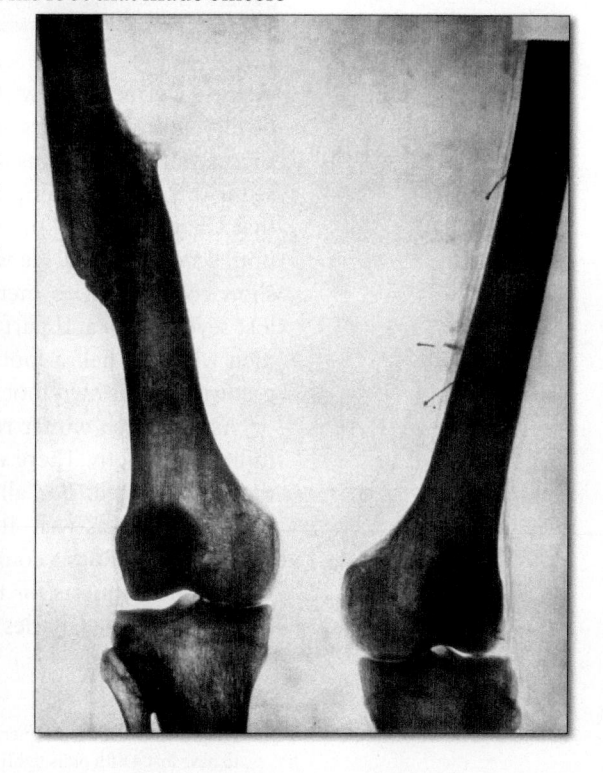

---

24 Carlson, *Eigenhändigen Briefe*, p.94.

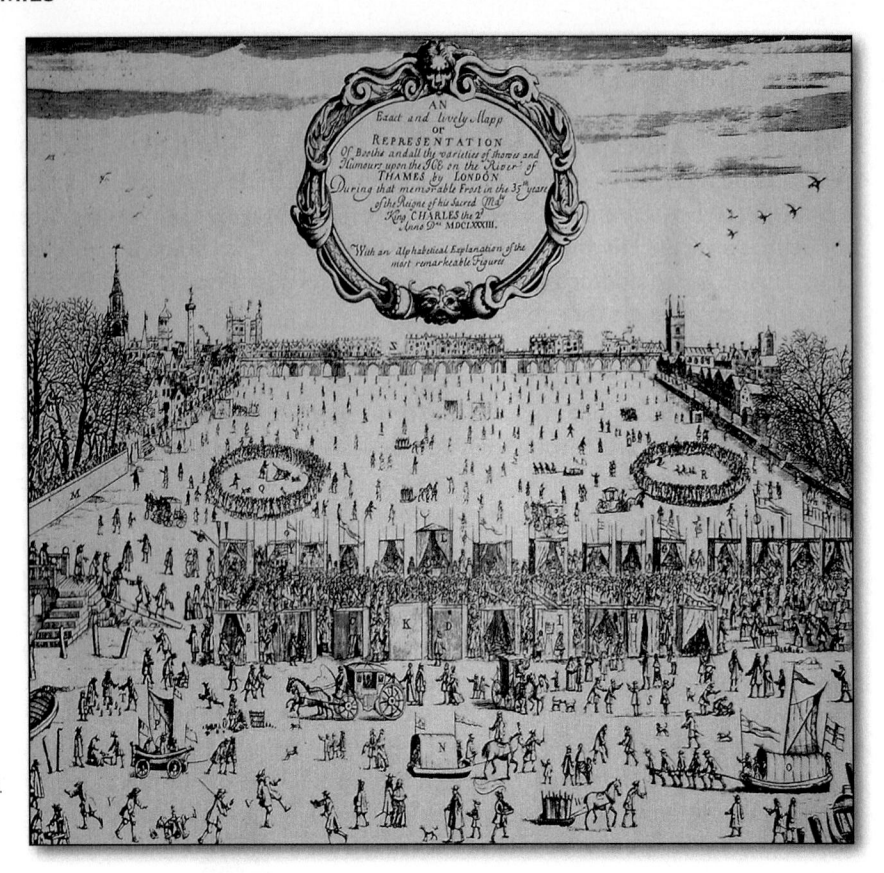

Frost fair on the Thames, 1683. (Frost Fair of 1683, public domain)

victory. Detractors saw the King's attempts as cavalier and reckless "daredevilry" but supporters were encouraged by his deep trust in God; that the successful outcome was a manifestation of His will and that Charles would see it through. In camp the drills would continue. One colonel remarked that Charles put regiments through their paces from four in the morning until seven at night. He would joke with officers who were tense and would show compassion to men who were wounded. For one young officer who lost several toes and part of his heel to frostbite, the King told him of other men who lost half a foot and could now walk better than before, all while gesturing to his own foot which he had propped onto his saddle.

As the harsh winter receded, Charles worked on bolstering his reduced military strength. There were more losses attributed to disease and weather than battle itself. For all the Swedes had suffered, the Russian army lost large numbers as well. It was a matter of replacing the losses that proved problematic.[25] Russia could call on a seemingly endless reserve of manpower; meanwhile, requests for reinforcements from Pomerania and Poland could not be fulfilled. Charles also made overtures to the Ottomans but only

---

25 Despite the weather, the guerrilla warfare, the loss of the supply train, Charles's army is estimated to have lost a fifth of its fighting size whereas Czar Peter's lost a third. Hatton, *Charles XII*, p.287. This estimate seems light when compared to other sources which suggest Swedish losses closer to half.

received letters of friendship in return. He could get no serious commitment. Russia tightened its grip on the region and blocked several routes that the Swedes could take effectively forcing them into a trap. Getting mail through proved difficult and the foreign land and weather prompted one soldier to remark "we live as if we are outside of the known world".[26]

The town of Poltava was a vital stepping stone on the road back north to Moscow and became the focus of the Swedes. Likewise, Peter determined that Poltava would mark the spot where his army would stand its ground and show the courts of Europe that a new power was ready to step onto the Continental stage. By the end of April 1709, a siege of the town was in place and Charles prepared for the battle he so desperately sought.

---

26 Carlson, *Eigenhändigen Briefe*, p.93, note 4.

Chapter 8

Poltava, 1709

"Everything is going well here. Only at the end of the year and only due to a special coincidence did the army unfortunately suffer losses which I hope in short time to rectify. A few days before the battle I received a fever in the foot which prohibited me from riding."
                      Charles XII to Ulrika Eleonora some six weeks after Poltava[1]

There are questions on whether the Swedish siege of Poltava was a military necessity. The Swedes themselves seemed to half-heartedly go through the motions of besieging and did not dedicate sufficient numbers of men or cannon. What purpose did it serve? It is most likely that Charles wanted to draw Peter into an open battle, an objective that eluded him since Russian soil was first invaded in early 1708. If this theory is assumed, it would also answer the question on why the Swedes allowed the bulk of the Russian army to cross the Vorskla river just north of Poltava with minimal resistance on 17 June. In hindsight, the day of the crossing would become known for something far more important than Swedish inaction.

Charles was inspecting the defences along the riverbank with a small entourage when a bullet, thought to be fired from a Cossack rifle, entered his heel and tore through the length of the left foot before exiting by the big toe. Those nearest the King were quick to voice concern and urged him to return to camp for medical attention. Charles ordered everyone present to keep quiet and with his usual stoicism continued his inspections. It was only after three hours of additional riding that he returned to his headquarters at which point he was noticeably pale from the loss of blood. Upon dismounting his horse Charles fainted and had to be carried to the surgeon. The impact of the King's condition on the Swedish camp was immediate. There was panic, fear, and talk of omens – the King was wounded on his birthday. There was no positive propaganda spin to be placed on the situation. Symbolically it was even worse – Charles had emerged from battle, time and again, unharmed and an aura of invulnerability had developed around him. In Lutheran eyes,

---

[1] Carlson, *Eigenhändigen Briefe*, p.72. While the King had exceptional optimism, the casualness with which he writes here may be his attempt to quell panic in Stockholm.

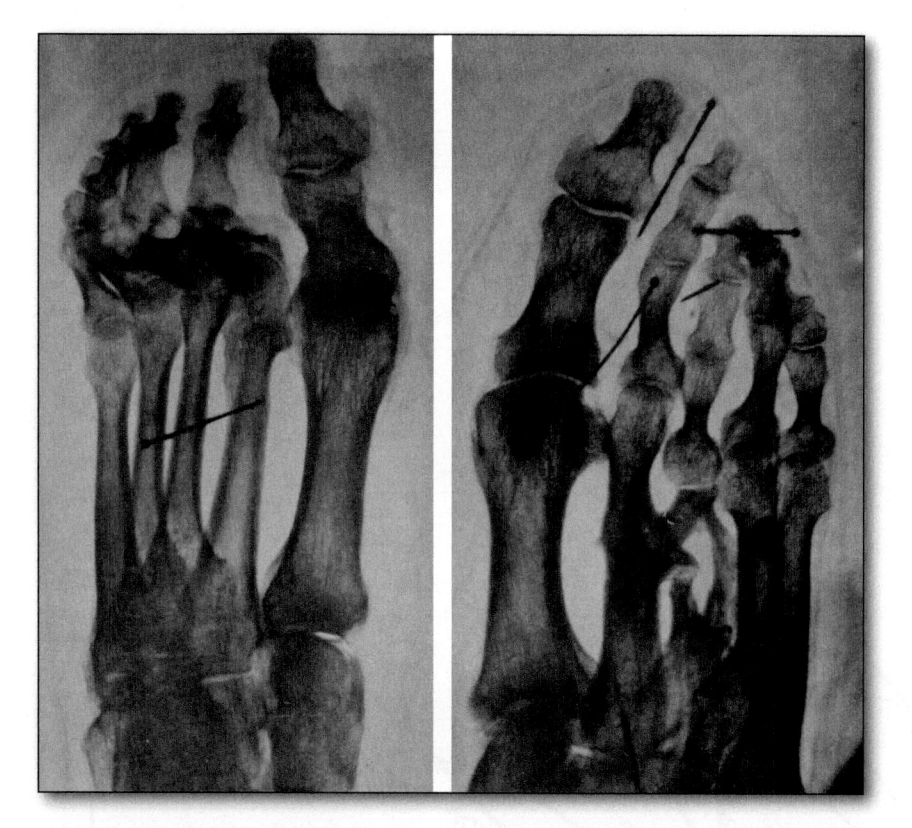

Underside of the King's feet via X-ray taken in 1917. (Author's collection, public domain)

the King held divine favour but for some reason it was forsaken on this day. What did that mean for the Swedish army at large?

Despite the work of the surgeons, infection set in with the summer heat and between the 19th and 21st there was little hope for the King's survival. The Russians also heard about his condition and hastened the construction of their field fortifications north of Poltava. In Charles's absence, Rehnskiöld assumed temporary command but critically did not commit any forces to deter or delay the Russian fieldworks. Charles managed to survive and, despite still being feverish, had a stretcher slung between two horses so he could be carried in front of his men. As the days progressed, he recovered his strength but his mobility was severely limited. For the coming battle, overall command would be given to Field Marshal Rehnskiöld but the King insisted on taking an active role in planning and preparation.

Count Piper and other members of the Field Chancery called for a return to Poland to assist Stanislaus, who was struggling to maintain his grip on the throne. Piper argued that the war with Russia could always be started anew at a later point. The Swedes could regroup, resupply, and apply the lessons learned from the current campaign. Charles and some of his military advisors were of the opinion that a successful engagement, even if it was not a sweeping victory, could help draw support from the Ottomans or even get the Russians to the negotiating table on more favourable terms to Sweden.

The Russians spent the time building several fortified encampments, each one getting larger and closer to Poltava with the last being a few kilometres north of the ongoing siege. The camp had earthen walls dotted

BY DEFEATING MY ENEMIES

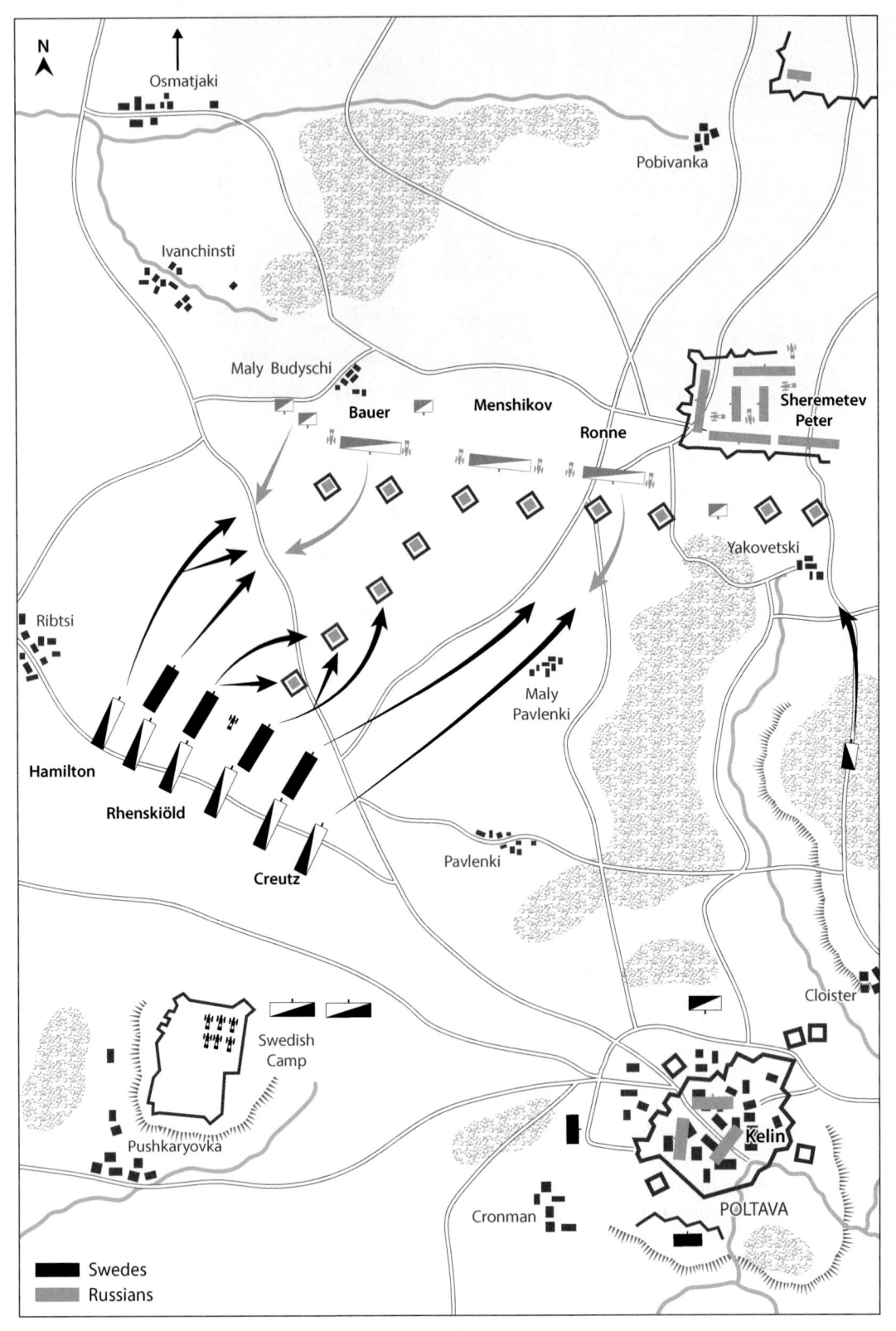

The Battle of Poltava, phase 1.

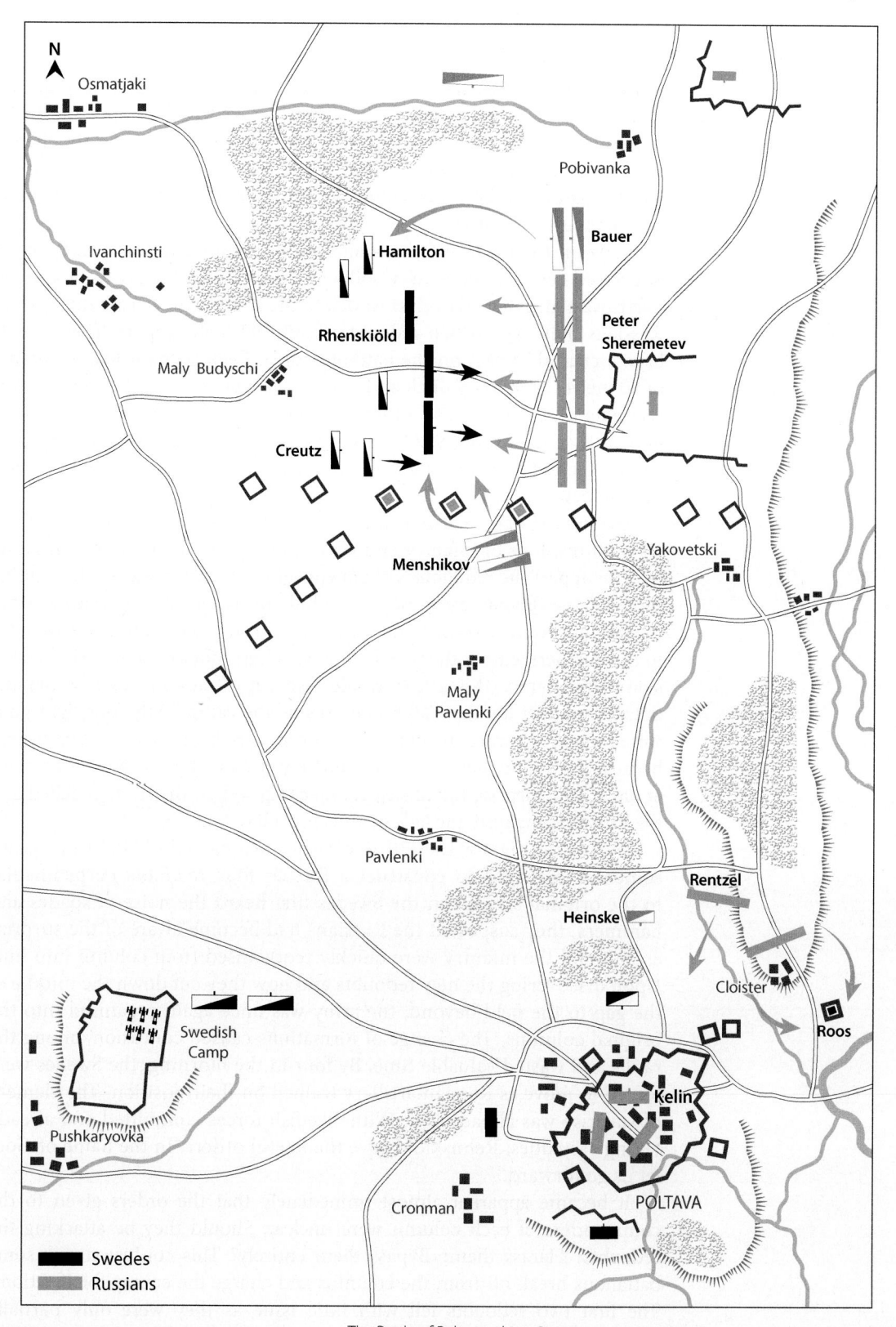

POLTAVA, 1709

The Battle of Poltava, phase 2.

with bastions for cannon. The southern wall was 1,200 metres long while the western side was about half that length. The northern wall was considered the weakest and the camp as a whole was backed up against a steep decline that led down to the Vorskla river. For the Swedes, the opportunity had presented itself to trap the Russians. After all, they had seen this before at Narva: a larger Russian force would see its numerical superiority constrained by camp walls and a river in the rear would severely hamper any chance at retreat.

Between the town of Poltava and the fortified camp was a narrow gap buttressed on both sides by woodland – the Budyschenski woods to the north-west and the Yakovetski woods to the south-east. Across this gap the Russians built six earthen redoubts about 200 metres apart. These would have a crucial impact on the battle to come. Each redoubt had a frontage of 50 metres with a dry ditch and *chevaux de frise* scattered before that. The redoubts were occupied by a total of 4,000 men. A cavalry force more than double that size, some 9,000 dragoons under Menshikov, were deployed behind the redoubts to exploit any weaknesses in the Swedish lines as they moved forward.

The initial Swedish plan drawn up on 27 June would have the army form 10 columns, four of infantry and six of cavalry, and then have Rehnskiöld lead them past the redoubts without engaging, so as to preserve the fighting force for the Russian camp where the bulk of the enemy lay waiting. Once the redoubts were bypassed, the cavalry would advance ahead of the infantry to the northern end of the field before wheeling about to engage the weaker side of the camp. This action would also cut off any means of providing outside support for the 30,000 men inside the camp. Only four light guns were brought forward in support – the rest were kept with the supply train because the Swedes needed to move quickly and silently to evade the bastions at dawn and surprise the unsuspecting camp. When the strategy failed and the Russians engaged, the lack of guns proved telling.

During the night of the 27th and early morning of the 28th, the Russians somehow managed to construct a further four redoubts perpendicular to the original six. When the Swedes first heard the noise of spades and hammers, they suspected the Russians had become aware of the surprise assault and the infantry were quickly reorganised from column into line. Upon discovering the new redoubts and how they cut down the middle of the gap to the field beyond, the army was once again organised into the original columns. The change of formations caused confusion among the ranks and wasted valuable time. By four in the morning, the Swedes were forced to move as Russian artillery trained on their position. The element of surprise was already lost. With Swedish forces committed and already taking casualties, Rehnskiöld gave the fateful order: "In the name of God, let us go forward."

It became apparent almost immediately that the orders given to the commanders of each column were unclear. Should they be attacking the redoubts? Harass them? Bypass them entirely? This confusion saw some battalions break off from the columns and charge the enemy fortifications. The first two redoubts fell with little issue as they were only partially

The Battle of Poltava. (Pierre-Denis Martin, The Battle of Poltava, 1726, Catherine Palace, public domain)

constructed. Any defenders that could not escape were wiped out. The third redoubt was better manned and better fortified and managed to repel six battalions under General Roos. The casualties were extremely high which threw the Swedes back in confusion and they retreated into the Yakovetski woods. In the meantime, some of Menshikov's dragoons charged from behind the original redoubts and sowed further disorder among the Swedish columns before being recalled to the main Russian camp.

Once the majority of the Swedish army passed the redoubts, they veered west and took cover below a ridge at the Budyschenski Wood line two kilometres away from the Russian camp. Rehnskiöld had to rebuke Lewenhaupt for attempting an immediate attack on the Russian earthwork's most exposed southern corner; the veteran commander wanted a concerted charge at full strength. It was then that he realised that Roos and his battalions were nowhere to be seen. He sent runners to try to find them. The absence of these wayward men, a third of the available infantry, caused the Swedes to delay their attack for two hours. The missing battalions never materialised and forced Rehnskiöld to move ahead with his plans short-handed. As the Swedes prepared to move forward, a stunning development unfolded before them. At nine in the morning, the Russian infantry abandoned their fortified camp and arrayed in line formation on the open field. The normally timid Peter had weighed his options and determined that his numerical superiority would be better assisted if it had room to manoeuvre. By leaving the camp, he could deploy his forces on a wider frontage. The first line had 24 battalions and the second had 18 for a total of 22,000 men among which were deployed 70 cannon. On the flanks were 9,000 dragoons under Bauer and 4,800 under

Menshikov.[2] The Swedes only had 12 battalions of infantry which resulted in a four to one disadvantage in manpower. The frontage of the Swedish line was thus shorter and risked the flanks being overwhelmed. Room to manoeuvre was also limited due to the terrain tapering off towards their end of the field. Creutz's cavalry had to deploy behind the infantry for lack of space. In another unexpected move, the Russians began to move forward and initiate the attack which unsettled the Swedish command. The order to countercharge was given to maintain initiative and create some breathing space between the infantry and the wood line. With both armies closing in, the pitched battle that the Swedes so desperately sought against the Russians was about to take place but came at a steep price: the Swedes were heavily outnumbered, had an absentee monarch, and possessed poor health and morale. Peter had played a perfect hand.

Just before they deployed from their camp, the Russians sent a detachment of five infantry battalions and five dragoon regiments to hunt down Roos and his lost men. Roos had become disoriented in the Yakovetski woods and came close to being surrounded. He pushed further towards the south-east and ended up taking refuge in an abandoned redoubt just beyond Poltava. Russian General Rentzel caught up to the Swedes and gave Roos time to consider surrendering. Roos complied, as his men had almost no ammunition left. Out of the 2,600 men that started the battle under his command, only 400 were left.

Back on the field, the disciplined fire which the Swedes walked into cut down man and horse with reckless abandon. Lewenhaupt noted afterwards that "it were impossible humanly to believe that any man at all of our sorely pressed infantry could emerge from it with his life".[3] Once within range, the Swedes loosed a volley and executed a *Gå På* charge. The impacted Russian regiments began to falter under the tried and true tactic. However, the Swedes in the centre were pressing too quickly, which gave the unoccupied Russians on the flank the opportunity to close in on the Swedes, similar to what befell the Romans at Cannae and the Saxons at Fraustadt. The issue was quickly identified but the Swedish cavalry that attempted to close the gap were repulsed by a Russian square. The Russian right wing had the veteran Semenovsky and Preobrazhensky guard regiments who pressed into the outnumbered Swedish left. The Närke-Värmland and Östergötland regiments broke and attention then turned to the isolated Uppland Regiment which was annihilated. The gaps in the Swedish line became too great and the attack stalled. The coordinated Russian fire between infantry, dragoons, and artillery proved to be too much. The Swedes started to flee en masse. Morale was broken. Lewenhaupt could not get men into line nor could Charles who, hampered by his wound, vainly yelled out "Swedes, Swedes!" Charles was now at risk of being captured. His stretcher had been initially damaged and then completely destroyed by incoming fire. Of the 24 guards charged with protecting the King, only three remained. He was put onto a horse but it was immediately shot dead. A Drabant then offered his, which allowed the King

---

2   Angus Konstam, *Poltava 1709: Russia Comes Of Age* (Oxford: Osprey Publishing, 1994), p.80.
3   *Ibid.*, p.82.

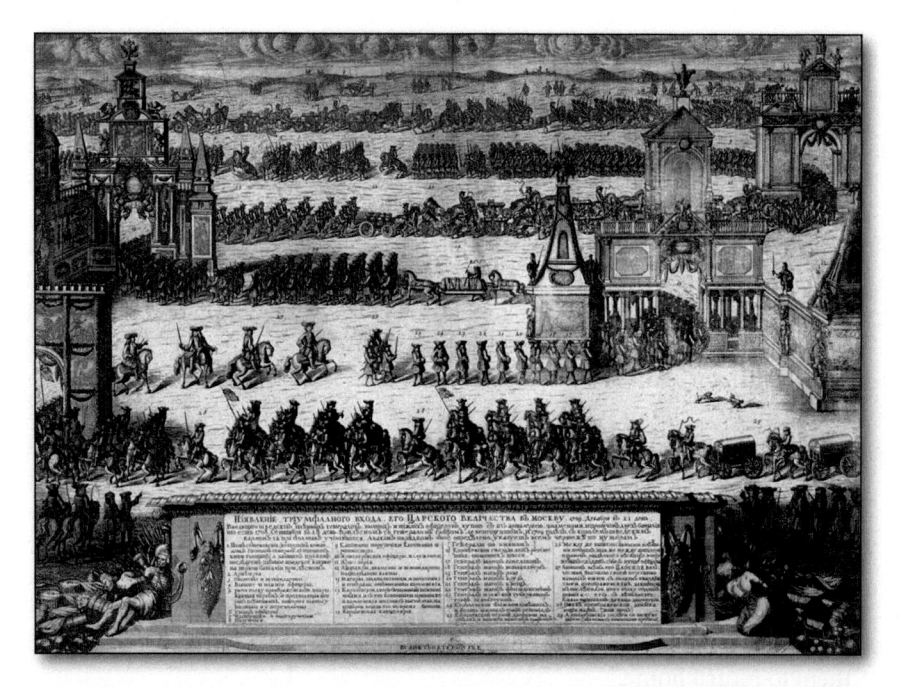

Triumphal march into Moscow. (Alexey Zubov, Triumphal Entry of the Russian Troops into Moscow, 1710–11, The State Hermitage Museum, public domain)

to escape. As he left the field, Charles did his best to reduce the panicked flight of his soldiers but as one general remarked to Lewenhaupt, "the devil could not make them stand". Rehnskiöld, Piper, Cederhielm, and Prince Maximilian were all captured on the field or shortly thereafter. They were toasted by the Czar as proper teachers in the art of war before being returned to their men and sent to Moscow. Russian losses were 1,345 killed and 3,200 wounded. The Swedes lost 6,900 with a further 2,800 marched into captivity.

The Swedes had been beaten in battle but the initial rout and panic gave way to a calm and orderly retreat towards the Dnieper river in order to stay ahead of any Russian pursuit. The main Russian force halted on the fields of Poltava but harassment continued from roving Cossacks. The plan was to return to Poland via Ottoman territory, assist Stanislaus in re-establishing control, and rebuild for a new attack on Russia. The lack of bridges over the river made the crossing slow and difficult. Passage would have been aided by the Zaporozhian river fleet but it was destroyed by the Russians as a harsh reprisal for the Cossack's altered loyalties. Both Perevolochna and the capital, Sich, were burnt and the population massacred. It was thus decided that Mazeppa and his Cossacks would cross first as their capture by the Russians would end in torture and execution, a fate worse than anything the Swedes would suffer. After initially refusing, Charles was also ferried across with his support staff and retainers. The rest of the army would follow thereafter with the rendezvous set for Ochakov. In total, some 900 Swedes and 2,000 Cossacks made the crossing.

Prior to passing the Dnieper, Charles gave Lewenhaupt command of the remaining army. Shortly after the first waves crossed over, General Menshikov appeared at Perevolochna on a ridgeline above the Swedes with 6,000 Russians and 2,000 Cossacks. Lewenhaupt had the larger force, but the extent of the Russian strength was unknown and the Swedes were still fatigued and low on supplies. Lewenhaupt and Creutz were entreated to surrender and given time to negotiate with the remaining officers of their army. Lewenhaupt's first query found that a good portion of Swedish soldiers were willing to fight but with the caveat that only if others did too. Defeatism was rife within the army, especially after the brutal loss at Poltava a few days earlier, but the condition had already plagued the men for quite some time: "Though we speak but little of peace at present, yet here are but few among us who do not heartily wish for it, for the officers as well as the common soldiers begin to be tired of their continual fatigues."[4] Lewenhaupt, not content with the non-answer, conducted a second round of questioning and found a few more officers willing to lay down arms. He now felt he had enough support to justify his decision to preserve the lives of his men and formally surrendered to the Russians. The low morale and fatalism finally had an adverse effect on the Swedes. As 1,161 officers and 13,138 of the rank and file laid down their weapons, they were forced to watch the remainder of their Cossack allies not fortunate enough to have crossed the river be executed. With that, the Swedish field army was gone. The survivors served as a prime attraction in the Czar's victory parade in Moscow and were then dispersed throughout Russia for a life of manual labour until the Peace at Nystad in 1721 allowed them to return home.

Historians who lean towards the extreme end of the "new school" in Carolean historiography have absolved Charles of any blame for the catastrophes at Poltava and Perevolochna, and instead placed it upon the shoulders of Rehnskiöld and Lewenhaupt. The two men were rivals and allowed their petty squabbles to interfere with the King's sound battle plan. Even at the time, both men understood that their reputations would be at stake and were quick to publish their own accounts of the battle and subsequent surrender. Given their deflection of blame as an act of self-preservation, their accounts should be viewed with caution. Charles was quick to defend his old mentor when he heard of criticisms levelled against the field marshal; towards Lewenhaupt the King was less sympathetic. While Charles did think of reasons why Lewenhaupt would have surrendered, he considered it a shameful act. More importantly, it had severely damaged the prestige of Swedish arms and as a consequence, Charles refused to have Lewenhaupt freed in a prisoner exchange. The general died in Moscow in 1719.

While Charles was unable to lead from the front, he was ultimately responsible for planning the surprise march past the redoubts. His orders were not communicated effectively which led to confusion in the attack. When the Russians emerged from their earthworks, Charles was unable to influence any change in strategy. The King even acknowledged one of his mistakes when he wrote of the surrender at Perevolochna:

> I was guilty of an oversight in that I forgot to give the other generals and colonels who were there the orders of which only Lewenhaupt and Creutz had knowledge. But for this, nothing would have happened as it did; for all the colonels were at a

---

4   Jefferyes, *Letters*, p.68.

POLTAVA, 1709

The Poltava Monument. (Swedish Army Museum, author's collection)

loss, not knowing what orders had been given nor which way they were to take their regiments, nor where I myself had gone.[5]

Beyond that, Charles had allowed himself to be manoeuvred by Peter into a battle that would have best been avoided. After halting at Mgliev, the King acknowledged to his closest advisors that he did not have a plan beyond the final objective being Moscow. The move south was not part of the initial thrust towards the capital and was necessitated in part by the scorched earth policy of the Russians. The move further south into the Ukraine was not planned either. This only occurred once they realised more supplies could be had and there was potential for alliances with the Cossacks and Ottomans. During the latter stages of the Russian campaign Charles was being reactive rather than proactive. Peter shadowed the movements of the Swedish army and never relinquished the initiative he took from the Swedes in the run up to Lesnaya. The subsequent decisions made by Charles can only be speculated at. The papers of the Field Chancery and regimental records, vital documents for understanding the campaign, were purposefully sunk in the Dnieper after Poltava.

Charles's overconfidence in his men achieving victory whatever the odds, coupled with his distrust and contempt of the Russians, saw him launch his army into a fight it had low odds of winning: "These are faults which the Swedes committed, and which plainly argues their presumption, however I think their punishment so much the greater since they were beaten and become slaves to a nation which they looked upon as the most despicable in the world."[6] Narva would not be repeated.

> Thus sir you see a victorious and numerous army destroyed in less than two years' time, much because of the little regard they had for their enemy; but chiefly because the King would not hearken to any advice that was given him by his councillors, who I can assure you were for carrying on this war after another method.[7]

---

5   Carlson, *Eigenhändigen Briefe*, p.121.
6   Jefferyes, *Letters*, p.82.
7   *Ibid.*, p.78, fn.

Chapter 9

Exile, 1709–1714

> "I hope that the difficulties that Sweden has for a while now found itself in will, with God's help, shortly disappear as long as everyone there keeps their courage. However bad it may now appear, I believe … that Sweden can obtain better results next year and restore the previous state of affairs."
>
> Charles XII to Ulrika Eleonora, 1710[1]

Via separate paths, the first remnants of the Swedish army and its Cossack allies reached Ochakov after 7 July. Charles immediately had letters sent to the governments in Stockholm and Warsaw telling them to prepare for his imminent return to Poland. While he mentioned the setback at Poltava, he was still under the assumption that the larger part of the army was but a few days behind and would arrive soon. He also ordered the Council in Stockholm to raise and equip reinforcements for the regiments that had suffered the most severe losses:

> The result is not a question of bravery or being outnumbered by the foe but rather the beneficial location and opportunity presented to the enemy that caused Swedish losses … The loss is great but we need to be careful and find a solution so that the enemy does not gain any advantages from this … It is required that the army be rebuilt in order to combat any attacks by the enemy. It is for this reason that we order you to, as quickly as possible, reconstitute the regiments of foot from new recruits and equip them with uniforms, muskets, flags, tents, and everything else that they previously possessed … It is important not to lose heart … Our work must be resumed with renewed strength and so restore the previous order and affect the desired ending."[2]

Shortly after the Swedes arrived in Ochakov, Yusuf Pasha, the Seraskier of Bender, approached Charles and Mazeppa with orders from Sultan Ahmed III asking that they and their forces move west to the fortress at Bender. The King and hetman had to comply given their status as refugees but they were treated like honourable guests as required by the laws of Islam. The demand

---

1 Carlson, *Eigenhändigen Briefe*, p.98.
2 *Ibid.*, p.353.

The Fortress at Bender. (Courtyard of the Fortress at Bender, Ivo Kruusamagi)

to relocate was not appreciated by the majority of Cossacks who were moved further away from the best routes home. For his part, Charles did not mind since Bender's location reduced the distance for a Polish return.

The stay within the cramped walls of Bender was a short one. Charles had a camp erected outside of the town's fortifications across the Dniester river. When the river suffered an extremely high flood, the camp was moved again to a new location – still within sight of Bender – and over time took on a more permanent construction. For his personal use, Charles had a two-story house built out of brick in 1712 alongside three others including the Chancery and stables. The tents used by the officers and men gave way to barracks dug halfway into the ground and organised by battalions in parallel rows. As the years passed, the camp became a de facto Swedish town. The Turks called it "New Bender" and one contemporary referred to it as *Carlopolis*. As was natural with camp life, the Swedes attracted numerous hangers-on and the population swelled on the outskirts of the encampment. Entrepreneurial Turks were quick to set up shops nearby and sell their goods and services. The Swedes paid in kind and maintained good relationships with the local population. Even the Janissaries were impressed and their respect for the soldiers and their king played an underrated role during the 1713 skirmish between the two sides, an event later known as the *Kalabalik*.[3]

---

3   *Kalabalik* is translated to tumult or ruckus.

EXILE, 1709–1714

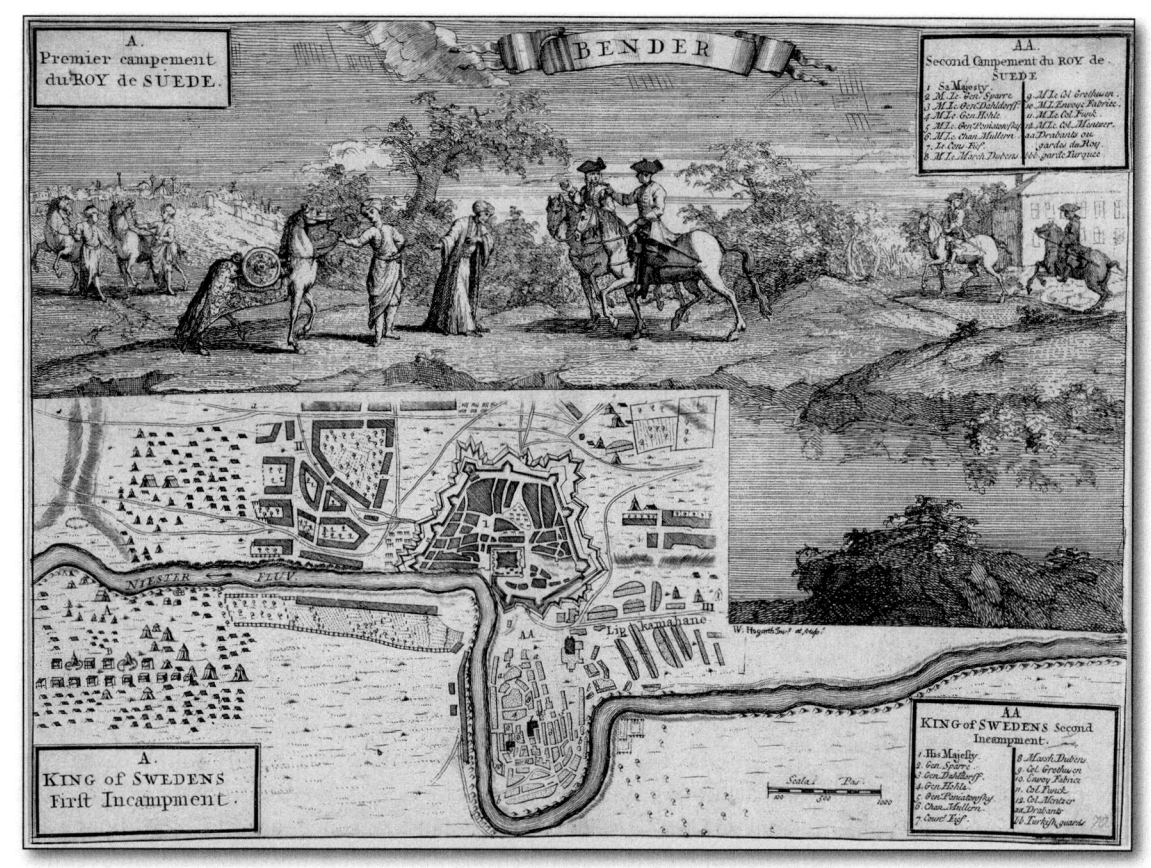

Swedish encampment at Bender. (Aubry de La Mottraye, Charles XII at Bender, 1723, Metropolitan Museum of Art, public domain)

In early August 1709 Charles had to come to terms with two pieces of terrible news. The remnants of his field army had indeed surrendered at Perevolochna, confirming the rumours that had spread in late July. He was also notified of the death of his beloved sister Hedvig Sophia, who had passed away in December 1708. The latter news only reached the Swedish camp shortly before Poltava, and the decision was made to keep it from the King who at the time was struggling with a severe infection stemming from the bullet wound in his foot. Charles remained stoic and calm upon hearing of the loss of his army but when he was told of his sister's death, he refused to believe "such a terrible rumour … that through smallpox we have lost all of our joy on earth."[4] He hid his face in his cloak and locked himself away as he ceaselessly wept. Such a piteous sight shocked his closest confidants, men who had served beside the King for so many years and never recalled seeing him in such a state. It was the first and only instance in his adult life where he would lose his famous self-control and openly display such emotion.[5]

---

4 Carlson, *Eigenhändigen Briefe*, p.96. In the same letter the King mentions the fresh loss at Poltava as the "particular instance" of his army having bad luck befall it. He does, however, hope to remedy the situation in the immediate future.

5 Years later, the King took his sword and slashed a newly completed portrait of himself. It is surmised that he could not bear to see what he had become over years of campaigning. He was alone at the time. This is discussed further in Appendix I.

123

Sultan Ahmed III. (Jean Baptiste Vanmour, Sultan Ahmed III, 1727–30, Rijksmuseum, public domain)

Though Charles would eventually come to accept his sister's death, it had a lasting effect on him: about two years later, he received a painting of his young nephew but after an initial glance refused to look at it again as the boy looked too much like his mother.

There were numerous attempts to have Charles return to Swedish territory as soon as possible. In letters addressed to the council and his own family, Charles wrote of his desire for a quick return to Poland. Similarly, among his early letters to the Sultan, Charles requested that: "your highness will put us in a condition of returning safely into Poland and our Provinces, under the guard of a body of your valiant horse".[6] He knew that news of Poltava would encourage his defeated foes to resume their war against Sweden. The King's very presence could serve as a deterrent but his reputation alone would not be enough to affect proceedings thousands of kilometres away.

Charles's immediate return was at first hampered by the wound in his foot, which had not yet healed and kept him from riding. The loss of the army at Perevolochna robbed him of a protective body of men which put the requirement for a royal escort on the Turks. As a secondary option, the King waited for a new Swedish army to march south from the German provinces via Poland and meet at Bender. Although the Turks had offered to escort the King north, there was disagreement over how the convoy would be utilised. Charles wanted to use the Turkish forces as a stand-in army to help Stanislaus fight for his position as king of Poland: "I find here all the encouragement imaginable, to hope for such a convoy as may enable me to force my way (in case of opposition) to your Majesty, where we may act in concert with new vigour, for the reestablishment of our affairs."[7] The Sultan insisted on a peaceful convoy with no attacks to be made on the Poles. If the convoy would be attacked along the way, would the Turks defend the Swedish king or hand him over to his enemies? Charles lacked the security he needed, and the instability in Poland caused by Russian and Saxon incursions coupled with the absence of a Swedish army forced Charles to stay in Bender longer than he initially desired.

Months ended up becoming years. In an attempt to affect change from his camp at Bender, Charles dove into Turkish politics and supported the more hawkish ministers in their efforts to have either the Tartar Khan or the Sultan declare war against Russia. The animosity between the Turks and Russians was well documented, with Peter having captured Azov in 1696 after several campaigns. As Russia expanded, Ottoman hegemony was in danger of shrinking and Charles hoped to use that fear to unite the Swedes and Turks

---

6   Adlerfeld, *Genuine History*, p.477.
7   Aubry de La Motraye, *Travels through Europe, Asia, and into Part of Africa* (London: privately published, 1723), p.419.

as allies against a common foe. The closest Charles came to success was with the Turkish declaration of war against Russia in late 1710. The resulting military campaign led to a near catastrophe for the Russians at Pruth, where Peter and his army were encircled by Turkish forces.[8] Through bribes and other means, the Czar managed to negotiate a deal with the Grand Vizier which allowed him and his army to march home with arms and artillery intact. When Charles learned of the peace agreement and the lack of any guarantees to Swedish demands, he quickly sent a diplomat to the Sultan to protest the "blindness and perfidy" of the Grand Vizier. It was to no avail. However, Peter failed to completely follow through on the terms imposed on him at Pruth,[9] which led to subsequent declarations of war from the Porte. There were four declarations of war in total but the last three were more akin to symbolic gestures and were never meant to be in earnest. Charles rued that such a golden opportunity had passed out of his control – fate had intervened against him once again.

Following the Swedish retreat into the Ottoman Empire in July/August 1709, Czar Peter immediately moved his armies north into Livonia and west into Poland. The absence of a large enemy force with Charles at its head gave Peter the opportunity to strengthen his grip on the Baltic provinces and reconstruct the anti-Swedish coalition with Russia being first among equals. The Treaty of Thorn, signed on 9 October of 1709, restored Augustus to the Polish throne and resumed cooperation between the Saxons and Russians. This effectively destroyed the Treaty of Altranstädt that Charles had worked so hard to establish. On 22 October, the Russo-Danish alliance was reformed and the Peace of Travendal torn up. Within a month, Denmark and Saxony had re-entered the conflict and all the hard-fought Swedish gains were lost. The diplomat James Jefferyes, who was released from Russian captivity and eventually returned to the King's side at Bender, predicted such a scenario in a letter sent in the immediate aftermath of Poltava and Perevolochna:

> This strange reverse of fortune has wholly changed the face of affairs in these parts, the Muscovites who have an army of 100,000 men of foot are now ready to enter Poland, the infantry as I am informed is to march to Livonia probably to besiege Riga while their cavalry advances towards Lemberg without doubt to raise new factions against the Swedes in Poland and to renew King Augustus right to that Crown; should Prussia and Denmark also join with them in these measures, 'tis more than probable that Sweden which because of this long and tedious war is exhausted of men and money will be forced to succumb.[10]

The situation was dire indeed. Courland fell to the Russians at the end of October with Estonia and Livonia likely being next to capitulate. Russian troops had moved into Poland to support Augustus's return to the throne

---

8　For greater detail on this campaign, refer to Nicholas Dorrell, *Peter the Great Humbled: the Russo-Ottoman War of 1711* (Warwick: Helion & Company, 2017).
9　He was to return Azov to Turkish control and pull Russian troops out of Poland. He eventually gave way on the former.
10　Jefferyes, *Letters*, p.76.

which led to the abdication and flight of Stanislaus in early 1710. At this low point Charles was sent a peace offer but it was rejected outright – the Czar demanded Livonia, Ingria, Estonia, Karelia and Kexholm to firmly secure Russia's place on the Baltic. The Danes were to have Scania returned and Augustus would be fully recognised as king of Poland, albeit without his desired Livonian territories. While denied in 1709, Peter would get most of his demands fulfilled in 1721.

Despite dedicating himself to diplomatic affairs and the remote governance of Sweden's war effort, Charles, for the first time since the start of the war, found himself with time to spare. He referred to his stay in Bender as the "lazy dog days" and threw himself into pursuits that could not have been undertaken while on campaign. Charles enjoyed a good game of chess but never took a loss as seriously as some of his opponents. It is interesting to note that Fabrice commented upon Charles's preference of using the King in his attacking play. Charles had a fondness for domestic reform and set about restructuring the Chancery into six offices to improve its effectiveness and introduced a capital tax that looked at wealth regardless of the person's position in the estate hierarchy. He also returned to the study of architecture and urban planning. Charles exchanged frequent letters with Nicodemus Tessin the Younger, the architect responsible for some of Stockholm's most well-known baroque buildings including the royal palace, Tessin palace, the current *Stadsmuseet*, and the gardens at Drottningholm. A contemporary of Christopher Wren, Tessin visualised a redesigned capital with grand avenues bookended by stately buildings that pulled design cues from antiquity. Charles submitted his own ideas, being particularly interested in the royal stables, and the schematics with Tessin's alterations are still preserved at the National Museum in Stockholm.[11] Reviewing building plans gave Charles some respite from the hardships of war and designs for the new royal palace were sent to the King during the dark days of the siege of Stralsund to help "drive away sad thoughts". Perhaps tinted with flattery for his royal patron, Tessin remarked of Charles: "He would have made a great king had war not come."

Charles was also keen to learn more about the Far East – a fascination which he inherited from his parents. He ordered and paid for three expeditions to the Orient which covered Asia Minor, the Holy Land, and Egypt. The first of these set off in January, 1710 with subsequent departures in 1711 and 1714. The men that returned brought with them hundreds of sketches, samples of plants, and region-specific material culture. The Kng had a chest full of papers placed in his own chamber so he could review them at his leisure. These drawings included images of Constantinople, the Hagia Sophia mosque, the ruins of Palmyra, the Pyramids, the fortifications of Rhodes, and the Holy City of Jerusalem. Of all the drawings and artefacts collected, relatively few survive today. Most were lost during the *Kalabalik* when the King's house burnt down. Cornelius Loos, an officer in the Drabants, was one of the men

---

11 Martin Olin, 'Tessin's Project for Royal Stables on Helgeandsholmen. A Study of Charles XII as a Patron of Architecture', *Konsthistorisk Tidskrift*, 72:1–2 (2003), pp.159–170. The author contends that Charles was not a visionary but more of an amateur.

EXILE, 1709–1714

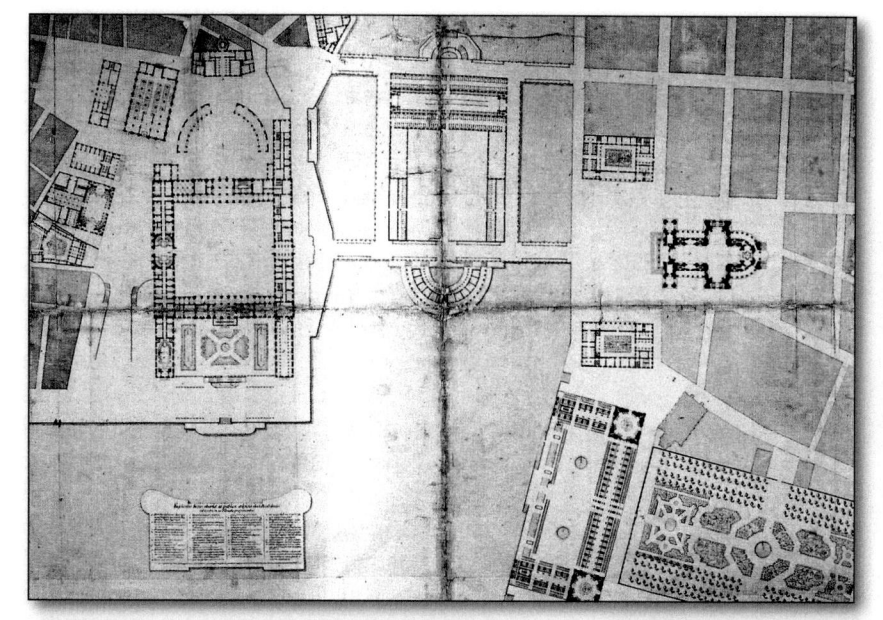

Plans for a redevelopment of central Stockholm, 1713. (Nicodemus Tessin the Younger, Plan for Central Stockholm, 1713, copy from 1774, public domain)

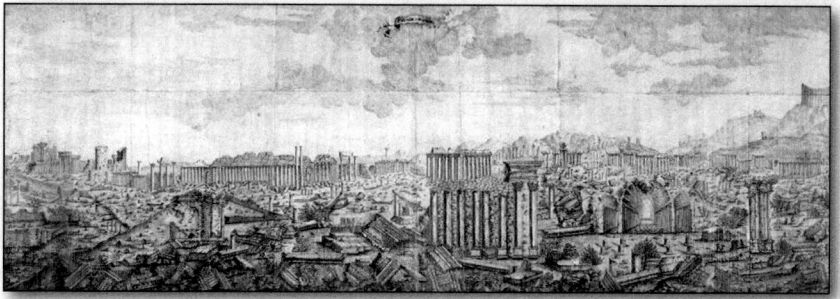

Ruins of Palmyra, 1711. (Cornelius Loos, Ruins of Palmyra, 1711, Nationalmuseum (Anna Danielsson), public domain)

Istanbul, 1710. (Cornelius Loos, Sultan's Palace at Istanbul, 1710, Nationalmuseum, public domain)

who left on the expeditions because of his skill at illustration. At Bender, he helped illustrate a drill book for the infantry and cavalry which incorporated the latest tactical theories from Charles himself.[12]

As the years in exile progressed, Charles railed against Stockholm's inability to alter the state of affairs. The letters sent from Bender seemingly become more desperate and irritated at the apparent lack of will to follow the

---

12   Hatton, *Charles XII*, p.315. The book still survives in the Swedish War Office archive.

Magnus Stenbock. (Georg Engelhard Schroder, *Magnus Stenbock*, 1708, Nationalmuseum, public domain)

King's commands. After being notified that General Stenbock agreed to a 14-day truce with General Flemming of the Saxons, Charles became enraged: "We could not have expected that you, without being subjected to our command, would take such an unanswerable and unheard of step of agreeing to a truce or even enter negotiations with the foe."[13] The physical distance between Charles, Stockholm, and the German provinces where the action was occurring, negatively affected the enforcement of his absolute power. It is worth noting that the government in Sweden continued to operate as it had throughout the war. The council and local governments maintained successful domestic policies – there were no widespread rebellions and reinforcements via the *indelningsverk* continued to be provided – but they had to become more involved in foreign policy, a matter in which the King had reserved final say for himself. Charles stressed that his decision was final, but an increasing number of actions were taken without his consultation because answers were needed quicker than could be afforded by mail sent across the Continent. Charles failed to empathise with his councillors on the difficulties they encountered.

The King's second grievance lie in the Porte's unwillingness to fight a costly war against Russia on his behalf. His one negotiating piece was the Swedish army that had won a dazzling victory against the Danes at Helsingborg on 27 February, 1710. Talk continued to materialise of a Swedish expeditionary force that would move into Poland and then travel to Bender to link up with the King and return him north. It was a bargaining chip that on occasion held weight and encouraged the Sultan to support Swedish plans. The final grand Swedish victory of the Great Northern War, at Gadebusch in 1712, helped bolster the King's power to negotiate once again, but the successful army could never be released to head south and ended up surrendering at Tönning after a three month siege in May 1713. The last political capital that Charles had to enforce any action on the Turks was lost.

The Kalabalik

Augustus knew of the political schemes emanating from Bender and sought to secure his grip on Poland and prevent a Swedish invasion. While he could not make any inroads with the Sultan, Augustus was able to influence Devlet-Gerei, the Tartar Khan, and Ismail Pasha the new Seraskier of Bender. True to his double-dealing form, Augustus convinced them that Charles needed

---

13 Carlson, *Eigenhändigen Briefe*, p.382.

to join with the Saxons and Turks to form an anti-Russian alliance. The best way to do this was to bring Charles north under escort but then allow the escort to disperse so that Charles could be "captured" and brought before the Elector for conversation. Devlet-Gerei seemed convinced that this was an honest plan and wanted to act quickly. If Charles would not go north under his own volition, he would need to be forced. Unfortunately for the parties involved, Swedish intelligence got wind of the plan and Charles refused to leave his camp and petitioned the Sultan for support.

Six weeks before the commencement of hostilities, Charles laid out a list of grievances of his perceived treatment at Bender. Among his points, he noted that "It is against the foundations of any religion to deny any guest asylum for as long as needed until they themselves have the means to leave." Likewise, "if one has been a guest for so long, they cannot be expelled like cattle until a discussion has been had with the Sultan". In his last point, Charles openly stated his belief that the Turks wanted to expel the Swedes hastily and without support so they can fall into the hands of the enemy. To avoid this fate, he would stay put until he can get assurances otherwise. He ended defiantly noting that "…we are prepared to stand against any who would want to attack us".[14]

By January 1713, the Sultan too had tired of Charles's ingratitude and the King's recent request for a new monetary loan proved to be the final straw. Ahmed resolved to have Charles escorted to the nearest port, put on a French ship, and sent home. The orders were sent to Ismail Pasha but the Sultan, based on his post-*Kalabalik* testimony, was unaware of the conspiracy between the Seraskier, the Khan, and Augustus.

On 11 January, Devlet-Gerei sent a military host to the outskirts of the Swedish camp. Charles rebuked them in Turkish and proceeded to ride through their ranks without being harmed. The Janissaries, who had come to hold the King in high regard, wanted to protect Charles and asked that he surrender himself to them. The request was denied and the Swedes began to set up barricades around the four large buildings at the centre of camp. On the 31st, the Turkish army had swelled in number with the arrival of additional horsemen, Janissaries, and artillery. The host was so large that an eyewitness claimed one could not look beyond their ranks, even from the balcony of the royal house. The army marched up to the camp's walls in a show of force but took no further action. It was hoped that conflict could be avoided as both sides had mutually coexisted and developed bonds of friendship over the past four years. Charles wished for the same and wanted to prolong the stand-off to preserve the lives of his men and give the Sultan time to intervene. A psychological battle began when the Turks raised their mass of banners and fired warning shots harmlessly over the camp. Charles countered with the playing of trumpets and drums. Some men lost their nerves and surrendered and the whole of the Swedes' Polish and Cossack allies had already given themselves up to the Turks. Charles still believed the stand-off was nothing more than an attempt to bully him into submission

---

14 Carlson, *Eigenhändigen Briefe*, p.384.

The action at Kalabalik.

and he urged any would-be deserters to stand firm: "His Majesty did assure everyone from the highest to the lowest who should stand by him for two hours longer, and not desert should be rewarded by him in the kindest manner, but whoever should desert to the Infidels he would never see them more."[15]

When the Turks finally stormed the camp, Swedish officers ordered their men to lower arms and allowed themselves to be taken captive. The lack of violence seemed to be part of the King's plan to maintain a moral high ground. Charles and a small group of Swedes retreated to the royal house only to find it occupied with looters. A more serious struggle in self-defence began. On the way in, a bullet grazed the King's nose, cheek, and ear, the third to hit him in his life. In the close confines of the house, Charles suffered a deep cut to his hand as he tried to block a sabre. Still preserved in the royal armoury is an otterskin cap purportedly worn by Charles during the skirmish and is credited with protecting him from another sabre blow to the head. At some point during the fight, the roof caught fire and spread through the interior of the house. The Swedes evacuated the building and made a dash for the neighbouring Chancery. Charles, with pistol and sword in hand, tripped over his spurs and fell to the ground. He was quickly set upon by Turks who ripped away at his coat in order to claim their share of the bounty for his capture. It was an abrupt and anti-climactic end to the proceedings.

Charles XII's otterskin cap. It purportedly saved the King's life by blocking a sabre strike. (Charles XII's Otterskin Cap, circa 1713, The Royal Armoury)

When Charles was brought before the Seraskier, there were many apologies for the King's treatment and a letter from the Sultan countermanding his initial order of capturing the King by force arrived too late to influence the affair. The Sultan professed his ignorance of the Saxon conspiracy and meted out punishments to those involved. The *Kalabalik*, more than anything, proved to be an awkward blunder for all. Charles, still smarting from his embarrassing fall, said the skirmish was "too much for a jest and too little to be in earnest".

The passage of time has caused the scale of the *Kalabalik* to grow out of proportion. The contemporary narratives from witnesses like Naundorf and Fabrice exaggerated the numbers involved and instead of large-scale casualties, modern estimates suggest around 40 Turkish and 12 Swedish dead. One romanticised account mentions Charles running his sword through three Turks at once although Charles himself only estimated three dead by his own hand over the entire day.

---

15 Egidius Naundorf, *Charles XII in Turkey: Narrative of the King of Sweden's Movements 1709–1714*, p.122 as quoted in Hatton, *Charles XII*, p.358.

Charles and a hand-selected group of a hundred Swedes were moved further south to Adrianople in the aftermath of the skirmish. It was a humbling experience and the awkwardness of the King's position was commented upon: "I cannot express ... what a melancholy spectacle this was to me, who had formerly seen this prince in his greatest glory and a terror to almost all of Europe, now to see him fallen so low as to be the scorn and derision of Turks and Infidels."[16] By this point, both the Sultan and the King recognised that there would be no mutually beneficial outcome – Charles would need to return north. The move would have to wait as Charles broke several bones in his foot, a result of his fall during the *Kalabalik*, and remained bedridden for nearly 10 months.[17] During that time, events around Europe began to calm. The Peace of Utrecht was signed, ending the War of the Spanish Succession, the plague which hit the Baltic region particularly hard from 1709 to 1713 had faded, and, via a new treaty with the Turks, Peter had to remove Russian troops from the Commonwealth and promise not to interfere with Charles's return.

Some of the changes were not in Sweden's favour. The completion of the War of the Spanish Succession gave Denmark and Saxony greater autonomy on military movements as the Maritime Powers no longer felt obligated to aid Sweden. The Duchy of Hanover, now backed by the power of Britain with its Elector crowned as King George I, eyed Swedish Bremen and Verden. Prussia finally felt confident enough to start negotiations with Russia and other powers to lay claim to the rest of Swedish Pomerania. The anti-Swedish coalition, therefore, had the potential to expand beyond the three original antagonists. The loss of Stenbock's army at Tönning, despite the two earlier victories at Helsingborg and Gadebusch, stung Charles, who made no attempt to extricate the general from Danish captivity. Sweden's lack of an army made negotiations in its favour difficult and maintaining previous treaties impossible.

While in exile, Charles managed to gain a surer grasp of European politics by holding interviews with both foreign and Swedish diplomats. This knowledge was something he lacked in his early campaign years and he had relied heavily on advisors who were now no longer present. Hatton suggests that the King's decision-making ability had matured by this point: "In many ways his personality was set between 1700 and 1706 though his judgement, in my opinion, did not develop to its fullest extent till after 1709, during the years in Turkey."[18] His growth in judgement and his assessment of Sweden's position in a changing Europe can be interpreted via a letter to his sister Ulrika from 2 September, 1714. In it, the King argued that Sweden was not in a good current position to make peace. He therefore gave Vellingk the order to conduct separate and secret negotiations with the three major enemies. This had two purposes. First, it was hoped that prolonged negotiations would

---

16 Hatton, *Letters*, p.363.
17 These breaks are now known to us thanks to the 1917 exhumation and subsequent X-ray analysis (see image on page 111). Prior to this discovery, "old school" historians believed that Charles remained bedridden out of embarrassment and stubbornness.
18 Hatton, *Letters*, p.209.

EXILE, 1709–1714

The wig worn by Charles XII as Captain Peter Frisk. (Wig used by Charles XII during ride, 1714, Royal Armoury)

Medal commemorating the King's ride to Stralsund. (Medal Commemorating return to Stralsund, public domain)

stall any military offences against Sweden while its defensive capabilities were negligible. Secondly, the lack of trust between members of the anti-Swedish coalition was common knowledge and the aim was to place each state in a "prisoner's dilemma" and have them start peace negotiations individually in the hope of gaining greater benefit over the others. Peace was wished for, but Sweden would first need to improve its credibility both politically and militarily; otherwise it would not be treated well in negotiations either with individual states or via a larger peace congress with mediators. Charles maintained a positive outlook: "How large Sweden's current predicament seems to be, yet I believe that our fortunes will improve in the coming year since they have already been unsettled enough in the past few years."[19]

Once his foot had sufficiently healed, Charles selected a route for his return north. His ride would take him through Transylvania, Hungary, and

---
19 Carlson, *Eigenhändigen Briefe*, p.133.

then the Holy Roman Empire. He decided to ride incognito for fear of being captured for reward, despite assurances from the Emperor that he would be unmolested. A running joke among his courtiers was that Charles simply needed to don a wig and drink heavily and he would not be recognisable given his enduring spartan, teetotaller image. He did indeed choose a wig with long locks, a brown coat, and a black felt tricorn with gold braiding. His pseudonym was Captain Peter Frisk and he rode with just two other companions ahead of a second party of three in which the Swedes had placed a royal decoy. Speed was vital as Charles hoped to be safe in his North German territories before news reached European courts of his departure from Turkey (see map on page 144). He set out on 27 October and by 5 November was in Vienna, having reached it in part by post-coach and with one less companion. The pace improved after Vienna, and on the night of 10/11 November Charles arrived outside the walls of Stralsund. The journey took 14 days and covered 2,152 kilometres. Such was the pace, over 150 kilometres per day, that the King needed a new uniform and new boots to replace those that had to be cut from his swollen feet. To commemorate Charles's daring ride, a medal was struck with an inscription that could have been pulled from one of his many optimistically laced letters: "What worries you so? God and I still live."

Chapter 10

Rearguard, 1714–1717

"Is God not on my side any more?"
Charles XII, reputedly, during the Battle of Stresow just before being hit by a musket ball

The Swedish Empire that Charles returned to in late 1714 was a shadow of its former self. The vital Baltic provinces, from Livonia to Ingria, were all taken by Russia. Karelia and Finland suffered the same fate. Stanislaus was removed from the Polish throne and Sweden's puppet state was returned to Augustus' tenuous grasp. The Elector had never given up on his designs for Poland, and as early as 1707 there were reports from Saxony that he was producing coin and cannon with the Polish arms emblazoned upon them. Augustus re-entered Poland easily enough with Russian support but then had to fight several battles against the Tarnogród Confederation to cement his rule. Denmark had returned to Swedish shores, but after being repulsed at Helsingborg, contented itself with overrunning the territories of Holstein-Gottorp. The ending of the War of the Spanish Succession in 1714 freed up several smaller German states who could now look north for their territorial aspirations: Hesse-Kassel, Hanover, and Prussia. All three had, at one point or another, been allies with Sweden, but picking off rich coastal cities from the weakened empire proved tempting for the latter two.

Since Poltava, the Swedish army and navy fought desperate actions on land and sea to try to avert the possibility of an invasion of home soil. The last army of a tangible size won a final victory at Gadebusch in 1712 but was then quickly outmanoeuvred and forced to capitulate. Throughout the war the Swedes were usually at a numerical disadvantage, but they now found themselves without a credible standing army. Being on the defensive also meant that Sweden had to replace the pitched battle with siege warfare out of necessity. For reference, the last victorious engagement for the Swedes on land was in defence of Stockholm at Stäket in 1719.

The 21-year span of the Great Northern War gave the anti-Swedish coalition time to learn from their early defeats and revise their strategies, raise new armies, and, most critically, improve their training. Tighter discipline and an increased rate of fire proved to be a hard counter to the favoured *Gå På* tactics of the Swedes. It made their frontal assaults less effective and

Augustus of Saxony, Frederick I of Prussia, and Frederik IV of Denmark. (Samuel Theodor Gericke, Portrait of Three Kings, 1709, Castle Caputh (Ralf Roletschek), public domain)

far more costly in manpower which a beleaguered Sweden could not afford. To make matters worse, the plague had returned to northern Europe and hit Swedish territories particularly hard. The depopulation of widespread geographic areas and within key cities and towns exaggerated an already large coalition numerical superiority.

It was a desperate time. Contrary to the views of historians subscribed to the "old school" of Carolean historiography, Charles did not eschew peace negotiations. In fact, the King submitted several proposals and was even prepared to cede territory if it led to a guaranteed and secured peace. When these were denied and counter-offers proved too unrealistic to accept, Charles attempted to strike deals with individual states. Even with diplomatic talks ongoing, Charles still believed that military victories could help Swedish odds at the negotiating table and either force an enemy to exit the war again or bring them over as an ally. The concept of pushing military success during mediation was nothing new for Sweden. The kingdom's most renowned High Chancellor, Axel Oxenstierna, argued for a "peace with reputation" after 1632 while his brother further expounded the thought by seeking "the respect which preserves a country's security".[1] In this context the desperate defence of Stralsund and the two Norwegian campaigns make more sense, and eliminate the view that the King was willingly leading his people into an all-encompassing *Vernichtungsschlacht*.

The Loss of the Eastern Baltic

The city of Riga, strategically located near the south-western border of Livonia and Courland, was a target of the anti-Swedish coalition since the war began in 1700. The opening of hostilities saw Augustus and his Saxons lay siege to the city although he was in the end forced to withdraw due to a dogged defence led by Erik Dahlberg and the pending arrival of a fresh Swedish army. Given its strong fortifications and position on the Düna river

---

1   Roberts, *Essays*, p.19.

REARGUARD, 1714–1717

with access to the Baltic, Riga was considered the "Key to Livonia" and would need to be captured if any occupation of the province were to take place. A new siege would not be attempted until the dust settled at Poltava, after which Peter immediately ordered a large army to march northwards and take the city. Riga's proven defences were strong and well designed. It was garrisoned by 10,000 men and had over 550 cannon. With Dünamünde in Swedish possession at the northern end of the river, supplies could be shipped down to reinforce the garrison and allow for an uninterrupted holdout.

By the end of October 1709 the Russians had reached the outskirts of the defences, and in November the siege and bombardment began in earnest. A lucky shot managed to hit and destroy the ammunition depot within Riga. The resulting massive explosion inflicted high casualties and damaged morale. The noose tightened as heavy artillery was brought forward and 30,000 Russians accumulated behind the siegeworks by March 1710. The emergence of the plague within Riga complicated matters for both sides as it spread. Swedish attempts to sail down the Düna with supplies failed as the Russians established a firm blockade. By July, a surrender was achieved. Dünamünde, Pernau, and Reval would subsequently fall and hasten the capitulation of Livonia and Estonia. The provinces were solely in Russian hands despite Livonia being the primary motive for Saxony's entry into the war.

Also in March of 1710, 13,000 Russians marched out from Ingria and arrived at Vyborg. The defending Swedes had an advantage in available firepower to keep the enemy at a distance but Russian mortars were very effective at lobbing shells into the city. A stalemate ensued. Given Vyborg's position on the Gulf of Finland, the navy that claimed the sea lane could determine the outcome of the siege. A Russian fleet of 250 ships beat the Swedes to the Gulf and effectively sealed the fate of the city. Vyborg fell on 13 June. The loss of Vyborg and Kexholm ensured the perpetual security of St. Petersburg and meant that Karelia had become Peter's newest provincial acquisition in the Baltic. It would be from this territory that the Czar

Vyborg. (Erik Dahlberg, Vyborg, late seventeenth century, public domain)

launched his 1713 campaign to drive the Swedes out of Finland.

Following the treaties at Pruth and Adrianople with the Ottomans, Peter felt secure enough on his southern borders to pursue an aggressive strike on Finland. Helsingfors was captured in May and the desperate Swedes appointed General Carl Armfeldt to try and reverse the losses. He was poorly supplied and could not expect reinforcements beyond his eight infantry and four cavalry regiments, who were mostly native Finns. Åbo was captured in September. Losses at the battles of Palkane and Storkyro resulted in the capture of Vasa and Nyslott, leaving Armfeldt little choice but to pull out of northern Finland and leave the grand duchy in the hands of the Russians who started a brutal occupation known as the "Great Wrath". By the end of 1714 when Charles arrived at Stralsund, Peter controlled all of Sweden's eastern and Baltic territories: Finland (1714), Karelia (1710), Ingria (1704), Estonia (1710), and Livonia (1710).

Carl Armfeldt. (David von Krafft, General Carl Armfeldt, Nationalmuseum, public domain)

* * *

The situation in Northern Germany had also become complex. With Denmark having re-entered the war after Poltava and Hanover and Prussia both emerging as antagonists, the Swedes were hard pressed to cover all of their territory effectively. A respite became possible in 1710 with the introduction of the newly written Neutrality Convention. Per the agreement, Sweden's German territories would be recognised as neutral as long as Sweden did not conduct any military operations from these locations. The document was signed by all the major powers including France, Britain, the Holy Roman Empire, Russia, and Saxony. The council in Stockholm voiced their support but Charles, who needed to maintain the option of having an army march south from the territories to affect pro-Swedish policy with the Turks, refused ratification. Charles was convinced that a joint Swedish–Turkish force marching into Poland would help his kingdom's cause more than a truce in Northern Germany. The King believed that the strongholds would hold and that his men would lead a defence as vigorously as he himself would. It was not the first nor the last time that the King's optimistic trust would be misplaced.

Charles's dismissal of the Neutrality Convention made Sweden's North German territories fair game. The conclusion of the War of the Spanish Succession gave the new King of Prussia, Frederick William I, time to consider annexing Swedish Pomerania and establish a lucrative port at Stettin. Hanoverian territorial aspirations were also a driving factor as Prussia did not wish to be outgained by a rival German state. The city of Stralsund was the lynchpin of Sweden's German holdings and was adequately reinforced in advance of any new declarations of war. This turned Danish attention to the port city of Wismar which lay just south-east of the ducal lands of Holstein-Gottorp. A small force of 5,000 cavalry and dragoons were sent to blockade the city until the Danes could march up larger numbers of infantry and artillery. The Swedish garrison, mostly enlisted Germans and also numbering around 5,000 men, launched an unexpected sally. The attack proved to be pyrrhic as the Danish camp was devastated, but the Swedes lost some 2,000 killed, wounded, or captured. Nevertheless, Wismar held and a Swedish relief fleet arrived in January 1712. A second siege in 1715, coordinated between the Danes, Hanoverians, and Prussians, resulted in a successful capture of the city in April 1716. Having outlasted Stralsund, Wismar was Sweden's last German possession to fall.

Charles Returned, and the Loss of Stralsund

After recovering from his ride to Stralsund, Charles did not depart for Sweden as everyone in Stockholm had expected. He assured both the council and his family that the defence of the Swedish homeland was in good hands and that his leadership was needed in Stralsund where the next blow was slated to fall: "... the urgency requires that I stay here longer to try and salvage what I can."[2] He hoped that enemy attention would be drawn to his presence in Northern Germany rather than to Sweden itself. Finally, if his men could withstand a lengthy siege and do so with courage and élan, maybe the respect for Swedish arms would be somewhat restored and become a factor in the negotiations for peace. There was precedence – was not Peter willing to return all captured territory, bar St. Petersburg and the Neva river, upon hearing of the victorious Swedes setting out from Altranstädt in 1708?

As previously mentioned, Charles was willing to cede some territory, both temporarily and permanently, in exchange for new alliances and military support. This was something he would have never allowed earlier in the war but even now the terms would need to be finely tuned to ensure acceptable security for Sweden. Since the anti-Swedish coalition found itself in dominating positions, none of the states took up the offer. Charles began to search for allies, but Sweden's aloofness during his father's reign had damaged both longstanding and prospective relationships with other states. The Maritime Powers, no longer hindered by the war over Spain, lifted their support for Sweden. Envoys were sent to Louis XIV to try to re-establish the older Franco-Swedish alliance by renewing the guarantees of the treaties of Westphalia and Oliva. While Sweden obtained a subsidy of 600,000 *riksdaler*, no other support was forthcoming. With the Sun King's death in 1715, it became harder to negotiate with his successor's administration. Attempts for an alliance with the Holy Roman Empire also failed due to the fractured nature of its electorates: the Landgraviate of Hesse-Kassel allied with the Swedes via royal marriage but Hannover and Saxony were obviously at war

---

2   Carlson, *Eigenhändigen Briefe*, p.138.

BY DEFEATING MY ENEMIES

with Sweden. The Emperor would not be able to pacify those German states without force and he lacked the political will to do so. His attention soon turned to the Turks, which permanently tabled any alliance prospects.

In early July of 1715, the final siege of Stralsund began with 28,000 Danes and 27,000 Prussians approaching the city. Saxony had an established military presence as well. Hanover's interests, now represented by Britain, ensured that eight of the best warships of the Royal Navy's Baltic fleet were attached to that of the Danes. The additional ships helped the coalition maintain a dominant presence at sea. Nevertheless, any attempt to take Stralsund, or at least successfully blockade it from all sides, required possession of the island of Rügen two kilometres off the coast. Charles was aware of the island's strategic importance and arrived with 800 infantry and 2,000 cavalry, mostly enlisted Germans, to support the existing garrison. Facing them was a joint force of Danes, Prussians, and Saxons, 22,500 men in all, under the command of Leopold von Anhalt-Dassau. The coalition abandoned their first landing attempt on Rügen having seen the King's defensive position on the shore. They managed

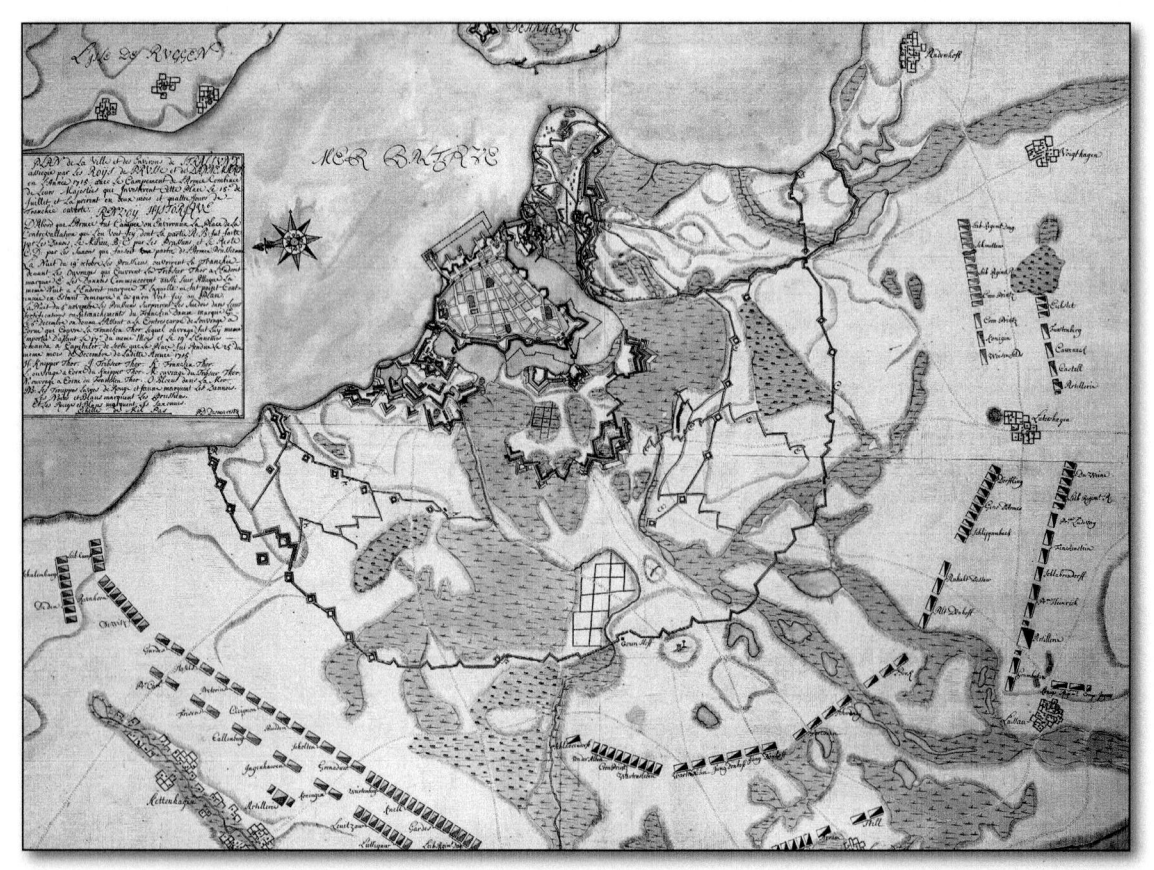

Charles XII with Stralsund in the background. (Axel Sparre, Charles XII King of Sweden, circa 1715, Nationalmuseum, public domain)

Siege of Stralsund. (P.D. Desmarest, Siege of Stralsund, 1715, Hessisches Staatsarchiv, public domain)

REARGUARD, 1714–1717

The Battle of Stresow.

141

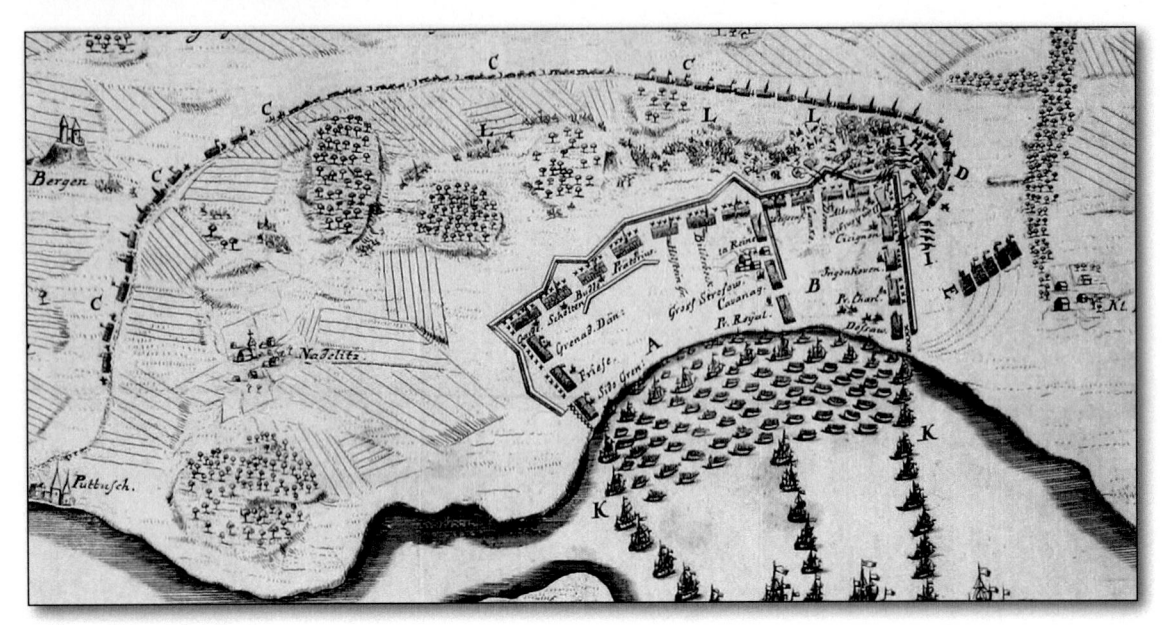

The coalition defences at Stresow and the Swedish direction of attack. (The Coalition Defences on Rügen, 1715, public domain)

to land near Stresow on 5 November without altercation due to heavy fog covering their approach. In response, Charles marched his men across Rügen and directed a column assault on the coalition's hastily erected beach defences, similar to the attacks launched at Narva and the redoubts at Poltava. The accurate musket fire from the Danes resulted in the first Swedish attack being repulsed with high casualties. A Danish cavalry sortie from the encampment caught their Swedish counterparts off-guard and scattered them. Charles had his horse shot out from under him and proceeded to regroup with his men and lead a second attack on foot. It was during this charge that Charles was struck in the chest by a musket ball, the fourth to hit him in his life. He was escorted away and the Swedes retreated en masse shortly thereafter. With that, the defence of the island was abandoned as the Swedes tried to escape capture. As Charles did not personally lead his men at Poltava, Stresow holds the distinction of being his first defeat while in command.

Charles returned to Stralsund but the city was now truly on its own. The defenders would have to rely on the strength of the walls as they numbered between 7,000 to 10,000 soldiers and were pitted against 30,000–50,000 attackers.[3] Major bombardment of the city started on 22 October resulting in cannonballs "flying through the town like feathers", and by the 25th portions of the outer defences had already fallen due to the moats freezing over which gave the enemy infantry ease of passage. Charles issued new terms for peace and included the permanent concession of Stettin and Wismar. He even offered to recognise Augustus as King of Poland, something that would have been anathema in earlier years. But with the death of Sweden's "protector" Louis XIV and stronger cooperation between the Danes, Saxons, and Prussians, Charles's entreaties came to nothing. He hoped the defences could hold until

---

3   Hatton, *Charles XII*, p.408.

spring so that the coalition would go into winter quarters and the Swedes could reinforce the city. It was not to be. The King led one final counter-attack on the captured outer defences before evacuating the city on 11 December. He was discreetly rowed to a waiting ship, the *Snappup*, which then set out for Sweden. Stralsund capitulated the next day. In the dark morning hours of 13 December, the King landed at Skåre and touched home soil for the first time in 15 years.

* * *

Charles, again, did not immediately set out for Stockholm – he would never return to the capital. In a letter to his sister, he excused his absence by noting that there was too much work to be done where he was. He also placed the blame for the fall of Stralsund on the lack of reinforcements from Sweden: "Those that are still there have probably surrendered. Stralsund will undoubtedly fall into the hands of the enemy because during the entire siege there were no reinforcements. I am still convinced that we will find ways to return everything to as it was before."[4] His optimism stemmed from the forthcoming invasion of Norway, for which planning was already underway. The King busied himself pouring over plans and, in a nod to his grandfather, spent time devising a feint to convince Denmark of an impending assault on Copenhagen over the frozen Sound. Similar to the defence of Stralsund, the Norwegian campaign that was launched in February 1716 had several objectives: force Denmark out of the coalition for a second time, divert enemy forces from a planned invasion of southern Sweden, allow Swedish troops to sustain themselves again on foreign soil at little cost to the treasury, and keep the British fleet closer to their own isles and therefore out of the Baltic. Regarding the latter objective, several of Charles's ministers opened secret negotiations with the Jacobites who were distressing the government in London with armed uprisings and covert operations aimed at putting the Catholic Stuarts back on the throne.[5] Charles never sanctioned negotiations with the Jacobites but he did not mind the frenzied conspiracies circulating among the British public as it ensured that the Royal Navy would need to keep an eye on the North Sea. Because of his perceived support, Charles became a target for pro-Hanoverian and anti-Jacobite pamphleteers who attempted to sully the King's character and reputation. They were quite successful, and some of

Charles XII with the *Snappup* in the background. (Henrik August Ankacrona, Charles XII, 1715, Nationalmuseum, public domain)

---

4   Carlson, *Eigenhändigen Briefe*, pp.149–150. Charles also mentions the death of his grandmother in this letter, but the sorrow is nowhere near the level of that of his sister from 1709.
5   For an in-depth look at British-Swedish relations, refer to Coroban, Costel, *Britain and Charles XII of Sweden 1709-1719* (Germany: Lambert Academic Publishing, 2013)

BY DEFEATING MY ENEMIES

Poltava to Skåre (see page 134).

REARGUARD, 1714–1717

Akershus Fortress, present day Oslo. (Author's collection)

their slander still affects public perception of Charles today. This is discussed further in Chapter 12.

The Swedes launched the Norwegian campaign of 1716 with four simultaneous movements. Charles and General Moerner would each lead 3,000–4,000 men straight to Kristiania, the capital. Eight hundred cavalry would move into Norway further south as a feint, while a single infantry regiment would march north to cut off any reinforcements en route to the capital. Despite running into some smaller enemy detachments which put up a strong resistance, the Swedes managed to join their two central armies and take Kristiania on 10 March. Despite the King's proclamation that no harm would befall civilians, the local population did not cooperate with the Swedes on matters of housing and food. The Danes also maintained control of the waterways heading into Kristiania and the strategically located fortress of Akershus did not surrender. Charles's grip on the capital was thus untenable and he retreated his forces on 18 April. This did not end the Swedish invasion, as Charles wanted to keep the Danish fleet occupied for as long as possible. The Swedes would briefly capture the town of Fredrikshald, south of the capital, but the looming fortress of Fredriksten on the cliffs above was heavily defended. A failed assault on 4 July, combined with a daring naval raid at Dynekilen by Admiral Tordenskjold which eliminated incoming supply ships, forced the Swedes to retreat further towards their own borders.

Logistics proved to be the determining factor of the short-lived campaign and the size of the army was not comparable to those that had previously fought on the Continent, which limited tactical options.

Rumours of a coalition invasion of southern Sweden were widespread since the fall of Stralsund. Denmark had already landed in 1710, albeit briefly, in the latest of a series of attempts to see Scania returned to Danish hegemony. Russian galleys were encroaching on Swedish waters from the east with Finland no longer acting as a buffer to the northern Baltic. With the conclusion of the first Norwegian campaign, the Swedes had no immediate opportunities to exert pressure elsewhere as a diversion and prepared for the worst. Hastily created plans outlined which towns should be evacuated, burned, or defended at all costs. Provisions and supplies were funnelled south in preparation. Charles moved to Lund, just north of Malmö, and established his headquarters in the town. Lund's location was a sound choice from which he could coordinate the defence of Scania – he could send and receive mail from the Continent and Stockholm in good time and march out to any enemy landing point on short notice.

Swedish fears of an invasion were not unsubstantiated. Denmark, Russia, and to a lesser extent Saxony and Hanover, spent the summer of 1716 in deep preparation. The Czar had 40,000 men at his disposal. Frederik IV committed 30,000. Both rulers also had enough men-at-war, transport, and supply ships waiting to cross the Sound although Frederik delayed the invasion by waiting for his remaining warships to return from Norwegian waters. The Czar's galley fleet was already harassing Sweden's eastern coastline and George I had his Baltic fleet prepared for the invasion despite anger in London over its perceived misuse for Hanoverian interests. Sweden's fleet would be no match for the combined navies, and if the coalition could land in sufficient numbers, there would not be enough Swedish soldiers to oppose them.

Fate would finally smile upon Charles, for on 8 September Peter called off the invasion. The move stunned Frederik and Augustus who had invested significant time and money on the plan. The mistrust that lingered among the coalition states finally boiled over. The Danes and Saxons had become wary of the Czar's growing power and influence in Western European affairs, and tried to limit his reach by barring Russian entry to the captured city of Wismar in 1716. Peter did not take slights lightly and perhaps withdrew his support as retribution. For his part Peter did not trust George I, who sought to gain from the invasion and was deeply involved with his Hanoverian electorate and its role within the Holy Roman Empire. Both Peter and George had a shared interest in the Duchy of Mecklenburg which led to further consternation between the two monarchs. The Russian military noted that the Swedish defences were strong and the Czar compared the whole venture to Charles's failed invasion of Russia and foresaw his own demise if he pursued the same course of action.

Publicly, Peter stated that it was too late in the season to launch an invasion and that the Danish delays pushed the timetable out too far. Frederik was indeed responsible for postponing the initial start date of the invasion as he wanted to bolster his fleet with the ships that were sent north to defend Norway. These valuable resources were tied up in the waters near

Kristiania during the Swedish presence in the capital. Despite Charles's first Norwegian campaign not forcing Denmark out of the war, it thus succeeded in pulling attention and resources away from a southern invasion of Sweden and therefore was not as ineffective as previously thought.

Home Front

With the threat of invasion suddenly removed, Charles had some time for himself; a luxury he had not had since his exile at Bender. He decided to stay in Lund due to its close proximity to both Norway and the Continent. The University of Lund became a regular destination for the King, who sat in on lectures of mathematics and philosophy. He had played with an octal numeric system as he believed 64 was the best number to work with, and he applied this study to military logistics. Due to the early death of his father and his subsequent accession to the throne, Charles never had a chance to study philosophy in his youth. Attending the lectures at Lund rekindled his interest and he found time to write *Anthroplogia Physica,* a short treatise which lays out 14 points on how man reacts to stimuli.[6] As the visiting Count de Croissy said: "He is so approachable and so free in conversation that I am not the least bit shy in speaking to him; indeed, the range of his conversation makes me feel I am talking to a philosopher rather than a king."[7]

Charles also returned to his architectural plans and increased his correspondence with Nicodemus Tessin the Younger. He even arranged a personal visit with the architect in early 1718. Discussions continued on the rebuilding of the royal palace and the designs for new stables that Charles took a particular interest in. There was also a new request from the King: that he be able to secretly move through the palace and reach the stables without being seen by the public. Charles disagreed with Tessin on certain design philosophies and came to embrace more simplistic features that sacrifice detail in favour of bold lines. This is particularly evident in his request for new regimental flags. The elaborate emblems were replaced with the royal cipher surrounded by a simple wreath. The materials were downgraded partly due to cost. The colour green was also absent from later flags as it had become strongly associated with Russia.

The King carried on with his daily tasks as usual. He would rise around three in the morning to work on memorandums before riding out to review the regiments between seven and noon. The afternoon was filled with official meetings before Charles finished the day in secret discussions after dark with his newest right-hand man: Baron Görtz. Georg Heinrich von Görtz was a native Holsteiner whose administrative talents were noticed by the King during the latter's sojourn in Turkey. Görtz's ability to find money from new sources to help fund the war effort greatly pleased Charles, who made him director of finance and commerce. Görtz was also promoted to undertake

---

6 Ernst Carlson, *Konung Karl XII:s Egenhändiga Bref* (Stockholm: P.A. Norstedt & Sons, 1893), p.467.
7 Hatton, *Charles XII*, p.408.

Charles XII and Baron Görtz. (Charles XII and Görtz, circa 1715, public domain)

diplomatic missions and actively worked towards Denmark's fall and Sweden's preservation. Despite having similar objectives, the ways of achieving them put the two men at odds, and oftentimes the successful negotiations conducted by Görtz were countermanded by Charles, forcing the minister to – in the words of Hatton – "walk a tightrope between the world as he found it and the King's outlook on that world".[8]

Görtz was very active in procuring support for the Swedish cause but one covert action led him into the clutches of British politics. The accession of the Protestant George of Hanover to the British crown did not go uncontested – the 1715 Jacobite rebellion was repulsed with a government victory at Preston. The exiled Jacobite leaders in France and supporters in London searched for allies. The Swedes, desperately short of money, seemed like viable candidates. As previously mentioned, Charles did not sanction any conversations with the Jacobites but Görtz and minister Carl Gyllenborg felt that Sweden's distressing situation merited contact. Perhaps a successful negotiation would change the King's mind. They therefore waited on informing the King until they accomplished something worthy of reporting. British agents became aware of the correspondence, which led to the arrest of Gyllenborg in England and Görtz in the Netherlands. The implication of the Swedes in a Jacobite plot caused a diplomatic uproar. Charles ordered Robert Jackson, the English minister in Stockholm, to be arrested in retaliation. The arrests gave George the ability to deny trade with Sweden, but fell short of allowing him to declare war with all of Britain's backing in a political challenge to the Act of Settlement. Both Görtz and Gyllenborg were eventually released and the correspondence with the Jacobites was discontinued.

Görtz's rapid rise to power and his closeness with the King made him many enemies – his Holstein origins put him in opposition to the Hessian party at court, his subversion of traditional avenues of government angered the council in Stockholm, and his enforcement of taxes and issuance of emergency coinage outraged the general public. The state of affairs continued to work against him. With Sweden fighting on the defensive and now pushed within its own borders, war could not feed war. Taxation was high. There were poor harvests and the plague of 1710–1712 had decimated Swedish communities. As an absolute monarch, Charles was considered to be above criticism so public outcry was directed towards Görtz as the next available figurehead. He was accused of administrative manipulation and

---

8   *Ibid.*, p.400.

of pushing the "true" Swedish servants out of the King's inner circle. Worst of all, Görtz was accused of alienating the King's affection for his subjects. These indictments bear similarities with another royal pairing fighting public upheaval during the Pilgrimage of Grace in 1536 – Henry VIII and his minister Thomas Cromwell. With the sudden, unexpected death of Charles in November 1718, Görtz lost his one protector. He was immediately arrested and executed in Stockholm on false charges, his reward for loyally serving the King.

While Charles continued to dodge questions about his own family prospects, he approved the marriage between Frederick, Landgrave of Hesse-Kassel, and his remaining sister Ulrika Eleonora. This brought the military of Hesse-Kassel into alliance with Sweden, and in Frederick they gained an able military commander who served with distinction in the War of the Spanish Succession. Charles and Frederick got on well enough and Ulrika became enamoured with her new husband. The injection of Hesse-Kassel's political interests into the Swedish court created two factions that would vie for future control of the throne especially with Charles still unmarried and without heirs. The Holstein-Gottorp party, with strong ties to the royal family since the 1650s, centred on young Charles Frederick, the only child of the late Duke of Holstein-Gottorp and Charles's older sister Hedvig. By all rights of succession, he was next in line for the throne should Charles not marry and have any heirs of his own body. With Ulrika still alive and more politically adroit, she could claim the throne in the interest of her husband and the Hessians. The death of the Dowager Queen, Hedvig Eleonora, in 1715, removed the strongest personality from the court and greatly weakened the power of the Holstein-Gottorp camp. For the time being Charles mediated between his family members and took the time to personally ask his sister to be more supportive and open-minded towards their nephew. He would have one final meeting with his family over two weeks at the end of March, 1718. Though he made some honest attempts at rapprochement, not settling the growing succession crisis may be one of Charles's biggest domestic failures as it had ramifications for his family's bloodline and the experiment with total royal power. By getting the government in Stockholm to support her accession, Ulrika renounced the absolutism which their father, Charles XI, had worked so hard to install.

Chapter 11

Death in the Trenches, 1718

> "We have always endeavoured to copy our life from him [Gustav II Adolf]; perhaps, God may likewise grant us the blessing of dying in the same manner."
>
> Charles XII addressing members of his party after visiting the battlefield of Lützen in 1706[1]

The year 1717 passed without major incident, as had the first half of 1718. The downtime was used to rebuild the Swedish army for a second Norwegian campaign. The previous invasion had failed because of insufficient logistics, but the army's small size prevented a full capture of Kristiania and also limited contingency plans. The failures were meticulously reviewed and corrected. The *indelningsverk*, tested so many times during 18 years of war, still produced soldiers when called upon. Despite being constructed with the defence of Swedish home soil in mind, the system was able to raise two new armies (~1710, ~1717) over the course of the war and provided a steady stream of reinforcements for depleted regiments with the burden of upkeep and costs distributed as evenly as possible. It is a testament to the foresight of Charles XI and his advisors, who tweaked an older system to produce such favourable results. By October 1718, Charles had his new army as he requested, 65,000 strong.

From the Age of Liberty (*Frihetstiden*) and beyond, those opposed to absolutism put forward the myth that Charles's last army consisted mostly of old men and young boys thus illustrating the wastefulness of war in the hands of a monarch who lacked any answerable authority. The numbers do not bear this out. Of the 65,000 men, roughly 18 percent were under the age of 21 and only six percent were older than 40. The numbers were supplemented by enlisted men recruited from the Continent.

The officer corps also had a larger number of foreign officers but these men brought the experiences of the War of the Spanish Succession with them. With the surrenders at Poltava, Perevolochna, Tönning, and Stralsund, Charles lost a large portion of the veteran officers who served with him on the earlier campaigns. Gone were Lewenhaupt, Stenbock, Maximilian,

---

1 Adlerfeld, *Genuine History*, p.320.

and Roos. The King did at least have two happy reunions. Carl Cronstedt returned to the colours after escaping Prussian captivity in October 1716, and within two years he rebuilt the army's depleted artillery corps. It would swell to 3,380 men and include heavier cannons cast via new forging methods. Cronstedt made several improvements to the accuracy and reload speed of the guns. One device allowed the cannon barrel to be raised and lowered at a faster pace, and by combining the ball and charge the number of firing steps were reduced. These efforts resulted in the *Geschwinder Schott* which could supposedly achieve 12 shots per minute. For his work, Cronstedt was made a baron by a grateful King. Also the veteran Rehnskiöld was a welcome presence among the inexperienced new army. Charles's old mentor and companion from the glorious campaigns before Poltava had, through Görtz's negotiations, been released from Russian captivity as part of a prisoner exchange in October 1718. There is no doubt that the King was overjoyed with his return, but the two men would ultimately only enjoy each other's company for a few days.

Some of Charles's officers, including Frederick of Hesse-Kassel, opposed another Norwegian campaign due to the difficulties encountered during the first attempt. They preferred an immediate return to the Continent, particularly Northern Germany. Both General Johan Meijerfelt and Frederick gave the King a list of counterpoints but the advice fell on deaf ears. Norway needed to be taken for the same reasons that justified the 1716 attempt. Furthermore, the new army needed to gain experience in the field. What better way to train, march, and fight than in Norway which was close to home and had similar terrain and weather? The King's death leaves doubts about his subsequent plans, but a return to the Continent following success in Norway seemed very likely.

Charles's approach to the second invasion of Norway was similar to the first in that he split his army so it could achieve certain objectives simultaneously. General Carl Gustaf Armfeldt, a specialist of mountain warfare and the commander of the doomed defence of Finland, was tasked with leading 7,500 men against Trondheim. He was to try to keep as many Norwegians engaged in the

Carl Cronstedt. (Helena Arnell, General Carl Cronstedt, 1740s, National Museum of Finland (Riitta Konttinen), public domain)

Frederick I. (Martin van Meytens, Frederick I, 1730, Nationalmuseum, public domain)

north as possible and so limit the arrival of reinforcements. The main bulk of the Swedish army, 36,000 strong, was to be divided into three unequally sized groups. It is worth noting that the preferred balance of infantry and cavalry was upset for the thrust into Norway. Instead of the usual one to one ratio, the infantry comprised of nearly two thirds of the entire force. The smallest detachment, mostly cavalry, was continuously repositioned along the border while Charles transferred from Frederick's detachment to his own as soon as the army marched into Norway. Both of these feints proved successful and kept the Danish-Norwegian forces guessing as to where the main thrust of the Swedish army would come from. As a result, progress into Norwegian territory in October was met with little opposition and is a testament of the King's ability to plan feints and launch quick marches to limit the enemy's intelligence and counter-attacking options.

Despite a majority of the newly raised army being comprised of fresh recruits, Charles expected that the standards set by its immediate predecessors would be maintained. When the King heard of discontent and poor discipline within Armfeldt's contingent, he sent a scathing letter that demanded the army fight as the original did – aggressively in the spirit of *Gå På* – and do so without questioning. In his mind, duty and courage were the sole requirements of the soldiers and officers, something that, as the King highlighted, was lacking at Perevolochna. As with the 1716 campaign, he expected discipline to extend beyond the camp and battlefield – civilians were to be treated kindly. Charles set the example and amused himself on several occasions with the local population. Much like his horseback ride across Europe, his visits with locals created enduring legends about where he slept, rested, or ate. Many of these tales, found on metal placards across the countryside, are not true but prove that the King's personality continued to capture the imagination even 18 years after first being catapulted into European consciousness.

Charles XII, 1715. (David von Krafft, Charles XII, 1715, Nationalmuseum (Per-Åke Persson), public domain)

The King's letter to Armfeldt and his second in command was received and understood. The northern army continued its march on Trondheim despite difficulties in obtaining supplies. The Norwegians were able to reinforce Trondheim before Armfeldt arrived so he kept his army in the vicinity without engaging. After being informed in December of the King's death and the termination of the campaign, Armfeldt retreated over the Tydal mountain range but became engulfed in a blizzard. The combination of extreme cold, lack of supplies, and the difficult mountain passes, led to two thirds of his remaining men freezing to death. To posterity it became known as the Carolean Death March.

Norway's border forts held a critical role in defending the approaches to Kristiania. Bypassing them, as Sweden initially did in 1716, left the rear of the army exposed and threatened supply lines. Determined not to make the same mistake, the Swedes attacked the forts first. Charles was familiar with Fredriksten fortress, having unsuccessfully besieged it two years earlier. Besides the fort's solid construction and a garrison of

DEATH IN THE TRENCHES, 1718

Fredriksten fortress overlooking modern-day Halden. (Author's collection)

1,400 men, it was supported by three outer bastions that acted independently and could provide additional fire support from alternative locations. These were Gyldenlove, Overberget, and Mellemberget. Given the position of the bastions and the undulating terrain surrounding the fortress, the Swedes decided on an approach from the north-east. The first trench lines were cut into the soil on 24 November and by the 27th Gyldenlove was overrun, with Charles being among the first of 200 grenadiers to surmount the bastion. With Gyldenlove captured, the Swedes could push their trench lines closer to the outer walls of the fortress.

The Fifth Bullet

Digging trenches was a dangerous task for the besieger. Soldiers would be exposed, especially in the early stages of construction, to artillery and sniper fire as they raced to dig downwards and place protective cover on the parapet. As the trenches neared the target, muskets would come into range and add to the weight of fire. The first four days of the siege at Fredriksten saw 27 casualties among those working in the trenches. The next two days had 89. The uptick in numbers reflects the Swedish approach as they would have just cleared Gyldenlove and begun to encroach on the fort itself. With the construction of the denoted "old line" trench, the bastions of Mellemberget and Overberget also came into line of sight. The evening of 30 November would see the Swedes create a second trench, the "new line", which ran parallel to the "old line". A communication trench was cut between the two so the Swedes could move back and forth under cover. Upon completion of the "new line", the Swedes would be in position to launch sapping operations

Model of trench system. (Swedish Army Museum, author's collection)

against the outermost walls of Fredriksten. Positive projections estimated the fall of the fortress within a week's time.

At 6:00 p.m. on 30 November, with Charles present, work began on the "new line" as Philippe Maigret, a French siege expert in Swedish service, led 400 men into position from the attached communications trench. Fascines were deployed to block incoming fire as men dug rapidly into the hard, rocky soil. Completed gabions were brought forward to be placed on the trench lip and filled with the displaced earth. In the brief four-hour life of the "new line", seven men were killed and 15 wounded from enemy fire. Charles had momentarily left the operation to have a meal at his headquarters near Gyldenlove. Upon his return, he moved into the "old line" along with seven other officers. He then kicked two footholds into the sidewall of the trench and pulled himself up to rest his arms on the parapet. This put his boots at the same height as the officers in the trench and exposed his head and shoulders above the cover granted by the trenchline. This had a purpose as he wanted to observe the fire coming from Fredriksten and he also wanted the men in the new trench to see him and be encouraged by his presence. It was not a new practice with Rehnskiöld noting: "…in rain and cold his Majesty insisted on being present in the approaches so that everything might run that more smoothly and work proceed at greatest speed."

DEATH IN THE TRENCHES, 1718

The Swedish approach to Fredriksten Fortress.

155

Charles XII's felt hat with projectile hole. (Charles XII's Hat with Projectile Hole, 1718, The Royal Armoury, public domain)

Pamphlet of Charles XII's funeral procession, 1719. (Pamphlet of Charles XII's Burial Procession, 1719, The Royal Armoury (Jens Mohr), public domain)

Descriptions on night-time visibility vary as the moon was mostly blocked by cloud cover. Fires were lit and hung from the walls of Fredriksten to help illuminate the field, but had an adverse effect by outlining the walls for the attackers. Occasional flares shot into the sky added brief moments of light. Charles propped up his head by resting his cheek on his left hand. As the minutes passed, officers in the trench requested that Charles climb back down to safety. The resulting dismissive wave of the hand, so common over his career as a response to the hazards of his wellbeing, was accompanied by "Do not be afraid." The lack of tonality removes any possibility of inferring if it was sincere or teasing. Charles continued with his observations. Sometime after 9:00 p.m. a projectile passed cleanly through his temple, killing him instantly.

The left hand fell away as Charles's head sunk down onto his shoulders and into the collar of his cloak. His feet slipped from the trench footholds but his bodyweight was supported by the parapet. Contrary to later descriptions and illustrations, his hand did not "instinctively" grasp the hilt of his sword – death was instantaneous. The sound of the impact, likened to throwing a stone into wet mud or slapping two fingers against an open palm, aroused the attention of the officers in the trench: "Lord Jesus, the King is shot!" was the first reply. The trench was sealed off to prevent anyone else from seeing the dead king. The body was covered with two cloaks and Andre Sicre, Frederick's adjutant, placed his own wig and gold-laced hat upon the King's head to make it seem like the casualty was an officer. A party of stretcher-bearers were brought in to, unbeknownst to them, carry the King's body first to Studekollen and then to the headquarters at Tistedal. Along the way, the uneven road caused some of the bearers to slip and fall and the body rolled off the stretcher to reveal the royal corpse, much to the company's dismay. Charles was placed in a makeshift wooden coffin for transport to Uddevalla where his surgeon Melchior Neumann embalmed the body and prepared it for a more dignified transport to Stockholm.

The body would rest at Karlberg, one of Charles's primary childhood homes – and now, fittingly, a military academy – before it

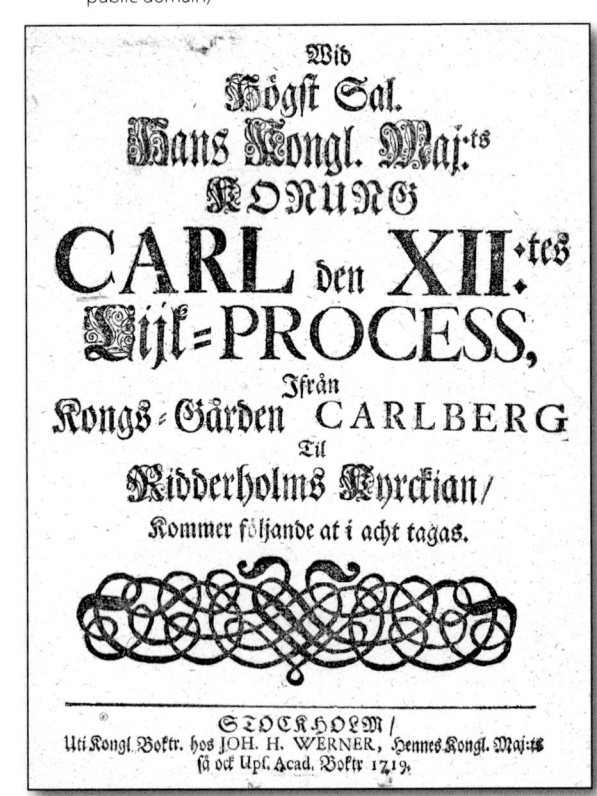

DEATH IN THE TRENCHES, 1718

Charles XII's funeral procession. (Funeral of Charles XII, public domain)

Close up of the King's coffin. (Funeral of Charles XII, public domain)

proceeded in a solemn funeral procession to *Riddarholmskyrkan* on 26 February. The coffin was interred in a black marble sarcophagus, topped with a lion pelt and crown in gilded brass. Charles lies above the vault that holds the rest of his Carolean family and directly across from the great Gustav II Adolf, thus forming symbolic bookends to the beginning and end of the Swedish Empire.

Unused concept sketch of Charles XII's sarcophagus.

Death Theory

One of the most enduring historical mysteries left to posterity is the circumstance of Charles's death. Was it an "honest enemy bullet" or was there something more sinister – regicide from within the ranks? The popularity of the murder theory has fluctuated over the centuries; the Age of Liberty, the parliamentary Hats and their 1741 war with Russia, the return of absolutism under Gustav III, the near intervention in the Crimean War, romanticism and the rise of nationalism, and the emergence of the modern welfare state – are all changes in the socio-political affairs of Sweden to which Charles's popularity, and thus the argument over his death, is tied.

Despite remaining unsolved for 300 years, there is a surprising amount of material to draw upon ranging from eyewitness accounts, second- and third-hand retellings, armoury and supply records, statements given in delirium, and even dream sequences. While the validity of some sources may be fairly questioned and others outright dismissed, even accepted facts have proven to lead to further conjecture. Analysing the source material is a study unto itself and unfortunately beyond the scope of this work. The following paragraphs will serve to merely highlight some of the unique evidence, stories, and modern interpretations that exist within the historiography.[2]

The officers who occupied the trench with Charles on the night of 30 November did not suspect foul play in the moment, nor did they assume the shot came from anywhere else but the left.[3] Maigret, a bystander in the trench at the moment of the King's death, believed that due to the size of the entry wound, the shot must have come from a weapon too heavy to carry; in other words, a canister round fired from an artillery piece. Fredriksten was easily within the effective range for musket and canister fire although Charles would most likely have been facing the fortress to observe the new

---

[2] For further reading refer to Carl Nordling, 'The Death of Karl XII: A Case of Political Murder', *Scandinavian Studies*, 71:1 (1999), pp.81–92; Peter From, *Karl XII:s död: gåtans lösning* (Lund: Historiska Media, 2005); Svante Ståhl, *Karl XII:s död* (Stockholm: Karolinska förbundet, 2003).

[3] There was a period of time when it was assumed the shot came from the right – see below.

DEATH IN THE TRENCHES, 1718

View from the current memorial to the fortress. (Author's collection)

trench being dug before him. Canister ammunition was also employed at the bastions of Mellemberget and Overberget which were 450 and 600 metres away respectively and positioned off to the King's left.

The debate over the size and type of ammunition used ultimately becomes an issue of millimetres. The King's felt hat survives in the Royal Armouries and the hole in the material was measured at 19.5 millimetres, although this too can be inconclusive – the felt may have shrunk over time or the hole could have been enlarged from frequent handling. If the projectile was indeed 19.5 millimetres in size, who had access to such ammunition? Depending on the source material, this could have been just the Norwegian defenders or the Swedes as well. X-rays taken of the King's corpse in 1917 revealed lead splinters in his foot where a musket ball had passed through and left seemingly irremovable debris behind. The skull showed no such traces. Was the projectile thus jacketed which would indicate the use of special ammunition? If so, who possessed such talent or stature to utilise it? Or, was the surgeon simply good at his craft and successfully cleaned out any remnants of lead during the embalming process?

In the decades following the King's death, two notable admissions of guilt were made by men with close ties to Charles and his last campaign: Andre Sicre, Frederick's adjutant and Carl Cronstedt, head of the artillery. Both statements were made during fits of delirium due to fever and ill health and were quickly recanted by the horrified men as they came to their senses. The statement from Cronstedt is taken seriously by Carl Nordling who points out that the general had an unmatched ballistics expertise and could have constructed a close range shot using a reduced powder charge that would have mimicked all the traces of a projectile fired from further away. Sicre and Cronstedt were both aligned to Frederick and the Hesse faction at court, which places ultimate responsibility of an assassination at the feet of the future king of Sweden. Given the hasty end of the Norwegian campaign, the sudden arrest and execution of Görtz, and the accessions of Ulrika and Frederick to the Swedish throne, Frederick's motives can be questioned and he is most closely associated with the regicide theory.

Perhaps the most bizarre of all accounts on the King's death comes from Melchior Neumann. He served as a field surgeon in the Swedish army and had operated on Charles's injured foot just before Poltava. He would ultimately be responsible for embalming the King's body and would have seen the entry and exit wounds up close and with an experienced eye. On the interior cover of a book, Neumann inscribed a personal dream in which the dead king became reanimated, grabbed his hand and said: "You will be the witness of how I was shot." Neumann asked: "Your majesty, were you shot from the fortress?" to which the King responded: "No, someone came creeping."[4] Two further cryptic lines questioning the source of the bullet and God's all-seeing eye reveal that Neumann was clearly troubled by the death and harboured a fair share of doubt over the origin of the projectile.

The attempt to establish or invalidate the murder theory was the motivation behind three of the four openings of Charles's sarcophagus. The group tasked with the first opening in 1746 reviewed the body and came away convinced that murder had indeed occurred. The 1859 opening muddied the waters further although it left quite the impression on the future King Oscar II, who was present and gleefully noted "… how utterly unfounded were the

Laurel leaves and hair taken from the 1859 opening. (Laurels and Hair taken from 1859 opening, The Royal Armoury)

---

4   Nordling, *The Death of Karl XII*, pp.86–87.

suspicions that the hero had fallen by an assassin's hand. God be thanked for the certainty that his illustrious life had a better and worthier close."[5]

The 1917 opening, and currently the last, utilised X-ray technology on the King's remains which greatly increased the understanding of his injuries – known and unknown – and confirmed the direction and planar route of the projectile. Up until then, one commonly held theory was that the shot came from the right and not the left, a suggestion that was not challenged until the mid nineteenth century. There were no enemy positions on the right so any support of this theory would promote regicide. The aforementioned hat in the Royal Armoury has a hole created by a projectile on the same side as the button. Regulations stated that hats would be worn with the button on the left. Would Charles, a strict adherent to military uniformity, have worn the hat in any other way? Even then there was debate on whether or not the hole in the hat was indented outwards or inwards. There was no mention of felt being found in the skull during the embalming process. Does that mean the felt was carried cleanly through the skull by the projectile or did it never enter the skull at all and thus suggest a shot from the right? Continued questioning here is trivial but it illustrates the point that presented evidence can be made to fit either narrative.

The study from 1917 failed to fully confirm or invalidate the murder theory. It did, however, all but confirm that the shot came from the left, passed nigh horizontally through the skull (there is a slight elevation left to right) and had a diameter between 18–20 millimetres. In recent decades more work has been done with ballistics testing to determine the velocity of the projectile and its effects on the human skull. The earlier issue of evidence being inconclusive continued to be problematic with Peter From and Svante Stahl both taking different interpretations from the surviving Danish-Norwegian artillery documents. While a shot from a pistol has been ruled out on account of its short range, a traditional musket ball, jacketed bullet, and canister shot are all accepted options. There remains one final ammunition anecdote in the form of the *kulknappen* (button projectile). Charles's ability to emerge from danger unharmed time and again led to a belief in his invulnerability to normal ammunition. The only way he could be harmed was by shooting him with a bullet fashioned from something off his person – in this case a button from his uniform. At first relegated to folklore, the theory gained attention in the 1940s thanks to Albert Sandklef. The button in question exists in a museum in Varberg although its provenance remains murky and while the *kulknappen* theory has its adamant supporters, it is largely dismissed.

The 300th anniversary of the King's death in 2018 sparked renewed public interest and led to new publications addressing the topic, with some authors making more outrageous claims than others. Michael Roberts, in all of his prolific work on Swedish history, turns his eye to Charles XII in one singular lecture, *The Dubious Hand,* and after reviewing the back and forth of the historiography surrounding the King's death, concludes it is best that historians leave the theorising alone – it is simply not worth the time.

---

5   Oscar Fredrik, *Charles XII*, trans. George Apgeorge (London: Spottiswoode & Co, 1878), p.121.

The End of the War

The death of Charles XII removed the most glaring obstacle that stood between Sweden and an immediate peace – or so it has been assumed. The immediate fallout was favourable for those inclined to diplomatic solutions. The day after the King's death, Frederick, in his capacity as generalissimo, organised a council of war at Tistedal. The decision was made to abandon the Norwegian campaign and return to Swedish soil. Fredriksten fortress thus remained uncaptured having survived two sieges by Swedish forces. Frederick had already voiced his misgivings of a second attack on Norway so an abrupt ending of the campaign under his leadership was not shocking. He would, however, have been more concerned with a hasty return to Stockholm to prepare for the inevitable power struggle between the Holstein and Hesse factions at court. Sweden would continue to fight in the Great Northern War for another three years as it attempted to secure better terms for peace. Diplomatic missions between 1719 and 1721 focused on achieving agreements with the smaller states and in the process form a united front against Russia which was now being recognised by other European powers as a major threat in the east. Stockholm's policy was, in a sense, a continuation of Charles's policy and perhaps a vote of confidence in the diplomatic direction the King was taking post 1715.

The British were among the first to recognise the plight of Sweden, with James Jefferyes and even the Duke of Marlborough commenting on Russia's ascendancy in the aftermath of Poltava. Writing to the Secretary of State for the Northern Department in London, Jefferyes noted: "…but certainly so many potent enemies at once will put the Swedes to their last shift if God Almighty cast not an eye of compassion on that poor nation".[6] Even harsh critics of Charles and the Swedish war effort reversed their position in light of Russia's advances in the waning years of the conflict. Daniel Dafoe included an editorial in his *Review*: "I cannot wish the Muscovite success against the Swede, because that growing Prince may once become formidable to Europe and I look upon the Swedes to be the great barrier against any attempts the future race of so great and increasing a monarch may make upon Europe."[7] Britain came to see Sweden's survival as a necessary buffer against Russia's push in the Baltic and reformed an alliance in 1719 to provide naval support. In November of that year, Hanover and Sweden reached an agreement: in exchange for one million *riksdaler*, Sweden would relinquish the Bishoprics of Bremen and Verden to Hanover. The latter had already secured the rights to the territories over Denmark in 1715.

A peace with Prussia followed in January, 1720. The fledgling kingdom secured Stettin and a portion of Western Pomerania south of the Penee river. Sweden would retain the rest of Pomerania, albeit much smaller since its original conquest, until it was finally lost in the Napoleonic Wars of the following century. Denmark followed suit and made peace in June. Sweden

---

[6] Jefferyes, *Letters*, p.85.
[7] Rothstein, *Peter and Marlborough*, p.228.

DEATH IN THE TRENCHES, 1718

renounced its support of Holstein-Gottorp and lost its exemption from the Sound tolls. Frederick fought adamantly to prevent the latter but, given his rivalry and hatred for Holstein, easily acquiesced to the former. Denmark was in no position militarily to exact further concessions from Sweden and was actually forced to return Stralsund along with its strategically important isle of Rügen as well as Wismar. As for Scania, Denmark's *casus belli* in 1700, it remained Swedish.

Frederick's willingness to accept less favourable terms for a lasting peace allowed him to achieve what Charles could not – the narrowing of antagonists down to one. Russia remained, and Sweden was working towards establishing a large anti-Russian alliance among itself, Britain, France, and the Holy Roman Empire. However, issues in the South Sea and the loss of war lust against Russia within the Empire saw each potential ally back away. Sweden was left to the mercy of Peter who, in his dominating position, could force his exact terms upon Stockholm. Despite the Swedish victory at Stäket in August 1719, the frequent galley raids on the Swedish coastline were a firm reminder of who was in charge. The Peace of Nystad was signed in August 1721 and put an end to the Great Northern War. Sweden would never regain the Baltic provinces nor Karelia or Kexholm. The rest of Finland was returned to Sweden only to be gradually nipped at after the Russo-Swedish wars of 1741–1743 and 1788–1790. Finland would be totally lost to Russia in 1809 under Gustav IV who saw Charles XII as an idealistic hero, wore the late King's uniform, and even had the sarcophagus opened to look upon the royal corpse. Had Gustav even the slightest of Charles's military talents, perhaps he may have fared better than he did.

Charles's refusal to marry until an impossible peace arrived meant that the succession crisis was entirely of his doing. Upon learning of her brother's death, Ulrika claimed the throne for herself and through some political wrangling managed to secure the consent of the Estates. Her accession came at the cost of renouncing absolutism, returning power to the *Riksdag*, and rewriting the constitution to ensure the election of subsequent monarchs.

Gustav IV Adolf at the opening of Charles XII's sarcophagus. (Erik Gustaf Gothe, Gustav IV Adolf at the Opening of Charles XII's Sarcophagus, 1802, Nationalmuseum (Madeleine Andersson), public domain)

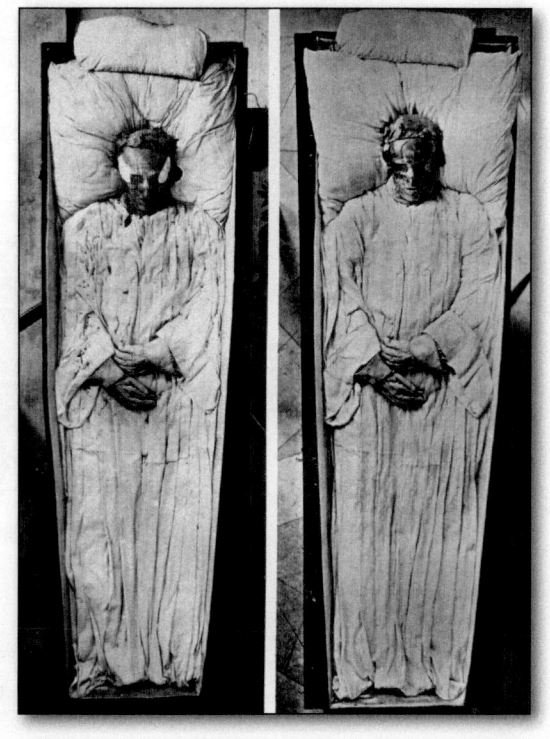

The body of Charles XII photographed before and after the 1917 examination. (Author's collection, public domain)

BY DEFEATING MY ENEMIES

Ulrika Eleonora. (Georg Desmarees, Ulrika Eleonora the Younger, Nationalmuseum, public domain)

Charles Frederick, Duke of Holstein-Gottorp. (David von Krafft, Charles Frederick, Nationalmuseum (Erik Cornelius), public domain)

A romantic and inaccurate portrayal of Charles XII's final return to Stockholm. (Gustaf Cederstrom, Bringing Home the Body of Charles XII, 1884, Nationalmuseum (Linn Ahlgren), public domain)

Having failed in several attempts to create a joint reign with Frederick at her side, she abdicated in his favour at the end of February, 1720. The reign of Frederick I ushered in the Swedish *Frehitstiden* which coincided with the wider European Enlightenment. However, it also signified an end to the old ways. The royal Carolean bloodline was cut off and Sweden returned to its former status as a second-rate power on the fringes of Continental affairs. The abrupt shift in Sweden's destiny is summed up in the famous, oft quoted, epigram:

> The glory of the Age is past and gone,
> We to our former nothingness are fated.
> King Charles is dead, King Fredrick consecrated,
> And Sweden's clock has moved from XII to I.

Chapter 12

The Warrior King Reassessed: 1718 and Beyond

King Carl, the youthful hero,
In smoke and dust he stood;
He drew his belted longsword and into battle strode.
'Come, let us try its war-bite, what Swedish steel may do.
Make way you Moscoviters, fresh heart, the lads in blue!'

Esaias Tegnér, 1818

"Karl XII, however, joined in the slaughter with glee. As a young man, already a crowned monarch then, he had practised by beheading sheep, cows and horses, and near Kristianstad he shot a cow, simply for his own amusement. Like a coward, he abandoned his country, having first impoverished it; and finally, driven by a last remnant of shame, he appointed a plenipotentiary, whom he could blame instead. But as sovereign his actions were reckless and his person sacrosanct."

August Strindberg, 1910[1]

Charles XII once quipped that if he put to death everyone who criticised him, there would not be many left alive in Sweden. The King was well aware of how he was perceived, both at home and abroad. His early successes placed him on the front page of circulated newspapers and made him the focus of poems, songs, paintings, and medals. The apogee was reached at Altranstädt where he held court to all of Europe. The loss at Poltava and subsequent time spent in exile with the Ottomans removed the lustre and by his untimely death he was barely mentioned in the very newspapers that once lauded him. He had become a footnote at best and demonised at worst. From the eighteenth century to modernity a theme has emerged, that Charles "has almost invariably … been given one of two extreme roles: admired role model or object lesson".[2] Crowned with the laurels of victory, he was

---

1 August Strindberg, 'Faraodyrkan', *Afton-Tidningen*, 29 April 1910. The posting of the article 'Pharaoh Worship' marks the start of the Strindberg Feud.
2 Nils Ekedahl, 'A Literary Charles XII', in John B. Hattendorf (ed.), *Charles XII Warrior King* (EU: Karwansaray Publishing, 2018), p.375.

portrayed as a Caesar, a northern Alexander, the second coming of Gustavus Adolphus. In the eyes of the opposition, he was the warlord, a sadist, a despot – the mad king who sought nothing but glory and destroyed himself and his kingdom in the process. This duality of hero and villain allows for anyone to seek, and justify, their preconceived opinions within the original source material and the literary depictions that followed over the centuries.

The gravity of Sweden's *Stormaktstiden*, as viewed through the lens of liberal and conservative Caroline historiography, tends to be placed squarely upon Charles's shoulders, even 300 years after his death. Unlike the pristine legacy of Gustavus Adolphus, which benefits from him dying at the height of success, that of Charles remains at the whim of socio-economic and geopolitical events. For as Sweden turns, so too does the perception and depiction of Charles XII. What follows is a brief chronological review of the shifting public attitudes towards Charles and his accomplishments.

Charles XII in the guise of a Roman hero. (Charles XII on Horse, Hans Thorwid, Nationalmuseum)

Eighteenth Century

From the perspective of the English, conflicting views of Charles XII were already materialising during his lifetime due to a series of events that occurred on the British Isles. King James II, a Stuart inclined to Catholicism and the belief in Divine Right, was deposed by the Glorious Revolution of 1688 in favour of Protestantism and a more constitutional monarchy. During this time, a two party system emerged in English politics. The Tories, connected to tradition, favoured a strong monarchy and had members side with pro-Stuart attempts to claim the throne. Their rivals, the Whigs, used the revolution to promote Parliamentary rule over that of the monarch. Political intrigue led to intermittent conflict known as the Jacobite Risings which flared from 1688 to 1746. As claimants and parties fought for power in government and occasionally on the battlefield, an additional war of propaganda attempted to win over the general public. As Charles stormed across Eastern Europe, his popularity made him a target for the papers and pamphlets of both political machines. Whereas the Tories saw him as a strong, capable leader and encouraged him to support the Jacobean cause, the Whigs attacked everything about him with accusations ranging from his poor table manners to his infliction of inhuman cruelties.

A shift against Charles occurred in 1714 with the accession of the Elector of Hanover to the British crown. As a member of the anti-Swedish coalition, George I's enmity towards Charles was now inherited by Great Britain. George tried to use the Royal Navy for Hanover's territorial ambitions, with varying degrees of success. The discovery of the Swedish-Jacobite plot allowed him to stir up public resentment. Whig pamphleteers went into high gear against Charles as rumours swirled that the King himself would lead a Jacobite rebellion through the Scottish Highlands. Daniel Defoe, an anti-absolutist, chimed in with the publication of *The History of the Wars of His Present Majesty Charles XII* in 1715, and was very critical of Charles's brazen attempts at capturing glory and power. The combination of Sweden's capitulation in 1721 and the success of the House of Hanover in Britain saw the Whigs win out over their parliamentary counterparts. As a result, their portrayal of Charles as an absolutist tyrant remained strong in British historiography until the early twentieth century. One final blow was to land nearly three decades after the war when the futility of Charles's actions was explored in Samuel Johnson's poem *The Vanity of Human Wishes* – for all of the King's efforts to obtain victory and glory, the tragic results rendered him as a mere warning for others.[3]

Sweden meanwhile, locked in the waning years of the Great Northern War, suffered under a combination of Russian coastal raids, high taxes and rolling famine. Public discontent grew and with it the need for an outlet. By the end of 1718, Charles lay dead in the trenches of Fredriksten and his loyal minister, Baron Görtz, was arrested and executed shortly thereafter. Görtz took the fall for his master but it is clear where the blame was meant to be placed. The first experiment with absolutism ended with the accession of Ulrika Eleonora and power was restored to the *Riksdag*. The ensuing period, known as the Age of Liberty, saw a distancing between parliament and the Crown to the point that Charles served as the ultimate example of power gone awry. To be an absolutist meant to be 'un-Swedish' and as the last veterans of the Great Northern War died off, so too did any surviving support for the King.

The release of Voltaire's *Histoire de Charles XII, Roi de Suede* in 1731 helped blunt some of the harsher depictions of the King resulting from the successful propaganda campaigns in Britain, Russia, and Sweden, but the overall image of a warrior king remained. Voltaire greatly admired Charles and saw him as virtuous beyond compare. His biography, however, takes a moralistic tact by showing that war and the pursuit of glory can destroy even the best of lives. In contrast, Voltaire's later publication on Peter the Great focuses on the Czar's domestic works rather than his military successes. In this way, Peter too is made a hero. Charles makes war for the sake of war while Peter makes war for the progress of his nation; this juxtaposition of noble but doomed warrior versus an off-putting but surviving reformer favours the latter in a philosophical and practical sense and thus elevates Peter above his rival. Joran Nordberg, a former chaplain in Charles's army, published a biography of the King in 1740 to correct several perceived mistakes in Voltaire's work. The timing was perhaps too coincidental as the publication occurred just before the outbreak of the Russo-Swedish war (1741–1743) which was encouraged by the Hats party in the *Riksdag*. They sought to use Charles as a symbol of standing up to the Russian menace.

---

3   See Appendix II.

THE WARRIOR KING REASSESSED: 1718 AND BEYOND

Nineteenth Century

In 1809, as the Napoleonic Wars raged in Europe, the Swedes surrendered all of Finland to Russia. The disaster forced the abdication of Gustav IV Adolf, a known admirer of Charles XII who on one occasion ordered the opening of the King's sarcophagus so he could see his predecessor for himself. The loss of Finland simultaneously fostered nostalgia for the *Stormaktstiden*. Charles XII now returned to public consciousness as the conquering hero and his exploits against the hated Russians at Narva trumped all.

Johan Molin's iconic statue of the King in Stockholm's Kungsträdgården was funded through an organised protest against Russian political and military aggression, and was revealed with great pomp and circumstance in 1868 on the 150th anniversary of his death. With one hand resting firmly on the hilt of his sword, Charles gestures defiantly towards the east – towards Russia.

Charles XIV John welcomed into Elysium by his predecessors. (Carl Andreas Dahlstrom, 1844, Skokloster Castle (Jens Mohr), public domain)

Molin's Charles XII. (Author's collection)

A Romantic depiction of Charles XII. (Julius Kronberg, Charles XII, 1893, Royal Armoury (Goran Schmidt), public domain)

The emergence of Romanticism in the early nineteenth century coupled with the centennial of Charles's death led to an increasing amount of sympathetic works. Esaias Tegnér and Erik Gustaf Geijer both wrote commemorative poems of the King which amounted to hero worship. Rather than an absolute tyrant, Charles was now compared to the Norse God Thor, and rather than being dead he merely sleeps in triumphant glory.[4] Echoing on the romantic theme of a flawed hero, the King as a tragic figure was continued in Verner von Heidenstam's novel *Karolinerna* (1897) where Charles stubbornly refused to admit defeat despite the empire collapsing around him. More importantly, the theme of sacrifice starts to shift from Charles to the men under his command.

August Strindberg's play from 1901 entitled *Karl XII* reversed the allocation of sympathy and placed it upon the Swedish people. Charles was portrayed as the villain who nearly led his kingdom into the abyss for his own vainglorious motives. Strindberg took his negative opinion of the King even further with a series of articles printed in the *Afton-Tidningen* in 1910.

Anti-absolutist views such as those of Strindberg became part and parcel of the "old school" Carolean historiography. To those ascribing historians,

---

4   Olov Westerlund, 'Karl XII i Svensk Litteratur', PhD diss, University of Lund, 1951.

The sarcophagus surrounded by the spoils of victory – a common setup for national heroes in the nineteenth century (Riddarholm Church, pre-1907, public domain)

Front page of the *Afton-Tidningen* with Strindberg's article 'Pharaoh Worship' (Afton-Tidningen, 1910, Wikimedia Commons, public domain)

Charles was deeply flawed and would stop at nothing to achieve his aims even if his obstinacy meant the destruction of Sweden. The authors of biographies applying this methodology include Anders Fryxell (1850s–1860s), Robert Nisbet Bain (1895), and Oscar Browning (1899).

Twentieth Century

By putting an increased emphasis on the study of primary source material, historians of the "new school" were able to evaluate the life of Charles XII in a new light. Decisions made by the King were re-examined and placed within the context of Swedish–European events to the point that many assertions made by the "old school" could be challenged and revised. The works of Eveline Godley (1928) and Ragnhild Hatton (1968), the latter in particular, have led to a correction in the assessment of the King's personality and actions although an overall consensus is still lacking.

Frans Bengtsson wrote his biography of Charles XII in 1935 at a time when militarism and nationalism were rampant. Factions within the Swedish military, fuelled by Russian animosity, wanted to ally with Germany which led in part to Charles being adopted by far right movements who recognised a historical parallel – the gothic hero attempting to curb Russia's rise. As a case in point, Adolf Hitler was gifted a small replica of the King's statue for his 50th birthday.

After the Second World War, with demilitarisation and the rise of the Swedish welfare state, Charles once again became a *persona non grata*. He represented wasteful spending in both money and lives – the exact opposite of what a modern Sweden wanted to project. Written at the high-water mark of the welfare state, Lars Widding's *Karolinersviten* portrays the King as a sadist. In a throwback to "old school" reasoning, Charles is shot by the novel's protagonist who could no longer endure the miseries inflicted upon him. In 1988, Peter Englund's bestselling book on Poltava used the battle and the loss of the empire as a way to mark the rise of a modern, peaceful Sweden. Charles is barely mentioned.

The current memorial to Charles XII at Fredriksten Fortress. (Author's collection)

Twenty-First Century

Bengt Liljegren published a balanced and popular account of the King in the year 2000 which also marked the 300th anniversary of the start of the Great Northern War. Driven by the tercentennial commemorations, the last two decades have seen a surge of interest in the war and a substantial increase in English-language publications. Amateur historians, teachers, students, re-enactors, and miniature wargamers are digging deeper into the history of the conflict, its armies, and its personalities. Charles XII has returned to public consciousness but still remains clouded by three centuries of propaganda, literary motifs, and myth. A cursory glance at the comments under any book review or social media post can quickly identify viewpoints that are extreme, biased, and often factually incorrect. As more studies are conducted and more books emerge, a new generation of scholars will share their impressions of the warrior king. If Ekedahl's hero–villain dictum holds true, it is not yet clear which way the pendulum will swing.

Conclusion

The Swedish Empire's foundation and early expansion came via a particular series of circumstances that never again materialised. The power vacuum at the end of the Thirty Years' War and the inwardness or exhaustion of rival states allowed Sweden to punch above its weight. And yet, the foundations were weak from the beginning. Charles X knew this but his wars, despite giving Sweden its greatest territorial extent, further complicated matters economically and diplomatically. Charles XI countered a decline by conducting reforms within his own borders but they came at the cost of strong alliances and the kingdom's political reputation. The unintended consequences created by his predecessors simply added to the complications experienced by Charles XII during the Great Northern War. These cannot be forgotten when assessing the King's actions during the early years of the war. There exists, ultimately, a sense of inescapability as a recent interpretation shows: "The Swedish 'age of empire' always rested upon exiguous economic and demographic foundations, and these were exposed by the dynamism of the Petrine state during the Great Northern War. Charles XII's military leadership could do no more, faced with the Russian behemoth, than delay the inevitable."[1]

Generalship is one matter, kingship is another and it is not wrong to suggest that the empire could have been sustained in some reduced form had Charles simply been more willing to compromise. Upon hearing of the disaster at Poltava, the Duke of Marlborough bluntly stated that "His [Charles] continued success, and the contempt he had for his enemies, has been his ruin."[2] Charles had his opportunities to gain favourable terms: immediately after Narva in 1700, at the outset from Saxony in 1706, and via the Neutrality Convention of 1710. In all instances he refused to bend, seeking guarantees and security that would not or could not be provided. This intractability changed as the war progressed but by the time Charles was willing to make exceptions, his enemies were in stronger positions militarily and diplomatically. They now had the ability to demand further concessions from Sweden and Charles could do nothing more than reject such impossible

---

1 Hamish Scott, 'The Great Northern War (1700–1721) and the Integration of the European States System', in John B. Hattendorf (ed.), *Charles XII Warrior King* (EU: Karwansaray Publishing, 2018), p.27.
2 John B. Hattendorf, 'British Policy towards Sweden, Charles XII, and the Great Northern War, 1697–1723', in John B. Hattendorf (ed.), *Charles XII Warrior King* (EU: Karwansaray Publishing, 2018), p.176.

demands. Although the government in Stockholm worked on agreements with allies and foes alike, Charles reserved final say on foreign policy for himself. Even when he appointed Baron Görtz to carry on with negotiations, Charles had a tendency to override his minister's efforts. The "new school" of Carolean historiography goes to great lengths to prove how the King's hands were tied by difficult circumstances and how he conducted his decisions with firm reasoning. Nevertheless, absolutism places final authority upon one figure and it is clear who should shoulder the blame. This too must be recognised in the overall assessment of the King.

As a military commander, Charles showed exceptional skill which matured even further as he aged. Like his father and grandfather, he fought aggressively and valued close-range combat over long-range firepower. This found a natural outlet in the *Gå På* doctrine and the resulting military victories against difficult odds garnered a solid reputation for Swedish arms. The King espoused quick movement and did not hesitate to push through unfavourable terrain. At Pultusk and Punitz he left his infantry behind and attacked solely with mounted units. At Grodno and Holowczyn he navigated marshland, streams, and rivers to surprise enemy contingents. His desire to maintain the initiative has led to accusations of rashness and that he purposefully marched his men into enemy fire. With the Swedish army tending to be outnumbered, Charles simply took advantage of his men's discipline and superior training to launch shock assaults which damaged the foe psychologically on the approach and then rendered their numbers useless as Swedish cold steel met the front ranks.

The King's willingness to endure the same stresses and fatigues suffered by the men under his command cannot be overemphasised. Charles did not ask anything of his men that he himself would not undertake and this, in turn, earned him trust, respect, and praise in equal measure. He was the first to jump off his boat at the storming of *Humlebaek*, he built trenches at Thorn and removed the protective haystacks placed around the walls of his tent, he led the river crossing at Holowczyn, and he was among the first to take the Gyldenlove bastion at Fredriksten. The effect on morale was not only positive, but critical and it is perhaps best summarised by General Löwen: "He bound you to him … you would follow him anywhere."[3]

That Charles XII became singularly associated with warfare was a historical inevitability given the duration of his reign spent in the field. And yet, Charles enjoyed working on domestic policies and wrote frequently of his desire for peace. Conversely, Queen Christina is commonly associated with the patronage of the arts and sciences but also stated:

> A war is better than a disgraceful peace. Our rise has come through war. It were an eternal disgrace to our position and our country if others saw that we took no better care of our interests; and we should be inexcusable to our posterity … When therefore we see the danger, and know too that God has commanded His people to wage war, why shall we not do it?[4]

---

3   Axel von Löwen, *Memoires*, p.55 as quoted in Hatton, *Charles XII*, p.379.
4   Roberts, *Essays*, p.22.

CONCLUSION

Charles was well educated from birth and used quiet moments at Bender and Lund to further indulge his curiosities in mathematics, languages, science, and architecture. It was Tessin's assessment that Charles would have made a great king had war not come, and it cannot be denied that the King was well equipped for an opportunity that never came.

Had Charles not inherited a crown, he would be placed among the great generals of the period and left at that. The added weight of ruling an empire and, whether appropriate or not, bearing the responsibility for its downfall, changes the narrative. In his opening to *Sweden's Age of Greatness*, Roberts uses a fireworks analogy to describe the lifecycle of the empire. The apex was reached in 1660 and the rocket was beginning to descend back to earth. However, Charles served as a booster and provided one final surge upwards before the dramatic finale. It seems unfair to solely place upon Charles the responsibility for the empire's collapse, as to do so ignores nearly 40 years of struggle and a near insurmountable set of odds not encountered by any of his vaunted predecessors. If blame is to be placed at the King's feet, it may be found in his unwavering belief in his schemes – that his plans, and by extension his men, would succeed through sheer force of will in spite of whatever was arrayed against them. In some instances this confidence was reinforced by hard-won successes: the deposition of Augustus did finally occur after five years of struggle and the Turks initially showed support for Swedish interests. However, misplaced confidence also led to critical blunders such as believing Lewenhaupt's supply train could hold its own and that the ragged Swedes could still successfully engage the Russians at Poltava. It was during the failed assault on Rügen, while Stralsund strained under a siege, that Charles finally realised that will and faith alone could not lead to victory.

This book ends, as it began, with the inclusion of a quote from Voltaire. In his mind, Charles was ultimately "A man extraordinary rather than a great man, and fitter to be admired than imitated. His life, however, may be a lesson to Kings, and teach them, that a peaceful and happy reign is more to be desired than so much glory."[5] Ideally, the Charles that emerges here, from this text, is to be respected and pitied. He is neither the infallible hero nor the villainous destroyer. When the trumpets of war sounded, he was not found wanting. He strove for the remainder of his life to defend the interests of Sweden as he saw them. Frederik IV and Augustus proved to be no match for the King, but in Peter I Charles was fated to share the stage with a giant of early modernity, another monarch who would deploy all the resources of his state to enforce his will. It was a knight errant versus a new age Solomon. It took one decisive battle to unmake the Swedish advances and shift the fight from offence to defence, from battlefields to negotiating tables. Peter thrived while Charles continued to hunt for one more elusive victory. To borrow from an old fable, Charles was an oak, noble but rigid and lasted only to a point in the tempest before he snapped; Peter was a willow, whose strategic and political grasp allowed him to sway unaffected in the turbulence of early eighteenth-century Europe.

---

5   Voltaire, *History*, p.237.

Appendix I

Personality, Traits, and Myth

As this book is a military biography, the battlefield exploits of Charles XII and his commanding role in the Great Northern War receive the most attention. A good biographical treatment must also consider other facets of the main character which may not directly pertain to the central storyline. The following themes expand upon what was either briefly covered in the main text or entirely omitted in the interest of flow and presentation.

Appearance

Given how many paintings of Charles XII survive, the modern viewer can reconstruct the King's appearance with relative certainty. As the eldest prince of the royal family, Charles featured predominantly in paintings that were circulated within Sweden and among the royal courts of Europe. The paintings of David Klocker Ehrenstrahl depict a youthful exuberance and Charles is often shown alongside his beloved sister Hedvig Sophia, surrounded by allegories foretelling future greatness. In addition to Ehrenstrahl's early works, artists Johan Schwartz and David von Krafft provided further portraits of Charles during his lengthy stay on the Continent. What results is a complete visual timeline from birth until death and the King's ageing and weathering from campaign life can be traced from portrait to portrait.

Charles was not a vain monarch and insisted that his portraits be painted as realistically as possible. As a youth, he hated his fair complexion and happily approved of some of the later paintings that would be sent off to Stockholm from the fields of Poland and Saxony. His 1706 Altranstädt portrait reveals a sun-beaten face – something that shocked the court back home. Despite this, a student who saw the King in person remarked that "Charles is much better looking than on the portraits we have seen."[1] It is known that the King enjoyed most of his depictions but in one rare instance near the end of his life, Charles lost his famous composure and slashed a portrait. It was painted by the competent David von Krafft so a lack of quality was not the issue –

---

1   Hatton, *Charles XII*, p.408.

Charles would approve of the repainted version. Perhaps he saw something in his own face that betrayed a weariness he could not accept.

Despite all of the surviving paintings, a comment made in 1707 claimed that no portrait ever looked exactly like the King and that it was difficult to recall his appearance once he was out of sight. Charles did not have a singular image defining feature like a Hapsburg jaw or aquiline nose – nothing that could really be overemphasised by the political cartoonists emerging in the late eighteenth century. It could be argued that when all of Charles's features are placed together – a high forehead, balding crown of hair, a persistent half smile – only then does one get a definite image of the warrior king. Compared to his rivals, Charles did not stand out either. The physical difference between him and Augustus was already commented upon. Charles stood at roughly 1.75 meters tall and thus dwarfed by the towering height of Peter the Great at over 2 meters. His body shape was quite recognisable and he was easy to pick out at costumed masques.

It was around the 1701–1702 timeframe that Charles adopted his signature look. He took to wearing a plain black felt hat without piping, a black cravat in lieu of lace, a blue cavalry uniform with no finery, and knee high riding boots that he was rarely seen without. The clothes were nicely tailored but similar, if not exact, to what was worn by men of the cavalry and dragoons. His one allowance for comfort were the fine undergarments worn beneath the coat and camisole. He abandoned the wig quite early in the war, preferring to "wear his own hair". In a letter from 1717, he thanked his sister for gifting him a karpus (cap) and wig to protect against the cold but wrote that he would not wear them as he was unaccustomed to such finery and "warmth around the ears".[2]

Injuries/Health

Charles was considered sickly as a child but would prove to have a hardy constitution. Out of five princes born to the royal couple, he was the only one to survive to adulthood. The most threatening disease he contracted as a youth was smallpox. Upon his emergence from the bout, he was quite pleased with the pox scars on his face as he felt they made him look manlier. Charles would go on to devise his own cures for illness and ailment. He commonly fasted to rid himself of a cough or cold and felt that hard exercise, riding in particular, could help combat fevers. He suffered from the latter on campaign, especially during the march on Russia in 1708 and again in 1713 in the hotter climes of the Ottoman Empire.

When he was too injured to ride or partake in military drill he tended to put on weight but nothing significant that would ever amount to being overweight. His portrait painted at Stralsund just after the years in Turkey shows the extent of his weight gain especially when compared side by side with earlier and later paintings. Charles was noted for not having the

---

2 Carlson, *Eigenhändigen Briefe*, p.165.

extreme range of courses served at his meals and would often be content with bread and beer in the field. His food preferences were surprisingly health-conscious: he leaned towards leafy greens, such as watercress, as well as a variety of fruits.

Part of the King's enduring image was his willingness to put himself into harm's way. This naturally created a series of close calls and injuries over the course of his military career. At Thorn he witnessed the officer next to him have both legs removed by a cannonball and shots would pass through his tent during the night. He had ordered that the blocks of hay stacked against his tent walls as a buffer be removed. By that point Charles had already felt the bite of a musket ball. He would ultimately be hit five times in his life: at the storming of the Russian defences at Narva, during observations near Poltava, while fighting the *Kalabalik*, during the battle of Stresow, and finally at the siege of Fredriksten. In addition to bullet wounds, he suffered gashes from sabres and broke several bones.

Charles had many instances of being de-horsed – a dangerous action that could see the rider thrown at high speed or crushed under the weight of the animal. The latter happened to the King in 1702 when his horse tripped over a tent support and fell on top of him. Charles suffered a broken femur but Adlerfeld noted: "… he alone seemed not to feel it … he told them it was nothing, and would be easily cured; no one heard him complain or give the least token of that pain which he must necessarily endure."[3] With Charles refusing to be motionless for long, the break did not set properly and resulted in a limp that accompanied him for the rest of his life. The extent of the break was revealed by the X-rays taken in 1917. Another notable fall happened at Stralsund which probably resulted in broken ribs or a punctured lung, as reports mentioned Charles coughing up blood.

Knowingly or not, Charles bridged the gap between folk remedies and new medical science. During his asylum in the Ottoman Empire, Charles paid the Sultan's medical advisor to obtain a treatise on vaccination as a means to prevent smallpox – a surprisingly modern take. But when writing to his sister about the plague in Stockholm in 1711, he comments about the hearsay that the plague will not thrive where it smells of sulphur.[4]

Marriage/Sexuality

The premature deaths of his mother and father removed a hand that would have controlled his availability on the marriage market. In his first years as king, there were attempts at identifying a potential spouse among several key states. Charles seemed drawn to one woman in particular – Princess Sophia of Denmark. The pairing, a king of Sweden and a Danish princess, would have mirrored that of his parents and the notion this was sought intentionally out of duty and respect is not far-fetched. His royal yacht, used to transport him into the opening stages of the Great Northern War, was simply named

---

3   Adlerfeld, *Genuine History*, p.99.
4   Carlson, *Eigenhändigen Briefe*, p.108.

Sophia. With the two kingdoms officially at war, the marriage talks fell apart. There were several occasions in later years when Sophia's name would re-emerge but by that point the King had abandoned any hope of marriage until the war was over.

Charles wanted to set an example for the rank and file of his army and argued that he could not wed and enjoy the comforts of marriage while his men were at war. It is true that the King tried to avoid talk of marriage altogether and would leave conversations when the topic came up. "Sweden will never lack of a king" was his terse reply.[5] Charles's grandmother, Hedvig Eleonora, who sought above all else to preserve the family's royal prerogative, would goad him on in letters which finally prompted a response from an exasperated King: "I have neither the time nor the opportunity for marriage. Even when I come home, there are too many things to be done to permit me to think of a speedy marriage."[6]

Charles was raised in a family comprised predominantly of women – his grandmother, mother, and two sisters. Even when Charles was given his own rooms and royal duties at the age of six, he remained close to them and would accompany his family at all manner of events and outings. It is clear that Charles held a romantic notion of marriage contrary to the expectations of a royal needing to put diplomatic duty first. Baron Carsten Feif recalled Charles's comments on marriage before the 1718 Norwegian campaign: "As for myself, when God gives peace, I also will marry. But I will seek a wife not for reasons of state, but one whom I like well and believe I will love for ever so that I need not keep what the French call maitresse: in simple Swedish a whore."[7] New Drabant recruits for the campaign were preferred to be bachelors, however Charles gave them the option to resign if they wished to marry.

The lack of a marriage and any legitimate hint of mistresses led to questioning of the King's sexuality. Nothing is revealed in any surviving source material and it thus seems that a lack of relationships falls solely to time constraints and a commitment to duty. However, the questions persist and as recent as 2014, an experimental film presented the King as a teetotalling homosexual.[8]

Religion

By the time of Charles's birth, Sweden was a devout Protestant state and a guarantor of the Peace of Westphalia which helped secure certain freedoms for practising Protestants in the Holy Roman Empire. Both of his parents held strong religious convictions although they applied them differently to the royal supremacy. For Charles XI, his creation of an absolutist monarchy lay on the unquestionable premise that he was appointed by God alone to

---

5   Hatton, *Charles XII*, p.212.
6   Carlson, *Eigenhändigen Briefe*, p.124.
7   Nordberg *Anmärckingar*, pp.50–51, as quoted in Hatton, *Charles XII*, p.466.
8   Roy Andersson, *A Pigeon Sat on a Branch Reflecting on Existence* (2014; Magnolia Pictures), film.

rule over his subjects. For Ulrika Eleonora, faith was used as a teaching device to create a more humane relationship between sovereign and subjects.

Charles's education began with Bible study and the memorisation of religious proverbs. Charles kept a copy of the Bible at his bedside in the field and would attend sermons regularly despite them sometimes affording him his only opportunity to catch a moment of sleep. In addition to daily devotions, the King observed several days of fasting each year. Critical decisions were often made after private prayer and reflection in addition to more secular council. An updated Swedish translation of the Bible was completed in 1703 and became known as *Karl XII:s bibel* (*Charles XII Bible*), despite the work being started in the reign of his father.

Charles was the only Swedish monarch born to absolutism and was utterly convinced of his holding of divine approval. The early, sweeping victories in battle reinforced the belief that God was with him. Contemporary observers noted how the Swedes would march into battle by saying *Med Guds hjalp* (With God's help), a refrain similar to the Germanic *Gott mit uns* (God with us). As Swedish successes faltered, the belief in divine approval became fragile. Hatton points out that Charles began to substitute the word *fate* for God in his letters. Thus, Poltava was an unfortunate fate and not a case of losing God's favour. Perhaps Charles could not reconcile his religious belief with Sweden's misfortunes. During the failed assault on coalition defences at the battle of Stresow, Charles purportedly asked aloud if God was still on his side. Shortly afterwards he was struck in the chest by a musket ball. Nevertheless, Charles remained devoted to his faith until his death.

As the Swedish army marched on Saxony, there was a fear that Charles intended to plunge deep into the affairs of the Holy Roman Empire – memories of the Thirty Years' War and marauding Swedish armies were still fresh in public consciousness. The fear seemed substantiated when Charles questioned the mistreatment of Protestants in the territory of Silesia. As a guarantor of Westphalia, he was obligated to intervene and his stay in Saxony allowed him to flex Sweden's diplomatic muscle. A second treaty was signed at Altranstädt which returned over 100 churches to the Protestants and halted counter-reformation efforts undertaken by the Emperor. Charles was praised for his labours but any further hopes of support were dashed when he evacuated Saxony and set off towards Russia.

Charles was open-minded in regard to other faiths, most notably with Islam. During his stay in Bender, he praised Muslims for their devotion, for keeping their word, for granting asylum, and withholding from strong drink. Cederhielm noted that Charles "did not want to force any man's religion."[9]

Alcohol

Upon returning from a hunt, Charles imbibed too much wine to slake his thirst. His slurred speech, something not becoming of a royal in the eyes

---

9   Hatton, *Charles XII*, p.523.

of Hedvig Eleonora, resulted in Charles being scolded by his grandmother. He thereafter resolved to never drink again. This story and the teetotalling myth that emerged from it, carries on to this day. The question is not if the King drank alcohol – he did – but rather how strong the drink was. This was already commented upon by observers: "… his Majesty's drinking no other liquor but water; this custom His Majesty has since thought fit in some sort to reform and begins now to drink small beer, but that of so mean a sort, that were it not for the name, he might as well make use of the pure element."[10] Charles would have beer on campaign and notably helped himself to a cup of wine while his house burned down during the *Kalabalik*. During his incognito return from exile, he would drink wine to fool observers who, even then, were convinced of the King's alcoholic abstinence. It must be remembered that contemporary drinks were at lower alcoholic volumes compared to their modern equivalents, so defining Charles as a teetotaller is rather subjective.

Money

Charles delighted in surprising people with monetary gifts. During social occasions before the war, he would slip small bags of coin into the pockets of unsuspecting courtiers. In the field he was quick to reward acts of bravery and duty – a crown for each stretcher bearer carrying the wounded Prince Maximilian of Württemberg, and 100 crowns to a soldier who chased down a Russian officer and recaptured two Swedish standards. He was also known to provide monetary reimbursement to civilians who offered up their home and table, and the army was instructed to pay fairly for goods and services rendered while on the march.

---

10 Jefferyes, *Letters*, p.38.

Appendix II

The Vanity of Human Wishes

The Vanity of Human Wishes, by Samuel Johnson, 1749, an excerpt:

On what Foundation stands the Warrior's Pride?
How just his Hopes let Swedish Charles decide;
A Frame of Adamant, a Soul of Fire,
No Dangers fright him, and no Labours tire;
O'er Love, o'er Force, extends his wide Domain,
Unconquer'd Lord of Pleasure and of Pain;
No Joys to him pacific Scepters yield,
War sounds the Trump, he rushes to the Field;
Behold surrounding Kings their Pow'r combine,
And One capitulate, and One resign;
Peace courts his Hand, but spread her Charms in vain;
"Think Nothing gain'd, he cries, till nought remain,
"On Moscow's Walls till Gothic Standards fly,
"And all is Mine beneath the Polar Sky."
The March begins in Military State,
And Nations on his Eye suspended wait;
Stern Famine guards the solitary Coast,
And Winter barricades the Realms of Frost;
He comes, nor Want nor Cold his Course delay;
Hide, blushing Glory, hide Pultowa's Day:
The vanquish'd Hero leaves his broken Bands,
And shews his Miseries in distant Lands;
Condemn'd a needy Supplicant to wait,
While Ladies interpose, and Slaves debate.
But did not Chance at length her Error mend?
Did no subverted Empire mark his End?
Did rival Monarchs give the fatal Wound?
Or hostile Millions press him to the Ground?
His Fall was destin'd to a barren Strand,
A petty Fortress, and a dubious Hand;
He left the Name, at which the World grew pale,
To point a Moral, or adorn a Tale.[1]

---

1 Godley, *Charles XII*, pp.237–238.

Colour Plate Commentaries

The uniform of Charles XII preserved at the Royal Armories in Stockholm is one of only three remaining examples of Carolean military dress, and the most complete. Barring a few accessories, it is also the only surviving set of clothes that once belonged to the King. This stands in stark contrast to the more than 270 items listed in the wardrobe collections of Peter I at the Hermitage.

Unlike the Czar's iconic uniform, which is modelled after an officer of the Life Guard (Preobrazhensky regiment), that of Charles appears to be a plain cavalry uniform. While it has an overall appearance similar to the generally accepted style of the Carolean uniform model, it does, on closer inspection, have features that are not found among the rank and file. The gilded brass buttons and enlarged coat pockets are two examples.

There is no display of rank and the uniform is free from ostentation. Whereas many officers lined their hats with lacing of silver or gold thread, that of the King consists of untrimmed black English felt. With the woollen cloak and jacket removed, some allowances for comfort can be identified. The fine linen undershirt is embroidered with a red "C" and the material, stitching, and overall quality of tailoring identifies the owner as someone of high rank.

The tight-fitting jacket and *kamisol* (long-sleeved vest) help confirm the King's overall body proportions. This, in turn, lends credence to the numerous artistic renderings of Charles which depict him with broad shoulders tapering off towards the waist. Measurements taken of the clothing and the body put the King's height at 5 feet 9 inches, or 1.75 meters. His hat size is 57 (European).

The bloodstained gloves are a combination of heavy moose skin around the cuffs, while thinner deer skin was used for the hand portion to grant flexibility. Charles wore his gloves regularly and would sometimes not bother to remove them when hastily signing documents.

The riding boots are made of blackened cowhide and are a size 42 (European). Given the overall wear and creasing in the leather, the boots were heavily used and thus not part of the rest of the uniform that was first worn on that fateful day in November, 1718.

Charles wore out his uniforms very quickly. That he was killed wearing this particular set for the first time has allowed it to be preserved in a remarkable state, although the clay mud of the trenches still cling to the lower edges of the cloak.

Select Bibliography

Åberg, Alf and Göte Göransson, *Karoliner* (Belgium: Bra Böcker, 1976)
Andersson, Ingvar, *A History of Sweden,* Translated by Carolyn Hannay (Stockholm: Natur Och Kultur, 1962)
Bengtsson, Frans, *The Sword Does Not Jest*, Translated by Naomi Walford (New York: St Martin's Press, 1960)
Bleile, Ralf and Joachim Krüger (eds.), *Princess Hedvig Sofia and the Great Northern War* (Dresden: Sandstein Verlag, 2015)
Boswell, James, *The Life of Samuel Johnson*, 2 vols (Boston: W. Andrews and L. Blake, 1807)
Browning, Oscar, *Charles XII of Sweden* (London: Hurst and Blackett Ltd, 1899)
Carlson, Ernst, *Die Eigenhändigen Briefe König Karls XII*, translated by F. Mewius (Berlin: Georg Reimer, 1894).
Carlson, Ernst, *Konung Karl XII:s Egenhändiga Bref* (Stockholm: Norstedt & Sons, 1893)
Chance, J.F., "England and Sweden in the Time of William III and Anne", *The English Historical Review*, 16:64 (October 1901), pp.676–711
Chandler, David, *The Art of Warfare in the Age of Marlborough* (Staplehurst: Spellmount, 1990)
Coroban, Costel, *Britain and Charles XII of Sweden 1709–1719* (Germany: Lambert Academic Publishing, 2013)
Dorrell, Nicholas, *Peter the Great Humbled: The Russo-Ottoman War of 1711* (Warwick: Helion & Company, 2018)
Englund, Peter, *The Battle That Shook Europe* (London: I.B. Tauris, 2013)
Ernstell, Eva-Sofi, *En kunglig fasad: Karl XII i Livrustkammaren* (Stockholm: Livrustkammaren, 1998)
Fabrice, Friedrich Ernst von, *The Genuine Letters of Baron Fabricius Envoy from His Serene Highness the Duke Administrator of Holstein to Charles XII of Sweden*, translator unknown (London: Tully's Head, 1761)
Fredholm von Essen, Michael, *Charles XI's War* (Warwick: Helion & Company, 2019)
Fredrik, Oscar, *Charles XII*, Translated by George Apgeorge (UK: Bentley, 1878)
Frost, Robert, *The Northern Wars 1558–1721* (Harlow: Longman, 2000)
Godley, Eveline, *Charles XII of Sweden: A Study in Kingship* (London: Collins, 1928)
Grimarest, Jean-Léonor, *Les Campagnes de Charles XII, roi de Suede*, 4 vols (Stockholm, 1707)
Haintz, Otto, *König Karl XII von Schweden,* 3 vols (Berlin: Walter De Gruyter & Co, 1958)
Hallart, Ludwig Nicolaus von, *Das Tagebuch des Generals von Hallart uber die Belagerung und Schlacht von Narva 1700*, edited by Friedrich Bienemann (F. Kluge, 1894)
Hattendorf, John (ed.), *Charles XII Warrior King* (EU: Karwansaray Publishers, 2018)
Hatton, Ragnhild (ed.), *Captain James Jefferyes's Letters from the Swedish Army 1707–1709* (Stockholm: Norstedt & Sons, 1954)
Hatton, Ragnhild, *Charles XII of Sweden* (New York: Weybright and Talley, 1969)
Höglund, Lars-Eric and Åke Sallnäs, *The Great Northern War 1700–1721 Colours and Uniforms* (Karlstad: Acedia Press, 2000)
Kirby, David, *Northern Europe in the Early Modern Period: The Baltic World 1492–1772* (New York: Longman, 1990)
Klein, Barbro, "The Testimony of the Button", *Journal of the Folklore Institute*, 8:2/3 (August–December 1971), pp.127–146
Kling Jr, Stephen (ed.), *Great Northern War Compendium*, 2 vols (St Louis: THGC Publishing, 2015)
Konstam, Angus, *Poltava 1709: Russia Comes of Age* (Oxford: Osprey Publishing, 1994)
Kurat, Akdes Nimet, "Der Prutfeldzug und der Prutfrieden von 1711", *Jahrbücher für Geschichte Osteuropas*, 10:1 (April 1962), pp.13–66

SELECT BIBLIOGRAPHY

Liljegren, Bengt, *Karl XII: en biografi* (Lund: Historiska Media, 2000)

Lindgren, Raymond, "A Projected Invasion of Sweden, 1716", *Huntington Library Quarterly*, 7:3 (May 1944), pp.223–246

Lisk, Jill, *The Struggle for Supremacy in the Baltic 1600-1725* (London: University of London Press, 1967)

Lockhart, Paul Douglas, *Sweden in the Seventeenth Century* (New York: Palgrave Macmillan, 2004)

Marklund, Andreas, "The Manly Sacrifice: Martial Manliness and Patriotic Martyrdom in Nordic Propaganda during the Great Northern War", *Gender & History*, 25:1 (April 2013), pp.150–169

Megorsky, Boris, *Peter the Great's Revenge: The Russian Siege of Narva in 1704* (Warwick: Helion & Company, 2018)

Megorsky, Boris, *The Russian Army in the Great Northern War 1700-1721* (Warwick: Helion & Company, 2018)

Milne, June, "The Diplomacy of Dr John Robinson at the Court of Charles XII of Sweden 1697-1709", *Transactions of the Royal Historical Society*, 30 (1948), pp.75–93

Moerk, Ernst, "From War Hero to Villain: Reversal of the Symbolic Value of War and a Warrior King", *Journal of Peace Research*, 35:4 (July 1998), pp.453–469

Motraye, Aubry de La, *Travels through Europe, Asia, and into Part of Africa*, 2 vols (London: privately published, 1723)

Nisbet Bain, Robert, *Charles XII and the Collapse of the Swedish Empire 1682-1719* (New York: G.P. Putnam's Sons, 1902)

Nordberg, Joran, *Konung Carl den XII:s Historia*, 2 vols (Stockholm, 1740)

Nordling, Carl, "The Death of Karl XII: A Case of Political Murder", *Scandinavian Studies*, 71:1 (Spring 1999), pp.81–92

Oakley, Stewart, *War and Peace in the Baltic 1560-1790* (New York: Routledge, 2002)

Olden-Jørgensen, Sebastian, "Ceremonial Interaction across the Baltic around 1700", *Scandinavian Journal of History*, 28 (2003), pp.243–251

Olin, Martin, "Tessin's Project for Royal Stables on Helgeandsholmen: A Study of Charles XII as a Patron of Architecture", *Konsthistorisk Tidskrift*, 72:1–2 (2003), pp.159–170

Plokhy, Serhii (ed.), *Poltava 1709: The Battle and the Myth* (Cambridge: Harvard University Press, 2012)

Querengässer, Alexander, *Die Armee Augusts des Starken im Nordischen Krieg* (Berlin: Zeughaus Verlag, 2013)

Roberts, Michael, *Essays in Swedish History* (London: Weidenfeld and Nicolson, 1967)

Roberts, Michael, *From Oxenstierna to Charles XII: Four Studies* (Cambridge: Cambridge University Press, 1991)

Roberts, Michael (ed.), *Sweden's Age of Greatness 1632-1718* (New York: St Martin's Press, 1973)

Roberts, Michael, *The Early Vasas: A History of Sweden 1523-1611* (Cambridge: Cambridge University Press, 1968)

Roberts, Michael, *The Swedish Imperial Experience 1560-1718* (Cambridge: Cambridge University Press, 1979)

Rothstein, Andrew, *Peter the Great and Marlborough: Politics and Diplomacy in Converging Wars* (New York: St Martin's Press, 1986)

Sapherson, C.A., *Forces of the Swedish Crown 1688-1721* (Essex: Partizan Press, undated)

Sarauw, Christian Frederik, *Die Feldzüge Karl's XII* (Leipzig: Bernhard Schlicke, 1881)

Scott, Franklin, *Sweden: The Nation's History* (USA: Southern Illinois University Press, 1988)

Sinclair, George, "The Scottish Officers of Charles XII", *The Scottish Historical Review*, 21:83 (April 1924), pp.178–192

Sjöström, Oskar, *Fraustadt 1706. Ett fält färgat rött* (Lund: Historiska Media, 2008)

Snickare, Mårten, "The Construction of Autocracy: Nicodemus Tessin the Younger and the Architecture of Stockholm", *Studies in the History of Art*, 66 (2005), pp.64–77

Stamp, A.E., "The Meeting of the Duke of Marlborough and Charles XII at Altranstädt, April 1707", *Transactions of the Royal Historical Society*, 12 (1898), pp.103–116

Stiles, Andrina, *Sweden and the Baltic 1523-1721* (London: Hodder & Stoughton, 1992)

Upton, Anthony, *Charles XI and Swedish Absolutism* (Cambridge: Cambridge University Press, 1998)

Voltaire, Francois-Marie Arouet de, *The History of Charles XII of Sweden*, translated by Antonia White (New York: Barnes & Noble, 1976)

Westerlund, Olov, "Karl XII I Svensk Litteratur", PhD dissertation, University of Lund, 1951.

Wolke, Lars Ericson, *The Swedish Army in the Great Northern War 1700-1721* (Warwick: Helion & Company, 2018)

Zernack, Klaus, "Schweden als europäische Grosmacht der frühen Neuzeit", *Historische Zeitschrift*, 232:2 (April 1981), pp.327–357